THE LOST KING OF ENGLAND

THE EAST EUROPEAN ADVENTURES OF EDWARD THE EXILE

To Lois

THE LOST KING OF ENGLAND

THE EAST EUROPEAN ADVENTURES OF EDWARD THE EXILE

Gabriel Ronay

THE BOYDELL PRESS

First published 1989 by The Boydell Press, Woodbridge

The Boydell Press is an imprint of Boydell & Brewer Ltd
PO Box 9, Woodbridge, Suffolk IP12 3DF
and of Boydell & Brewer Inc.
Wolfeboro, New Hampshire 03894-2069, USA

ISBN 0 85115 541 3

British Library Cataloguing in Publication Data
Ronay, Gabriel
The lost king of England: the East European
adventures of Edward the Exile.
1. England. Edward the Exile
I. Title
942.01'8'0924
ISBN 0–85115–541–3

Library of Congress Cataloging-in Publication Data applied for

Errata on the dust jacket
Under 'Cover illustrations': the icon illustrated on the front was formerly in the church of St Boris and St Gleb-in-Plotniki; the illustration on the back is from a chronicle of 1283.

The paper used in this publication meets the minimum requirements of American National Standard for Information Sciences – Permanence of Paper for Printed Library Materials, ANSI Z39.48–1984.

Printed and bound in Great Britain

Contents

List of illustrations   vii

Foreword   viii

PART I: THE AGONY OF A KINGDOM

1. Of auguries and thingmen and Anglo-Saxon attitudes   3

2. Odin's bird of battle flaps its wings: Edmund Ironside's valiant struggle against Canute at London   10

3. Murder royal in the privy: a turncoat's tale   19

4. A 'letter of death': Canute's choice of murder by proxy   26

PART II: THE ROAD INTO EXILE

5. The resentful English look to the aethelings for deliverance: the restoration plot pre-empted by Queen Emma's 'evil coup'   37

6. Twenty-nine false leads and a cold trail   43

7. The Russian connection: the flight eastward along the Norsemen's route   50

8. The 'Polish red herring': two vital pointers and a crucial discovery   55

PART III: COUNTERS IN A EUROPEAN POWER GAME

9. At Yaroslav the Great's hospitable court: Nordic ethos and Byzantine statecraft on the steppes of Russia   61

10. Anglo-Saxon counters in a Continental battle for dominance   68

11. Hungarian princes join Kievan refugee colony: friendship among the exiles   71

12. A call from Hungary: the aethelings leave the Nordic orbit to participate in Prince Andrew's military adventure   78

13. In the rebel camp: riding to power on the backs of pagan Magyars   83

PART IV: HOME FROM HOME IN SOUTH-EASTERN EUROPE

14. Signs of royal favour: in search of the aethelings' footsteps at Mecseknádasd, 'The Land of Britons' — 91

15. Scandal at court: the fiery love of a Hungarian princess and its consequences — 102

16. Edward's marriage to a 'lady of royal descent': the riddle of Agatha's origin resolved — 109

17. Two tell-tale insertions in a Norman law collection: the glossarist's account of a political marriage in Russia — 115

PART V: HEEDING ENGLAND'S CALL: A TRAGIC HOMECOMING

18. The shadow of the Bastard of Normandy over England: the king sends for Edward the Exile — 125

19. An innocent abroad: the Emperor's double-cross foils Archbishop Ealdred's mission — 132

20. A tragic end to Edward's Continental odyssey: a murder most foul with two suspects and a belated conviction — 136

21. Edward's son groomed for the throne, but the king's deathbed words secure the crown for Harold — 143

22. 1066: the comet of revolution over England; death of a kingdom — 151

PART VI: THE 'LOST KING' OF ENGLAND

23. A kingdom for a bag of silver — 161

24. Tilting at Norman windmills: Edgar's progression from Berkhamsted to nowhere — 167

Epilogue — 173

Appendices

1. Florence of Worcester: *Chronicon ex Chronicis ab initio Mundi ad Annum Domini 1118* — 183

2. *Leges Edovardi Confessori* — 184

3. William of Poitier's account of the Norman Conquest: *Gesta Guillelmi Ducis Normannorum et Regis Anglorum* — 186

Notes to text — 191
Selected bibliography — 201
Index — 207

Illustrations

1. King Edmund Ironside, Edward the Exile's father, in single combat with Canute to decide the fate of England (*La Estoire de St Aedward le Rei*, Ms. Cantab. Ee iii 59) — 13

2. Edmund pierced by a lance (Ms. Cantab. Ee iii 59) — 21

3. Prince Andrew of Hungary and his brothers, Béla and Levente, advised by their uncle, King St Stephen to go into exile (the *Óbudai Képes Krónika*) — 73

4. King St Stephen of Hungary (an embroidered Coronation Cloak, c.1031) — 77

5. The coronation of Andrew I of Hungary in 1047 (from *Kézai Simon Krónikája* 1283) — 87

6. Crucial evidence of the Anglo-Saxon princes' sojourn in south Hungary near Nádasd (Ms. Somogyvári trans-sumptum 76/1404) — 92

7. The key sentence referring to the 'Terra Britanorum de Nádasd' in the 1404 land deed — 95

8. View of the mountain at Nádasd, site of the ruins of Rékavár castle — 99

9. The Holy Roman Emperor Henry (his 'Sacramentarium', Staatsbibliothek, München) — 113

10. Edward the Confessor on his deathbed (the Bayeux Tapestry) — 147

11. Harold presented with the crown of England in the presence of Archbishop Stigant (the Bayeux Tapestry) — 148

12. Illuminated pages from the Gospel of St Margaret of Scotland, the daughter of the 'Lost King of England' (Bodleian Library, Oxford) — 179

Foreword

King Canute of the waves and Edward the Confessor are household names in Britain, two firm landmarks on the road to 1066. The story of the two aethelings whose fate curiously linked together the two kings has, however, fallen through the net of national consciousness.* Canute wanted to murder Edmund and Edward, the rightful heirs to the English crown, while nearly forty years later the Confessor allotted one of them a key role in his desperate plan to avert a Norman take-over.

The drama of saving the lives of the two young princes greatly exercised the imagination of the chroniclers of the time, who rated it among the most momentous events of the eleventh century. It was a conspiracy of hearts which, but for a tragic stroke of fate, might have prevented the Norman Conquest, inviting speculation about one of the most crucial 'might-have-beens' of British history.

In spite of the aethelings' importance for British history, until now virtually nothing was known about how they escaped the later fate of the 'two princes in the Tower', and the events of their Continental odyssey were a closed book. Their years in Kievan exile were shrouded in mystery, and the surviving accounts of their peregrinations appear more as a gathering of legends than as authentic history. There is, in fact, no authoritative reference book that can furnish reliable facts about the two Anglo-Saxon princes' years in exile.

The *Encyclopaedia Britannica*, for example, merely notes that Edmund and Edward lived in exile in Hungary and that Edward's daughter, Margaret, was brought up at the Hungarian court. *Burke's Peerage* even gets the maternal forebears of Edward's daughter wrong. And the *Dictionary of National Biography* confines itself to stating that 'Edward and his brother Edmund, when yet infants, are said to have been sent to Sweden'. It adds that the aethelings 'passed to Hungary before 1038, when [King] Stephen died. No trace of the exiles has, however, been found in the histories of Hungary . . .'

---

* The title 'aetheling' given to Edmund Ironside's sons by the chroniclers was in general use amongst Anglo-Saxons. It was used to refer to sons and brothers of kings, and its original meaning was 'noble youth', deriving from *adel* (noble) and the suffix *-ing* which denoted youth.

A close examination of a wide variety of contemporary sources in half a dozen Continental archives has revealed new material evidence about their life and times, and their 'missing' years in exile can be reconstructed with considerable certainty.

These years were rich in political intrigues, chivalrous deeds and royal bedroom scandals, and some of the aethelings' adventures make the much-vaunted exploits of professional knights errant look positively tame. But there were more compelling reasons than the lure of a good adventure story that prompted this present endeavour to piece together the aethelings' exile career.

For a start, the roles of Edward and his son, Edgar aetheling, in the turbulent events preceding 1066 needed investigating, especially in view of the Confessor's gamble to keep the crown in Anglo-Saxon hands with their help. Another unresolved problem was Edward's sudden and mysterious death upon his triumphant return to England after forty years of exile. Was it murder or accident?

A further interest motivating this inquiry was the enigma of Edgar Aetheling. The son of an exile, born in exile, he became the Great White Hope of the English thanes, who elected him king after the disaster of Hastings to counter William the Bastard's claim to the English throne. The circumstances that shaped the character of the last rightful Anglo-Saxon heir required elucidation, for otherwise the actions of the man who became England's 'lost' king could not be understood.

Then there were the conflicting accounts of Edward's Continental marriage inviting patient investigation. The scrutiny of the unexplored political circumstances of it was not an academic hobby-horse medievalists so love to pursue in their private world of scholarship. It was concerned with a live issue, with practical, present-day repercussions: through an offspring of Edward and Agatha's daughter – the saintly Queen Margaret of Scotland – the Stuarts became kings of England, linking the ancient House of Wessex to the present Royal Family.

In the end, however, it was the excitement of uncovering under the dust of nine-and-a-half centuries the aethelings' trail that sustained this present inquiry. With the aid of new material unearthed in the course of the research, and a fresh approach to the available documentary evidence, new insight could be gained into the Anglo-Saxon princes' extraordinary life at the Kievan and Hungarian courts.

Passions, human foibles and foolish gambles showed up their fallibility and brought them closer to our day. The anguish of a tempestuous love affair between Edmund and a royal princess that shook the Hungarian court has lost none of its immediacy, even in the stilted rendering of an Anglo-Norman gossip-writer.

In spite of the romances and escapades, the aethelings' life in exile turned out to be an adventure story with a difference. Under the polished exterior of a professional exile, Edward revealed a constant preoccupation

ix

with home, a yearning for a country that was in fact more alien to him than the foreign countries that had given him refuge: for in the Promised Land he had been dreaming about during his forty years in the Continental wilderness, the poisoner's cup, not gratitude, awaited him. And as a direct consequence of Edward's tragedy, 1066 became inevitable.

PART I: THE AGONY OF A KINGDOM

1. Of auguries and thingmen and Anglo-Saxon attitudes

Astrologers, soothsayers, necromancers and the host of less orthodox diviners of the future in the kingdom of Wessex could offer nothing but doom-laden prophecies to those who consulted them about their prospects in the new year of 1013. The omens were universally bad and the predictions terrifying. Even the most reliable star-gazers foresaw nothing but death and destruction.

Yet as the year progressed King Aethelred (of the wounding sobriquet 'the Unready') began to look to the future with renewed confidence. Although in that year of grace, as so often in the preceding two centuries, the dragon ships of the Norsemen had appeared along the coast of England to pillage, sack and burn the defenceless settlements, a new stratagem had been evolved to deal with the raiders. Thorkill the Tall and his pack of 3,000 Jómvikings had been induced, by the staggering sum of 48,000 pounds of silver, to enter English service as mercenaries.

There was, of course, nothing new about yielding to Viking demands of tribute or the payment of Danegeld, but the use of Norsemen as protectors of the English on such a big scale was a new departure. Aethelred and the magnates who had put up the money reasoned in the Witan, the Anglo-Saxon assembly, that with this standing army of seasoned warriors Wessex stood a good chance of repulsing further Danish attacks.

But many people, and that included the educated élite in that superstitious age, believed blindly the auguries and set little store by the Jómvikings' reliability.[1] The buying-off of a marauding wolfpack and their reappearance in sheep's clothing could, they reasoned, hardly be called a turning-point in the battle against the Danish raiders.

Their gloomy prognostication was shared by those who sought to gain an insight into the future by interpreting for themselves the prophecies of the ancient seer Merlin, who was enjoying a great revival.[2] The Red Dragon, representing the people of Britain, would be overrun by the White Dragon coming from overseas, so the interpretation of Merlin's prediction ran, and the dragon ships of the Norsemen were cruising along the coast of England for all to see.

And that was not all, for Merlin's prophecies appeared to offer far more tangible proof of the fate awaiting the island race: 'A shower of blood shall fall and a dire famine shall afflict mankind. The Red Dragon shall grieve for what had happened. . . . The bellies of mothers shall be cut open and babies will be born prematurely. Men will suffer most grievously in order that those born in the country may regain power. He who will achieve these things shall appear as the Man of Bronze and for long years he shall guard the gates of London upon a brazen horse.'

Whoever the Man of Bronze destined to guard the gates of London was, in the opinion of the people he could not be Aethelred. Although, admittedly, he was of the ancient Anglo-Saxon stock, St Dunstan's widely remembered oracle, made on his coronation day, was depressingly clear: Aethelred could not deflect the sword of fate poised above his House.[3] His fate was sealed as this sword would rage against him all his life. What is more, his offspring too were doomed to die and, eventually, his kingdom would be taken over by a foreigner. And that portended not only the destruction of the House of Cerdic but of his kingdom. As St Dunstan's oracle was seen as a token of divine insight, not infernal craft like the auguries of heathen star-gazers, there was no denying its truth.

This sense of impending doom and fearful foreboding could, however, hardly be ascribed to the eschatological predictions of sighted diviners alone. These fears were rooted in the appalling reality of early eleventh-century England and the auguries and prophecies, whatever their source, were thinly-disguised projection of the present into an unpromising and menacing future.

The facts speak for themselves: three of the four English kingdoms had already been destroyed in the wave of Danish raids, and upon their ruins emerged the Danelaw, the Norse cuckoo in the Anglo-Saxon nest. This alien colony now stretched from York to the River Thames.

Sweyn Forkbeard, the warrior king of Denmark always eager for booty and battle, seized upon the defection of Thorkill and his band of Jómvikings to mount a fresh attack on the fertile lands of England. Although he hardly needed much persuasion to indulge in his favourite pastime, a near-contemporary account, the *Encomium Emmae Reginae*, contains a graphic description of how the council of his warriors argued to make war on England.

> 'Thorkill', they said, 'the chief of your forces, O King, departed with your permission that he might revenge a brother who had been slain there [England], and led with him a large part of your host. Now that he rejoices in victory and is in the possession of the southern part of the country, he prefers to remain there as an exile and friend of the English whom he has conquered through your power, rather than return with the host in submission to you and ascribing the victory to yourself.
>
> And now we are defrauded of our companions and of forty ships

4

which he sailed to England laden with the best warriors of Denmark. Let not, out Lord, suffer so grave a loss but go forth leading your willing army, and we will subdue for you the contumacious Thorkill, together with his companions, and also the English who are in league with them, and all their possessions. We are certain that they cannot resist long because our countrymen will come over to us readily.'

This was a fair appraisal of the situation. A part of the population of the British Isles was clearly well disposed towards the Danish invaders, while Aethelred's kingdom was weak and its people divided and demoralized. And while Aethelred was setting great store by his new mercenary force, Sweyn seemed reasonably certain that when they saw his banner, the Jómvikings would rejoin the ranks of the Norsemen.

The infectious eagerness of his warriors' council convinced Sweyn that he could now conquer the whole of England. Accordingly, he ordered a general muster and the warriors of Denmark flocked to his banner hoping for booty and glory.

Seeing his huge, enthusiastic host awaiting his signal, Sweyn told the warriors that he was determined to bring England under his rule by force or stratagem. He also decided to take his younger son, Canute, with him, even though the boy was still under fourteen.

Although it was in keeping with the Norse tradition to initiate a prince into the art of war at a very early age, Sweyn's decision to take Canute on this campaign must have had an additional reason. As a younger son, Canute could not hope to inherit the Crown of Denmark The conquest of England, however, promised not only plunder and fame but also a country to govern.

The campaign itself followed the course of countless previous raids, yet even in the somewhat stylized rendering of an alien monk, who over 100 years later set to rhyme the misery of the English in his *La Estoire de Seint Aedward le Rei,* [4] the suffering of the country from the Danish invaders is clearly discernible

> The country burns . . . all the inhabitants fly before Sweyn,
> All the property he keeps and amasses;
> And makes war the worse because he knew
> That against him could make no resistance
> The people of the country.
> Aethelred to Normandy
> Flies to save his life:
> Wherefore was Sweyn more fierce and bold,
> When the people lost comfort;
> And caused himself to be called king,
> And did outrage and great disorder;

Property he robbed out of all bounds,
Without pity and without right,
Then he came into the country of Saint Edmund,
Where he destroys all and confounds all;
He demands property for his exactions
Beyond the power [of the people] and without reason.
The people, poor and already destroyed,
Fly to the martyr Edmund,
And cry to their Lord,
And he avenges them with great readiness:
At night came to him the vengeance
That he was pierced with a lance.

Sweyn did indeed die during the 1014 campaign, but he died peace-fully in bed and was not pierced by some mysterious lance of the martyr St Edmund. This belief in St Edmund's divine intervention was so wide-spread that even the Norse *Heimskringlasaga*, recorded by the Icelander Snorri Sturluson in the early years of the thirteenth century, contains an account of it. In Sturluson's version, Englishmen believed that Edmund the Saint killed Sweyn with his flaming sword, the way that the holy Mercurius had killed the apostate Julian.

Sweyn's death offered England a brief respite. Aethelred was restored to his throne by the Witan and he recalled his Norman wife, Emma, and their two children – Aedward and Aelfred – from the court of Richard the Good in Normandy, where they had taken refuge during Sweyn's on-slaught.

But the damage done to the fabric of society by the ceaseless Norse incursions was too great to allow Aethelred to benefit from it. Under the strain of the attacks the very foundations of social order began to crack. Laws and moral standards were debased, rapes went unpunished, trea-son became common occurrence and disloyalty was so widespread that it could hardly be considered a crime.

In a remarkable sermon, entitled 'Sermo Lupi ad Anglos quando Dani maxime persecuti sunt eos, quod fuit in dies Aethelredi regis', Archbishop Wulfstan of York pilloried the treachery and moral cowardice of the country's rulers and chided the people for their wickedness, impiety and collaboration with the invaders. By threatening them with God's anger, he was hoping to rouse them from their moral turpitude and restore their self-respect:

Things have not gone well now for a long time at home or abroad.
There has been devastation and persecution in every district again
and again, and the English have been for a long time now completely defeated and too disheartened through God's anger.
And the pirates have been so strong with God's consent that often

in battle one can put to flight ten, and sometimes less, and some-times more, all because of our sins.

And often ten or a dozen, one after another, insult disgracefully the thane's wife, and sometimes his daughter or near kinswoman, whilst he looks on, a man who considered himself brave and mighty and stout enough before that happened. And often a slave binds very fast the thane who previously was his master and makes him into a slave through God's anger. Alas for the misery, and alas for the public shame which the English now have, all through God's anger . . .

But all the insults which we often suffer we repay by honouring those who insult us; we repay them continually and they humiliate us daily; they ravage and they burn, plunder and rob and carry on board. And lo, what else is there in all these events except God's anger, clear and visible over this people?

In January 1015, the sorely-tried English attacked and massacred garri-sons of 'thingmen', as the Danish mercenaries became known, stationed at London and Slessick. Young Canute, who took over the leadership of the Danish armies upon his father's death, was out of the country at the time. When the news reached him he felt it was a personal challenge to him and reacted accordingly. He gathered a mighty armada of ships, determined not only to teach the English a sharp lesson but to prove his leadership in battle.[5]

The description of Canute's battle fleet by the author of the *Encomium* (hereafter the Encomiast) captures its terrible magnificence and conveys, across nine centuries, the terror that these dragon ships instilled in the people of the British Isles.

The ships' rich, gold decoration bedazzled the coast-watchers and to those looking at them from a distance, they seemed to be made of flame rather than wood. The rays of the sun lit up the gold on the prows, the silver of the flashing arms and the flame-like reflection of the warriors' suspended shields. The impact of Canute's terrifying battle fleet was such that its appearance on the horizon was enough to cow the trembling inhabitants into instant submission. His warriors were, most of the time, not even required to join battle.

According to the Encomiast, whose inside information of Norse affairs and Canute's campaigns is repeatedly demonstrated, the English were particularly terrified of bulls' heads on the ships, with menacing horns dipped in blood-red gold, and dragons with frightening golden faces.

The combined fleets of the Danes and Norwegians, who joined Canute in his punitive campaign, sailed to Sandwich, then swung round to Kent and Wessex and began harrying Aethelred's meagre forces at several points in the south, including Dorset, Wiltshire and Somerset. As in the past, these pirate techniques were successful but not decisive.

The dragon ships spread terror and death as they plundered the country, but however ferocious the raids, they did not exceed the limits of a more sustained campaign of vengeance. Chroniclers described Canute's warriors as covetous, cruel war-lovers. They delighted in killing defenceless women and children, and burned down churches, as well as houses, without remorse. Together with rape and senseless destruction, it was all part and parcel of the traditional Norse harrying tactics.

Canute's own style of fighting, however, quickly veered away from the hidebound approach of his predecessors and soon began to show greater flexibility. He improvized and introduced elements of surprise, but terror remained an essential part of his campaign. He took his first calculated step in this direction at Sandwich, when his father entrusted a group of high-ranking English hostages into his care: he had some castrated and the rest mutilated; their noses and ears were cut off before they were set free. These acts of gratuitous savagery were never forgotten by the English. But it duly impressed the Norsemen; and that was perhaps just as important for young Canute.

An eulogy written by Ottar the Black, the Norse bard, laid particular emphasis on Canute's ferociousness: 'You were of no great age when you pushed off your ships . . . Chief, you made your armoured ships, and were daring beyond measure. In your rage, Canute, you mustered the red shield of sea. Young leader, you made the English fall close by the Tees.'

In the autumn of 1015, he gave further proof of his instinctive flair for the art of war and leadership with the surprise decision to disregard the Viking custom of leaving England with the onset of bad weather for winter quarters and to carry on campaigning. This extension of the fighting to the winter season was so unexpected that it gave him a further edge in the initiative, threw the English into disarray and turned his incursion into a decisive campaign.

Against this able and aggressive young Viking Aethelred cut a sorry figure. He behaved that winter like a man under a spell, as if he had decided that there was nothing he could do to prevent the prophecies from coming true. Eventually he took to his sick-bed at Cosham, near Portsmouth, leaving the fight against Canute's host to his son Edmund.

Edmund showed unexpected resolution in prosecuting the war against the invaders and his valour soon won him the epithet of 'Ironside'. His desire to beat Canute at his own game and free England from the invaders not through the paying of Danegeld but through military victory is clearly reflected in the life story of his famous brother, Edward the Confessor.[6]

> . . . Edmund Ironside
> Was the son of the daughter of Count Torin [Theodoric]
> The third son of King Aethelred,
> Eldest of the three. He said: 'By my faith,
> Noble father, from us departs

No portion of our enemies;
Our friends and our people they slay,
The country they burn and destroy,
Strange and unnatural.
Their sovereign fierce and cruel,
Whose name is Cnut, spares no
People, so as not to take their lives.
Much grief I have, and much saddens me
Both his disorder and his pride.
By your counsel and assistance
I go to crush his cunning.'
So did he, for afterwards in war
As far as the frontiers of his land
He drove him.

He became a worthy adversary of Canute, who soon learnt to respect the sword of the English prince. He gave hope to his countrymen and restored their pride. Before long, people were wondering whether Edmund Ironside was the 'Man of Bronze' of Merlin's prophecy, destined to recover the country from the aliens. The irresistible desire of the people to see the prophecy come true made them look to London whose gates were to be guarded for long years by the bronze saviour of the ancient oracle. A number of events, some fortuitous others predictable, indeed put London in the centre of the struggle for supremacy between Canute and Edmund Ironside in 1016. But with hindsight – not foresight – it is clear that the tribulations of the island race were just beginning in earnest and not ending, as prophesied by Merlin.

2. Odin's bird of battle flaps its wings: Edmund Ironside's valiant struggle against Canute at London.

1016 was the year of continuous warfare in England. There were battles, sieges and lightning raids after Canute's battle fleet left the Isle of Wight, where it had been moored during the winter storms. He left his ships at Poole harbour, and in the early spring months the fighting between the Danish host and Edmund's army ebbed and flowed from Warwickshire to York without a single decisive encounter between them.

But in the recollection of the Nordic sagas, it was the Year of the Raven, Odin's bird of battle, portending great Norse feats of arms. Canute's army brought with it from Denmark the ancient Raven Banner made of white silk and showing, according to the Norse accounts, no visual portrayal of Odin's bird. But every time battle was joined, the raven appeared on the flag, its behaviour indicating the outcome of the fighting. When victory was imminent it flapped its wings, opened its beak and moved its feet vigorously, but when defeat was staring the Danes in the face, it hung its head and did not move.

Throughout 1016, the raven showed unusual excitement encouraging the heartening Canute's warriors, and this curious Nordic superstition was affirmed as true, even if his readers should find it difficult to believe, by the monastic Encomiast.[1]

The sudden death of Aethelred in April introduced fresh elements of uncertainty into an already highly volatile situation. With many high-ranking Anglo-Saxon hostages in Canute's camp in southern England, the Witan's choice of a successor to Aethelred must have been influenced by the memory of the fate of English hostages at Sandwich. The lords, bishops and nobles of southern England offered the crown to Canute although, according to tradition and custom, the nearest male heir of the House of Cerdic should have been made king. Afterwards, the nobles and church dignitaries of southern England gathered at Southampton to swear fealty to their Danish sovereign in a sorry spectacle of cowardly collaboration.

But Edmund Ironside, as if acting out his fateful role in London as predicted by the oracle, successfully countered the subservient move of the southern England Witan. An assembly of northern notables meeting in London, where Edmund was staying at the time of his father's death, helped the young prince to thwart Canute's take-over plan. According to Florence of Worcester, the northern Witan and the burghers of London proclaimed Edmund Ironside king. However, as neither the southern nor the northern Witan could reasonably claim to represent the whole country, the fate of the crown, and the Anglo-Saxon kingdom, could only be decided by war.

Canute immediately moved against London. His plan is reliably recounted by the Encomiast:

> The king, ordered the city of London, the capital of the country, to be besieged because the chief men and part of [Edmund's] army had fled to it, and also a very great number of common people, for it is a most populous place. And because infantry and cavalry could not accomplish this, for the city is surrounded on all sides by a river, which is in a sense equal to the sea, he caused it to be shut in with towered ships, and held it in a strong circumvallation.

Canute intended to isolate the city from the north by blocking the Thames both above and below the city. Further, a canal was dug near what is now London Bridge to allow the narrow Viking ships to reach a stream west of the city, and with the help of a further ditch the Danes made sure that no one could enter or leave London.

With the vigorous backing of the townspeople, Edmund Ironside repulsed several attacks on the town's fortifications and bravely defended the gates of London, as prophesied by Merlin, although most certainly not from a 'brazen horse'.

Before the town was fully sealed off Edmund secretly slipped out to raise an army and relieve London. Canute prudently sent part of his army against Edmund's newly-recruited force. At a fierce encounter at Sherstone, Edmund Ironside was, to judge by most English and Norman accounts, cheated of victory by the treason of Eadric Streona, the ealdorman of Mercia, who sowed confusion within Edmund's host by allegedly holding aloft the severed head of a warrior resembling their lord.

Although the battle was inconclusive, Edmund's army received further reinforcements from the north and immediately marched on London to break Canute's siege. The Dane, with great flexibility, simply withdrew to his ships and raised the siege without giving battle to a much stronger army. On seeing the rapid change in fortunes, Eadric did not hesitate to switch sides again and was not only forgiven but granted a warm welcome by Edmund.

According to the Encomiast, Edmund entered the city of London in state. There the people flocked to him and swore allegiance, declaring that he, rather than the prince of the Danes, was their choice for king. Eadric was one of his main supporters, a man described as skilful in counsel but treacherous in guile.

After his success in relieving London, his forces dispersed, as was the habit of medieval armies at harvest time, and Edmund was forced to try and raise yet another army in Wessex. Canute exploited Edmund's temporary impotence to resume the siege of London, but in spite of waves of attacks from ships and from land, he failed to take it for the second time.

After a year of appalling destruction and ceaseless warfare, Canute was not much nearer to conquering England than when he first landed. His supplies must have dwindled, he had no secure base, and his opponent, Edmund, had succeeded in stiffening the resistance of the English. Although he had a battle-hardened army and a superb fleet at his disposal, the rising tide of English hostility towards the Danish invaders and the patriotic fervour aroused by Edmund's leadership made the contest for supremacy between the two less unequal.

Even the Encomiast, who wrote his work as an eulogy of Canute's wife, Emma, at her orders, readily admitted that the English had good reason to hate the invaders and that their resistance was natural and justified. He paid due tribute to Edmund's valour and, secretly, seemed to sympathize with his efforts to free his country.

Indeed, from all the surviving contemporary accounts Edmund Ironside emerges as a strong, impetuous, but valiant king, who could have provided England with a sense of unity and moral purpose so sadly lacking in the years of his father's rule.

In all, Edmund raised five armies that year and fought a superior Viking force to a standstill. During the summer, he also offered single combat to Canute to decide, in accordance with the customs of both the English and the Danes, who should rule England. It was a shrewd move which helped to boost his chivalrous image even among the Danes especially as Canute, showing his customary caution, at first refused to meet him.

Most Anglo-Norman chroniclers included in their annals the single combat incident although its form and place vary to some degree. According to Walter Map, the author of the twelfth-century *De Nugis Curialium* the fight was at the suggestion of Canute, not Edmund. They fought on horseback in a French-style tournament arranged with the pomp and circumstance fitted more to the post-Norman Conquest period than the early years of the century.

However, Henry of Huntingdon described a different kind of battle between the two. They fought with spears and lances and, when these broke, with swords. This typical Scandinavian *holmganga*-type duel also occurs in the account of Geoffrey Gaimar, the early twelfth-century Norman historian and 'gossip-columnist', although according to his version,

1. King Edmund Ironside, Edward the Exile's father, in single combat with Canute to decide the fate of England, an illustration from *La Estoire de St Aedward the Rei* (Ms. Cantab. Ee iii 59; by permission of the Syndics of Cambridge University Library).

Canute and Edmund fought on a ship anchored in the Severn, with their warriors and retinues lining the banks of the river.

But perhaps the most graphic description of the combat between the rival kings of England survives in the *La Estoire de Seint Aedward le Rei*.[2]

> ... Then according to the general wish,
> Edmund and Cnut fought
> In single combat, as the English
> And the Danes proposed.
> Cnut was fierce as a dragon,
> Edmund bold as a lion;
> Nor could one find in the whole world
> An equal to Cnut and Edmund.
> When the one and the other consent to it,
> The kings arm themselves with great courtesy,
> With coats of mail and shining helmets,
> And mount their swift war horses;
> Their lances soon break,
> The splinters of which fly far;
> Then they seize their furbished brands,
> Now begins the combat;
> The blows are hard which each gives,
> Each in striking stuns the other;
> Nor on this side can the Englishman boast,
> Nor on the other side the Dane,
> The Earl displays more skill,
> But Edmund was more vigorous,
> For young and hardened was he;
> The other, wise and older [*sic*].
> And less gifted with strength,
> Feels that Edmund was long-winded;
> And the longer the fight lasts
> The fresher and fiercer leaps on him,
> And is stronger in the battle,
> And strikes with the greater violence;
> Nor can Cnut long endure;
> But he feigns himself quite fresh and strong,
> Makes a fierce assault on Edmund,
> Strikes and strikes again: so that from the middle
> Of Edmund's shield he breaks off a piece,
> Of his armour breaks a link,
> With his brand of steel which cuts so well.
> Then he says: 'Edmund, friend,
> Now listen to what I tell you.
> Much would be the grief and loss

14

If a youth of your age
Should perish, good son Edmund;
All the world would be injured.
Lord and king am I of the Danes,
And thou art king of the English;
Thy father is dead, certainly it is a loss,
For he was peaceable and wise;
Thy brothers are in Normandy,
Thou remainest alone, and without aid.
Thou hast been elected king of England,
But thou hast not the consent of all.
Nor can you so as to drive me out
Expel me from the country;
Pity seizes me of thy beauty,
Courage, good sense and boldness,
Thy gentleness and thy youth,
Who hast not more than thirty years,
I desire not to seek to oppose thee.
I dare not for God's sake do the sin;
Believe my counsel, that never in the world
You have heard of a more loyal one, Edmund.
Let us be kings in common
Of both one and the other people.
Do you have a share in my country,
And I a share of yours without fighting.
I covet your friendship more
Than kingdom, country or city:
As we were enemies,
Let us henceforward be friends;
Let neither in peace or in battle
Fail the other in this life,
And there will be no one who fears not
Among these princes our companionship. . .'
Edmund, who was debonair,
At these words would not be silent:
'Bold and courageous,
If treason had not been sown here,
At once would you have brought me to consent.
But treason fear I much.'
'Fear not', replied Cnut;
Then each throws away his brand,
And unlaces the shining helm,
And they kiss each other with gentleness;
When they saw it, both one and the other people

15

Had great joy; no fear is there;
English and Danes make one company.

Contrary to the assertion of the poet, who linked together two separate events in his narrative, there was no offer of friendship or truce immediately after the single combat but an even greater determination to prosecute the war. On 18 October Edmund caught up with Canute's host retreating to their ships at Ashington, in Essex, and decided to attack straightaway.

Ealdorman Eadric, by now clearly in league with the Danes, urged the English not to fight and, though Edmund's force was considerably larger than Canute's, tried to make out that against a foe as hardy as the Danes they stood no chance. As battle was joined he tried to incite them to flee the battle field and went on railing at his comrades that they were facing certain death unless they took to their heels.

When he saw that his words were having no effect, he lowered his banner and retreated with his bodyguard. The disappearance of his flag was taken as a signal and resulted in the withdrawal of a large part of Edmund's army from the battle.

Whatever explanation is given of Eadric's behaviour – and most contemporary chroniclers considered it a deliberate attempt to undermine the English army's will to fight – his treachery robbed Edmund of victory in a crucial engagement of the war. Edmund fought on with the remainder of his army till nightfall against Canute and Thorkill the Tall, who had rejoined the Danish side as predicted by most level-headed Anglo-Saxons. But Eadric's flight had made the outsome of the battle a foregone conclusion. Not even Edmund's inspired words of encouragement to his soldiers could change that.

'Oh Englishmen', he told his host, 'today you must fight or surrender yourselves altogether. Therefore, fight for your liberty and your country, men of understanding. Truly, those who are in flight, inasmuch as they are afraid, if they were not withdrawing, would be a hindrance to my army.'

In the end, in spite of Edmund's great personal bravery, there was nothing for the English but to take flight under cover of darkness and to seek refuge at safe, nearby places. Although his army was badly mauled, Edmund retained the hope that eventually he might raise a more powerful force, and with their help try to turn the fortune of war in his favour.

The Danes did not pursue Edmund's fleeing army. They too had suffered heavy casualties in the battle, furthermore, they were not familiar with the lie of the land so they thought it safer to stay put. In effect, both sides were totally exhausted and, while Eadric's treachery deprived the English of outright victory, Canute was far from winning the upper hand. Edmund's success at London, the keypoint of the struggle for supremacy, assured him a fair position in the inevitable peace talks, which were dictated by the logic of the situation. Canute would certainly not have consented to the parley had he felt strong enough to continue the fight.

Ealderman Eadric's ambiguous position was used to open talks with Canute and, despite Edmund's great reluctance, those in his army wishing for peace prevailed and envoys were sent to the Danish camp with the peace terms. Both the *Anglo-Saxon Chronicle* and the *Encomium* confirm that Eadric helped to bring about the negotiations, which took place at Olney, near Deerhurst, in Gloucestershire.

A division of the country between the two kings became inevitable, sounding the death knell of the independent and unified Anglo-Saxon kingdom. Some chroniclers, however, insist that the accord of Olney resulted in peace and friendship, and this evaluation was, surprisingly enough, shared by Florence of Worcester.

The English negotiators offered a fair deal: Canute should rule the north and Edmund the south of the country. But they added that unless Canute accepted the accord as it stood Edmund would fight on with strengthened resolve and increased ferocity.

After long deliberation, Canute agreed to the peace terms, but insisted that, as a punishment, Edmund must pay tribute to his army. Without this payment there could be no talk of peace, he insisted.

The details of the agreement were preserved in a number of contemporary annals. The dividing line between the two kingdoms was to be the Thames, and Edmund was to rule Wessex and Canute the *northdael*, according to the *Anglo-Saxon Chronicle* (Ms. 'D'). However, other chronicle manuscripts give Canute Mercia instead of *northdael*, and the fate of Essex and East Anglia seems far from clear from the surviving accounts of the agreement. Florence insisted that London was assigned to Edmund, but Canute was allowed to winter in the unconquered city indicating that, like the levying of Danegeld on Edmund's truncated territory, this was part of the peace terms.

Of far greater importance both for the future of the English kingdom and the fate of Edmund Ironside's two young sons, was the question of succession. While the territorial division had to be clear and unambiguous if further fighting was to be avoided, the succession issue – involving an implicit acceptance of an inferior role by one of the contracting parties – might well have proved too difficult to solve in the emotional atmosphere of Olney and was, therefore, left deliberately vaguely worded in the peace agreement. After all, both Edmund and Canute were young men and, at the start of a long period of peaceful coexistence, succession probably did not seem a pressing issue to them.

The decision to become sworn brothers underlines their intention to put off *sine die* the problem by opting for an equivocal rather than a cut-and-dried arrangement. As befitting elective relations, according to the Norse *Knytlingasaga* and Henry Huntingdon's chronicle, they agreed that whoever outlived the other should inherit the dead brother's kingdom. This impression is confirmed by Edmund's acceptance of this Scandinavian custom which, as he well knew it, went against the Anglo-Saxon tradition of succession.

The acceptance of this ambiguous formula was to give hostages to fortune. For, although the peace halted the Norse depredations, the survival of the sole remaining English kingdom hinged on the physical survival of Edmund Ironside. And with the unscrupulous Eadric Streona ready for any mischief or treason to enhance his own position, this was a virtual invitation to murder.

In the event, Edmund Ironside's reign proved tragically short. Within a month of becoming Canute's sworn brother he was dead. His untimely demise sealed the fate of the Anglo-Saxon kingdom and appeared to fulfil St Dunstan's prophecy about the sword of fate hanging above the house of Aethelred the Unready.

William Malmesbury's appraisal of his worldly errand could serve as his epitaph: 'He would have shrouded the indolence of his father, and the meanness of his mother, by his own conspicuous virtue, could the fates have spared him . . . He died soon after [the division of England], on the festival of St Andrew, though by what mischance is not known.'[3]

As the Year of Grace 1016 was drawing to its close, Canute stood to become the undisputed ruler of England. Merlin's promising prophecy about the Man of Bronze who was to regain power for the Anglo-Saxons, did not come true. Indeed, the tribulations of a new generation of Aethelred's house – the children of Edmund Ironside – were just beginning. But then St Dunstan had clearly predicted that the sins of Aethelred shall be expiated only by long, continued punishment of his house.

3. *Murder royal in the privy: a turncoat's tale*

Edmund's death stunned the country. Even in an age when people often died suddenly and violently, the king's unexpected death gave rise to a welter of gossip and innuendo. He was young and healthy and of an unusually robust constitution, as his given name 'Ironside' showed. He was also strong and warlike, always in the vanguard of the fighting against Canute, a man of boundless energy who could govern, raise armies, pursue the enemy through the length and breadth of England, and inspire his country's resistance. The image that his countrymen perceived of him was certainly not of a sickly laggard who would die in his bed of one of his many ailments.

It was, therefore, a natural and legitimate question that people at the time, and in the ensuing centuries, asked themselves: whose interest would his death have served? The motive of the crime, if crime it was, can easily be established and the posing of the question *cui bono*? would, like a divining rod in the hands of a gifted dowser, lead the investigator straight to Canute.

Edmund alone stood between Canute and the subjugation of the whole of England, a single life in the way of the fulfilment of a dream of power and conquest. Furthermore, Canute was not squeamish in his methods and his ruthless resolve, shown in the months after Edmund's death, to eliminate all potential claimants to the crown of England revealed him in his true light.

But motive is not proof of guilt, the establishment of personal interest in the crime is not actual evidence that would stand up in a court of law. In a fair investigation of an act that had a direct bearing on the fate of the heirs of the English crown, the hidden motives and obvious biases of the chroniclers of the time must also be scrutinized and the question asked: whose interest would Canute's implication in the crime have served?

The Norse writers and bards had a vested interest in clearing their kith and kin's name, and the Anglo-Norman annalists had a similar interest in denigrating Canute. In unravelling the tangled strands of fact and fiction the most surprising realisation is that there is no evidence of Canute's direct involvement in any of the authoritative contemporary documents. That, however, does not rule out the possibility that Edmund was struck down in response to, or anticipation of, a hint from the Dane and the early practioners of the historical 'whodunit' genre have seen to it that there are a sufficient number of pointers in that direction.

The Encomiast used a euphemism to skate over the thin ice of Edmund's demise, contenting himself with a hint that whatever had happened was divine providence and in the best interest of England. A kingdom divided against itself could not survive for long, he averred, and the Good Lord, pitying the realm of the English, removed Edmund from the world of the living lest the kingdom should be continually wasted by renewed fighting.

Coming as it did from a hand that was explicitly employed to praise Canute's wife, not incriminate her lord, the linking of Edmund's death with the dangers of two kings ruling the same country is most significant. Although the general drift of the argument could be interpreted either way, the fact that he omitted to mention the name of the man widely rumoured at the time to have murdered Edmund is most suspicious. Indeed, considering his openly-acknowledged debt to Canute's house, it could be construed as a deliberate suppression of an act of treason that would have cast a slur on the husband of his patron.

Some contemporary accounts placed Edmund's murder in London, others in Oxford, but both versions claimed that Edmund 'perished by the treason'. Since Oxford was the seat of Eadric Streona and, according to the *Anglo-Saxon Chronicle* the earls Sigeferth and Morcar were murdered at his house there in 1015, Eadric's implication in the crime was obvious. Indeed, he was named as the murderer in most works.

A Latin-language account written within about a generation of Edmund's death said the king was murdered by Eadric in London.[1] A similar version can be found in the Icelandic Snorri Sturlusson's *Heimskringlasaga*: 'King Canute then made an agreement with King Edmund, that each of them should have half of England. In the same month Henry Strion murdered King Edmund.'

The intention of these acounts to place the blame squarely at the door of Streona, Edmund's turncoat brother-in-law and confidant, and thus exonerate Canute, would have been much more successful had it not been for two other extant Norse versions accusing Canute of direct involvement. The poet Sighvat recounted that 'Now all the sons of Aethelred were either fallen, or had fled; some slain by Canute', while the *Knytlingasaga* bluntly stated that Eadric killed Edmund, after having been bribed by Canute.[2]

The English versions, based mainly on the works of twelfth-century Anglo-Norman chroniclers, seemed to have become clearer and more elaborate in the retelling. They too pointed an accusing finger at Eadric, but provided no more than hints of Canute's own role in the murder.

The only notable exception among the near-contemporary keepers of England's historical accounts was Florence of Worcester, who apparently preferred to follow the line taken by the *Anglo-Saxon Chronicles* in record-

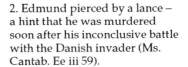

2. Edmund pierced by a lance –
a hint that he was murdered
soon after his inconclusive battle
with the Danish invader (Ms.
Cantab. Ee iii 59).

ing the simple, ascertainable fact of Edmund's death to trusting the more colourful reports and hearsay still extant in his time. There is no mention of Eadric, or actual murder, and reticence is the more significant as he is quite forthcoming about Eadric's other nefarious acts.

William of Malmesbury, on the other hand, succeeded in involving both Eadric and Canute in the murder, while at the same time protecting his integrity with a journalistic sleight-of-hand, boldly asserting, after having recounted all the damning details of the current accusations, that the cause of Edmund's death was uncertain.

The main outline of his case against Eadric is not unlike that of Henry of Huntingdon and a number of other Anglo-Norman chroniclers, who provide variations of the same basic story.

'Fame asperses Eadric, as having, through regard for Canute, compassed his death by means of his servants', wrote Malmesbury. 'Reporting that there were two attendants on the king to whom he had committed the entire care of his person, and, that Eadric seducing them by promises, at length made them his accomplices, though at first they were struck with horror at the enormity of the crime.'

All variants maintain that Edmund was murdered in a particularly beastly and painful fashion. They only differ in naming the murderer as Eadric himself, as his son or his two servants. According to Malmesbury, Eadric's servants drove an iron hook into his bottom as he was sitting down to relieve himself. In the *La Estoire de Seint Aedward le Rei*, Eadric slew him treacherously in the lavatory; Roger of Wendover has a similar story to tell, while Capgrave, drawing on a number of sources, accused Eadric's son of murdering Edmund with a sharp basulard which he stuck in the king's bowels.

John of Brompton gave three versions of the murder, the quaintest among them describing a rather advanced mechanical device that was used by Eadric to kill the king at Oxford. It involved a specially constructed wooden figure with a taut bow in his hands that was placed by his host in the king's bedroom. As Edmund touched the figure the arrow went off and killed him.

There can be little doubt that Geoffroi Gaimar's early twelfth-century history, *L'Estoire des Engleis* served as the source and inspiration of Brompton's story.[3] According to Gaimar, the contraption was so constructed that

> if anything touched the string soon one would hear bad news. Even a bason, if it struck it, it would split it with the arrow. Where this bow was prepared he had placed a new house, privy house they call it, men went there for that purpose.
>
> The king was taken there at night, as Eadric had commanded. Directly he sat on the seat the arrow struck him in the fundament. It went up as far as the lungs. The feather never showed of the arrow, which was in his body. And no blood came forth. The king cried a death cry, the soul fled from him, he was no more. There was no recovery ... May God, if it pleases him, do justice on the evil felon, the traitor, who thus murdered his lord.

The many variations on the manner in which Edmund was murdered according to extant accounts can in no way eclipse the crucial fact that his death served Canute's interests and that Eadric was a traitor and a Danish collaborator. The charges preferred against them could, perhaps, not be proved in a court of law without reasonable doubt, but the quaint innuendo of the Encomiast would have weighed more heavily than the silence of Florence of Worcester in convincing the judges that Canute and Eadric were far from innocent of Edmund's blood.

The people of England were, no doubt, perfectly aware of the facts. They mourned their king for a long time but accepted the inevitable. His death put an end to the country's hopes of ridding itself of the invaders, hopes so cruelly raised by his valour, leadership and military prowess.

The leaderless and demoralized country had no choice but to accept Canute's rule.

The seemingly endless waves of Norse raids had sapped the will to resist, the levies of Danegeld had drained the resources of not only the rich towns and monasteries, but also of the farming communities, and the people were desperate for peace.

Ingulph, the Abbot of Croyland, a discerning observer of the people of the British Isles, well reflected this mood in his chronicle and, eventually, came to welcome Canute's rule because he saw it as offering the country a measure of security and peace. In evaluating the first year of Canute's rule, he noted the fulfilment of these expectations: 'The storms of battle had ceased and the serenity of peace had begun to shed prosperity upon the times.'

But this peace did not extend to Aethelred's fated house. It was a royal house divided against itself, rent by dissension, shamed by scandal and reeling under the strain of losing two kings within a single year. Having been forced twice to seek refuge abroad, first by Sweyn's campaign then by Canute's war, they were once again facing the stark choice of probable murder or exile.

Only Emma (Aelfgifu), Aethelred's widow, showed great determination to break away from England's doomed ruling house and to move to the winning side as fast as her position and dignity allowed. Since she was the daughter of Duke Richard of Normandy, she found no difficulty in distancing herself from the defeated English. Although she had borne Aethelred several children, she was still beautiful enough to charm the much younger conqueror of England and lure him to her bed. Her beauty was acknowledged by the chronicler Henry of Huntingdon, who described her as 'Emma Normannorum gemma' ('the gem of the Normans').

Canute soon married Emma, and the Encomiast writing under her personal guidance, took great pains to explain the marriage as a political step, aimed at assuring racial harmony between the English and the Danes. But since the marriage of a Norman princess to a Dane could hardly reconcile the English to their conquerors, her nuptial bond to Canute could only have served her own private interests and boundless ambitions.

In her eagerness to sever all her links with the past and identify more fully with the new man in her life, she was perfectly willing to abandon her children to their fate and start a new family. Her new-found allegiance is well reflected in the tenor of the *Encomium*, whose author appears to have been instructed to suppress the very fact that Canute's queen had once been the wife of Aethelred or that she had been the first lady of the battered Anglo-Saxon royal house.

But she was judged harshly even by the Anglo-Normans who could find no excuse for her perfidy. William of Malmesbury, whose father came to England from Normandy during the Conquest, berated the Duke of Normandy because he married his sister, Emma, to the enemy and invader. And he wondered whether it was 'to the greater ignominy of him who bestowed her, or of the woman who consented to share the nuptial couch of that man who had so cruelly molested her husband'.

There was no love lost between Emma and her stepson, Edmund, and the suspicious circumstances of his death did not seem to have worried her too much or stopped her from marrying his deadly adversary. The rift dated back to Edmund's secret marriage to Ealdgyth, the earl Sigeferth's Swedish-born widow, in 1015 (in spite of Aethelred's strenuous efforts to prevent it). The scandal surrounding Edmund's secret love affair with the murdered earl's wife, held prisoner at Malmesbury, resulted in a further rift within the family and led to an icy relationship between the two women.[4]

Canute's determined efforts after the take-over to eliminate all actual and potential claimants to the throne of England bode ill for Ealdgyth and her tiny children, young Edmund, nearly one-year-old, and Edward, a newborn babe.[5] In fact, the strange remark in Gaimar's history that Edmund was given a royal funeral but 'his Queen did not know it' can only be taken as a hint that she and her children were already being held prisoner at the beginning of December 1016, or that she was then confined with Edward.

The manner in which Canute rid himself of Aethelred's sons must have filled Ealdgyth with fear for the lives of her children. The new king wrongfully banished the relations and friends of King Aethelred from the country, or had them treacherously put to death, wrote Edward the Confessor's biographer. Malmesbury too reported that Edmund's brothers were driven into exile by Eadric at the command of Canute.

The fatal consequences of the inheritance clause of the Olney peace accord were brought home to the defenceless Ealdgyth. Her children were taken away from her and there was no one who would protect the lives of Edmund Ironside's sons, the heirs of the Anglo-Saxon crown.

Gaimar, whose work was based on the *Anglo-Saxon Chronicle*, oral tradition and other contemporary sources now lost, reported that the prime mover against the two aethelings was none other than Eadric, the turncoat duke.

> Before ever [Ealdgyth] knew it
> Or any man could tell her,
> To Cnut they were brought directly.
> This did Eadric, the traitor.
> Thus he thought to increase his honour.

The lives of Edmund and Edward Aetheling hung in the balance. Canute summoned the nobles who had witnessed the pact between himself and Edward at Olney, as they were charged with the accord's supervision, but they did not speak up for the aethelings. If there was some clause favouring Edmund's male heirs[6] in the agreement, there was no one in the country who would stand up to demand its enforcement.

John Stow, the Elizabethan antiquarian, who appears to have been interested in the issue, gave an incisive analysis of Canute's action and the aethelings' predicament in his encyclopaedic book *General Chronicle of England*:

Canutus the Dane, taking an occasion, because in the covenant that was concluded concerning the dividing of the *Realme*, no assurance was made for the children of Edmund, he challenged all England to *himselfe* alone by the law they call it, *of growing to*, which was a most *easie* thing for him to *doe*, because there was no man that durst erect *himselfe* as patrone to defende the children's Right and Title, and by this subtile and *craftie* interpretation of the covenant, the Dane got the Monarchie of England . . .[7]

4. A 'Letter of death': Canute's choice of murder by proxy

Canute began his rule with a wave of executions and massacres. The elimination of all those who could in any way threaten or challenge his hold on England was intended to cow the rest of the population into supine submission. Amid the death-throes of the Anglo-Saxon kingdom the cries of the innocents were hardly noticed. After centuries of Norse depredations the English seemed to have run out of tears.

Yet even in the midst of all the fear and apathy in the New Year of 1017, the murder of Eadwig, Edmund Ironside's brother and a popular youth, aroused a sense of revulsion and impotent anger. But Canute brushed these tremulous protests aside and continued to consolidate his victory in his own fashion, accentuating the pathetic helplessness of the vanquished.

With Aethelred's sons Alfred and Edward in exile and Edwin dead, Canute had to resolve the threat posed by the existence of Edmund Ironside's children before he could settle down to enjoy in peace the fruits of his conquest. Although he had shown ruthless determination in eliminating everyone who could come between the Crown of England and himself, for the first time he hesitated.

It was certainly not squeamishness nor moral compunction that stopped him from having Edmund and Edward Aetheling killed. According to Anglo-Saxon tradition, the aethelings were the direct heirs to the Crown and their elimination, therefore, required a political solution.

He rejected Eadric's suggestion – recorded by Florence and Simeon of Durham – that the boys be murdered straightaway, and put them personally in the care of the Abbot of Westminster, while seeking to find a better way of ridding himself of their presence.

His ostentatious protection of the aethelings' lives and his show of respect for the Westminster sanctuary, so becoming to a recent convert to Christianity, went a long way to allay the fears of the pro-Ironside Londoners. Nevertheless, the Christman Gemot (Great Council) accepted that owing to his new position, Canute could not honour his duties as the 'sworn brother' of Edmund Ironside and look after his children.

According to Florence, the status of the aethelings was also discussed at the Gemot. Since the immediate exiling of Edmund's brothers gave an indication that the brothers of the contracting parties were formally excluded from the succession by the Olney Treaty, the reported discussion of the status of Edmund's children could be taken as a proof, however circumstantial, that some vaguely-phrased stipulations of their rights were included in the pact. In any case, their title of aethelings assured them, under the Anglo-Saxon custom, of a preference in the case of any future vacancy on the throne of England.

Because of this, and Canute's ostentatious gesture of protection, Florence's claim that the fate of the aethelings was actually decided at the 1016 Christmas Gemot, seems unlikely. The decision to send them out of the country in order to be murdered in secret must have been taken later, and certainly not by the Gemot. For no assembly, however supine, could accede to the murder by proxy of two aethelings of the true English line. That decision could only have been taken by Canute.

Gaimar claims that the decision to have them taken out of England, and thus deprive the English of a focal point of resistance, was prompted by Emma. Unfortunately, he omits to give his authority for this interesting aside on the way the aethelings' future was decided.

According to Gaimar, Canute rode to Emma's house to seek her advice before taking such a difficult decision. On learning that the aethelings were at the Westminster sanctuary, she warned Canute: 'Sir, believe me, you must take other steps. These are the right heirs of the land, if they live they will make war. While you can have peace if you take my advice: cause it to be known that they are taken to another land. Beware of their doing harm. Trust them to such a man that they may be kept from [doing] evil.'

Emma's suggestion, made perhaps with an eye on the succession of her yet unborn children by Canute, tied in neatly with both the new king's inclination and the old royal tradition of murder by proxy.

The sending of a dangerous rival or threatening heir abroad with a 'letter of death' ordering their destruction there was a stratagem well known in the Europe of the Middle Ages. Canute's choice of having the aethelings put to death by one of his Scandinavian vassals would have been the perfect solution to an awkward situation. It was certainly a politician's choice: no direct link with the murder, no untoward repercussions at home and the threat posed by the aethelings to his crown painlessly removed. Besides, his own countrymen would not saddle him with the guilt of a 'murder most foul', which the slaying of a sworn-brother's children would be in Scandinavian eyes.

It was a solution that ran in the family, as it were. Another King of Denmark, immortalized by Shakespeare, used a similar stratagem when he sent Amleth (Hamlet) to England with a 'letter of death' ordering his murder.

In his Book III, Saxo Grammaticus, the earliest historian of Denmark and recorder of its past, describes a virtual carboncopy plan by Feng, the defender of Jutland, to rid himself of the rightful heir to the throne of Denmark after having murdered Amleth's father and married his mother.

The usurper 'suspected that his stepson was certainly full of guile, and desired to make away with him, but *durst* not do the deed for fear of the displeasure, not only of Amleth's grandfather Rorik, but also of his wife. So he thought that the king of Britain should be employed to slay him, so that another could do the deed, and he be able to feign innocence. Thus, desirous to hide his cruelty, he chose rather to besmirch his friend than to bring disgrace on his own head.'

Most near-contemporary chroniclers, and especially the Anglo-Norman writers of the following century, recorded Canute's plan to have the aethelings murdered in Sweden, although inevitably there are a fair number of variations in the place of the children's destination. However, they all seem to agree that the King of Sweden refused to play the role of the executioner, took pity on the children and sent them on a further journey out of Canute's reach.

Gaimar's account of the events of 1017 provides a different timetable. Although he must have known the generally accepted version, current in the twelfth century, that the aethelings were sent directly to Sweden, with a letter of death, he insists that they were first taken to Denmark by a Danish nobleman called Walgar. He was to bring them up there in a style fit for the children of Canute's sworn-brother.

Reassuringly, the move to Denmark is also reported by Orderic Vitalis, the well-informed twelfth-century monk of Evroult. Unhappily, however, he got the name of the king of Denmark, to whom allegedly the aethelings were sent, wrong. Although Canute had a brother, called Harold, who actually ruled Denmark, he never had a brother called Sweyn, as reported by Orderic. The mere fact that the monk had heard about the first leg of the aethelings' exile to Denmark is, of course, more important than the confusion over who actually ruled Denmark at the time.

> They entrusted the two lads to him
> Who were king's sons, and noble,
> He received them, to nourish them well,
> To bring them up and keep them.
> He thought indeed that if he lived,
> He would bring them up in great honour.
> What shall I say? He departed,
> And went to Denmark.
> With the children he went.
> One was called Eadgar [*sic*]
> The other's name was Aethelred.
> This was the younger lad.
> Well were they kept and well nourished.[1]

The seeming contradictions contained in this version – that the aethelings were merely removed from England – are resolved by Gaimar with the introduction of Canute's murder attempt at a later stage in the children's life, indicating a knowledge of certain subsequent historical events left out of all the other chronicles.

That he actually got the names of Edmund Ironside's children wrong – even though the people and the events were virtually within living memory – is of no great significance. History was not recorded with great accuracy, even by the most scrupulous annalists of the time, and Gaimar's *L'Estoire des Engleis* was written with an eye on a popular readership among the Anglo-Norman aristocracy.

The recording of historical facts is a highly selective act at the best of times. This must have been even more subjective in the years of consolidation following the Danish conquest, when the needs of the conqueror and the conquered, the new and the old ruling houses, were diametrically opposed. A partisanship was demanded of the chronicler, a slant to reflect the new political imperatives and allegiances.

This partisanship required of the chroniclers of Canute's era to reflect the legality of the new dynasty, or at least to suppress certain uncormfortable facts concerning the rights of the ousted royal house. The Encomiast, for instance, did not lie; he simply excised such issues. Hence the dearth of ascertainable facts concerning the fate of the aethelings in contemporary sources.

With the exponents of the Anglo-Saxon line either massacred or forced to flee abroad to save their lives, the need to write a balanced account of the consolidation process was removed. A stylized or highly-selective rendering of events suited much more the interests of both the various monasteries housing the annalists and Canute. Naturally, the interests of the victorious side, upon whose patronage and good will the monasteries were dependent, were uppermost in the minds of the chroniclers, and the propagandist aspect of their writings can hardly be overlooked.

The omissions, distortions and contradictions in these chroniclers made some of the reputable Anglo-Norman historians question their veracity. With the apparent intention of putting the record straight they rewrote history with the aid of still-extant accounts and garbled heresay, and introduced, however unwittingly, fresh political bias. But the more traditional chroniclers simply copied the available accounts, in accordance with monastic custom, further hardening their material into seemingly cast-iron facts.

However, both sets of chroniclers – and this includes historians of such differing political imperatives as the Encomiast and Gaimar – are agreed that the aethelings were removed from the country and that the arch-traitor Eadric was put to death by Canute in a hollow gesture of goodwill towards Anglo-Saxon public opinion. Whether the execution of Edmund Ironside's reputed murderer was sufficient to counter the dismay felt over the disappearance of the aethelings is doubtful. Nevertheless, it indicated popular concern over their fate.

The Encomiast makes out that Canute was determined to punish those of his new subjects who had betrayed his sworn-brother Edmund. By presenting the massacres that ushered in his reign as virtually an act of divine retribution for treason, the writer managed to tell at least part of the truth about those terrible, bloody days, while ostensibly conducting a public relations exercise, whitewashing his patron's husband:

> Canute loved those whom he had heard to have fought previously for Edmund faithfully without deceit, and he so hated those whom he knew to have been deceitful, and to have hesitated between the two sides with fraudulent tergiverzation, that on a certain day he ordered the execution of many chiefs for deceit of this kind. One of these was Eadric, who had fled from the war and to whom, when he asked for a reward for this from the king, pretending to have done it to ensure his victory, the king said: 'Shall you, who have deceived your lord with guile, be capable of being true to me? I will return to you a worthy reward, but I will do so to the end that deception may not subsequently be your pleasure.'
>
> And summoning Eirikr, his commander, he said: 'Pay this man what we owe him; that is to say, kill him least he play false.' He indeed raised his axe without delay and cut off his head with a mighty blow, so that soldiers may learn from this example to be faithful, not faithless, to their king.

Florence of Worcester accepted somewhat naively this explanation of Eadric's execution but Gaimar links it directly to Eadric's role in the abduction of the aethelings from their mother after Edmund's murder and his suggestion that they too be put to death. His version of events, linking a notorious traitor's execution to an issue of popular interest like the aethelings' fate, rather than the more abstract notion of soldiers' duty to their kings, appears to be closer to the facts as established by the present investigation. The *Anglo-Saxon Chronicle* affirms that Eadric's execution took place in 1017, that is a few months later than in Gaimar's chronology.

> To London went this wicked felon.
> King Cnut was there and many a thane.
> Before the king he kneeled;
> In his ear he told him
> How he had dealt with Edmund,
> And of the children whom he had brought.
> When the king had heard it all,
> He was very sad and wroth.

He sent for the thanes;
He had the treason told them.
When he had proved it in their hearing,
He had Eadric taken, then he was led
To an ancient tower, situated so that
When the tide rises, the Thames beats it,
The king himself came after;
He sent for all the citizens.
He had an axe brought,
I know not if it had its equal under [the] heaven
In the forelock of the traitor
He caused a rod to be twisted round.
When the forelock was firmly held
King Cnut came straightaway.
He gave him a quick stroke
From the body he severed the head.
He had the body thrown down,
The tide came up outside.
He made them throw out the felon's head;
Both went towards the deep sea.
The living devil take them.
Thus ended Eadric Streona.
And the king said to his household,
So that many heard it:
This man slew my brother.
In him I have avenged all my friends.[2]

With the unerring instinct of the medieval minstrel, who combined the roles of reporter, gossip-columnist and historian, Gaimar focused upon the single event of the preceding century that still concerned and passionately interested the public of his time – the fate of the aethelings. Without knowing it, he contributed to the genesis of a legend that, in changing forms, has remained a favourite subject of royal propagandists, committed chroniclers and historical sleuths to this day.

The emotive force of the plot to murder the royal princes was such that the chroniclers of the post-1066 period could hardly resist the temptation to exploit it to fresh political ends and to use it as a peg for new values intended to show up the superiority of the Norman world. Florence of Worcester, Simeon of Durham, Roger of Hoveden, Bishop Ealdred, Henry of Huntingdon, Ranulph of Chester and William of Malmesbury, to name the more outstanding, all succumbed to the lure of the legend.

Their integrity attracted later generations of historians to the sorrowful story of the aethelings, greatly contributing to its conversion into a legend of a more enduring form. The horrified reaction of the honest Anglo-Norman chroniclers to Canute's attempted murder of two innocent princes drove home its proven propaganda value and, like several other powerful legends, it inspired more gifted writers with a political axe to grind. The theme of the 'doomed little princes and the usurper' can be traced through a chain of borrowings right up to Shakespeare.

Throughout the Middle Ages the story remained essentially unchanged. It followed Gaimar's account which already contained all the main component features of the legend: there is a good king, Edmund Ironside, and a ruthless usurper, Canute; there are merciless schemers and unscupulous courtiers ready to do the usurper's bidding; the henchman who murdered the good king also snatches the little princes from their mother; and there are the pitiful heirs to the throne doomed to an early death because of the usurper's lust for power.

The substitution of the aethelings with another, equally-charming set of royal princes provided the writers of the Tudor period with a most rewarding subject and a devastating propaganda weapon. Sir Thomas More was the first among the humanists to resurrect the parable of the wicked usurper and the doomed little princes as a vehicle for his fight against royal tyranny.

The metamorphosis of the aethelings' story into the murder of the princes in the Tower occurred while he was writing his *History of the Reign Of Richard III*. He never finished it. Its fictionalized construction and references to 'old wives' tales' as some of his sources, appeared to emphasize that Sir Thomas was dramatizing a period of history for political purposes. The Tudor butterfly that emerged from the aethelings' story in Sir Thomas's version proved more enthralling than the original legend. The link between the medieval users of the legend and Shakespeare was clearly Sir Thomas, but it was the Bard, with his known pro-Tudor bias, who brought the theme to its apotheosis in *The Tragedy of King Richard III*. It was his second and, from both political propaganda and dramatic point of view, the more successful attempt to adapt the story of the doomed little princes to suit an entertainment for his time.

For what interested Shakespeare's audiences above all were the sources of sovereignty and the personality of power. Shakespeare himself was interested in themes with proven propaganda value and dramatic impact. Nothing could have made all this more palpable than a play in which supreme power is opposed by innocence, and the need for legitimacy eventually forces the usurper to resort to infanticides.

His first try was *Edmund Ironside*, a chronicle-history drama of some 2000 lines which survives in manuscript form (BL Egerton 1994). The authentication of this hitherto-anonymous Elizabethan work as an early Shakespeare has provided the organic link between the two sets of princes and Shakespeare.

This crucially important work has been dated to circa 1590 and positively indentified as from Shakespeare's pen by E.B.Everitt [3] and Eric Sams [4], confirming the assumption of this investigation that in writing his *Richard*

III, the Bard was indeed indebted to the tribulation of Edmund Ironside's children.

Edmund Ironside treats factually the struggle for the crown of England between Ironside and Canute, and paints the historical background to the aethelings' tribulations. Significantly, the action takes place in the spring and summer of 1016, when Ironside's children were not yet orphaned.

Shakespeare must have intended to save the dramatic climax of the theme – the murder by proxy of the royal princes – for a later act or another play. But to develop the theme and advance the action from the summer of 1016 to 1017, when Ironside's orphaned children faced death from the usurper, Shakespeare had to employ more dramatic means. He made, it seems, *Richard III* a natural sequel to his *Ironside* by having the good king murdered early on by the usurper. And by also changing the key scene – from intended murder by proxy abroad to actual pitiless slaying in the Tower – he achieved a dramatically and politically more compelling climax.

Thus the five-centuries-old story of the doomed little princes became a drama of unrivalled impact, and King Richard the most horrendous child-murderer in English history. The aethelings' story had come into its own as a political propaganda weapon.

The aethelings' parable as pawns in the harsh struggle for power reappears in various shapes in at least two other plays – *The Life and Death of King John* and *Cymbeline* – spanning Shakespeare's entire creative life. Plays about ruthless usurpers and defenceless heirs to the throne were fruitful subjects, arousing spontaneous responses in Elizabethan audiences craving assurances on justice, legitimacy and sovereignity.

As for King Richard's reputation and historical truth, these should not be based on plays, however emotive and powerful, written for entertainment. Richard III, if indeed he had a hand in the murder of the two little princes, did no more than what Canute was trying to achieve with his 'letter of death'.

Yet ever since Shakespeare, anyone daring to question the hand behind 'the most arch deed of piteous massacre that ever yet this land was guilty of' is considered to be delving into history with crooked fingers. Such is the staying power of the aethelings' story immortalised by a genius of a propagandist.

PART II: THE ROAD INTO EXILE

5. The Resentful English look to the aethelings for deliverance: the restoration plot pre-empted by Queen Emma's 'evil coup'

In the first decade of Danish rule the Church and an influential section of the Anglo-Saxon nobility came to an understanding with the Conqueror. There was peace in the country and under Canute's protective sword the murderous Norse raids had been stopped, a protection which not many Anglo-Saxon kings were able to provide in the preceding two centuries. Those who collaborated with the foreign ruler could justly claim – not unlike the apologists of present-day dictators – that Canute's firm government had eliminated the degeneracy, feebleness and loose social order of Aethelred's rule.

This image of Canute as a 'stern but just' king was augmented by the contemporary portrayal of England's conqueror and his queen, Emma, as a handsome, happy couple, much given to good works and the patronage of the arts. There is a striking drawing of Canute and Emma, preserved in the *Liber Vitae* at Hyde Abbey, showing them with an outsize gold cross they had presented to the new Winchester Minster. Angels hold the pious couple's crowns, and a group of cowled and tonsured monks watch in prayerful atitude this admirable act of royal largesse. This benign image of Canute, endorsed by the Church as the illustration shows, was designed to reflect the mood of a country reconciled to its conqueror. His dynasty was now well established (Emma having borne him two children), and he had good reason to expect that the glamour of his ruling house would eclipse the memory of Edmund Ironside and his ousted heirs.

Yet in spite of the outward signs of reconciliation, popular interest in the fate of the aethelings did not fade. On the contrary, it became stronger with the hardening of the Danish grip on England.

One of the reasons was the seething resentment aroused by the arrogance of the invaders. The Danes had not only made themselves at home at the expense of the indigenous population, but took every opportunity to emphasize their superiority. The rights of free men were being eroded; farming communities were ill-treated by their new Danish masters, and ordinary people found themselves second-class citizens in their own country. They did not like it. The Encomiast, writing within living memory of these humiliations, regarded this hostility as 'natural and justified'.[1]

A careful reading of near-contemporary works reveals a long list of popular grievances. Violence, rape and dispossession were common occurrences; injustice and humiliation were the concomitants of their condition. But the arrogance of the conquerors semed the hardest to bear: the Danes 'often shamed' the English and 'held them cheap'.

The Danes insisted, for instance, on being greeted with obeisance by the natives: 'If a hundred met one Dane alone it was bad for them if they did not bow.' The Danes also expected privileged treatment at public places and preference in every walk of life. If a group of English villeins met a Dane at a bridge, they had to wait until the Dane walked across at his leisure. And if they did not bow to him, 'shamefully men beat them, so cheap were the English, so the Danes insulted them'.

The daily humiliations kept the pot of resentment simmering and, as a result of occasional Danish excesses, from time to time it boiled over. In their plight the leaderless Anglo-Saxons looked to the exiled sons of Edmund Ironside for deliverance. But they had no organization and their amateurish attempts at restoration posed no serious danger to Canute's rule. This focusing of the country's hopes on the aethelings drew fresh attention to them, underlining the fact that as long as they were alive the widespread desire to see an heir of the true Anglo-Saxon royal house on the throne would lead to further restoration attempts.

Gaimar gives the date of one of these plots as having taken place some twelve years after the sending of the aethelings out of the country. 'To England came the news that their heirs were grown up. Greatly the English rejoiced, for they did not like the Danes. They made ready ships and would send thither [Denmark], when this was told to the Queen, whose name was Emeline [Emma].'

Emma certainly watched like a she-tigress over the succession rights of her children by Canute – Harthacanute and Gunhild – and the Anglo-Saxon restoration attempt at around 1028 turned her with fresh fury against the aethelings. Gaimar is very persuasive in claiming that Emma was once again the prime-mover of the demand that Edward and Edmund Aetheling be wiped off the face of the earth, and John of Brompton, drawing upon contemporary oral tradition, bears this out.[2] Having had her sons by Aethelred banished to Normandy, Ironside and Eadwig murdered, and her marriage contract specifically stipulating that the throne of England should pass to Canute's children by her, to the exclusion of offspring by any other woman, she was obviously not prepared to take further chances with the aethelings.

'The two lads troubled her', according to Gaimar, as much for her son's as for her husband's sake, 'and she wished them much ill.' This ambitious woman was clearly prepared to go to any lengths to eliminate the exiled rivals and, inspired by the succession of English restoration attempts, she devised 'an evil plan'.

> To her lord she went, with bent head,
> 'Sire,' she said, 'you know not
> The sons of Edmund will be sent for:
> The English say they are the rightful heirs.
> They wish to receive them instead of you.'
> Canute replied: 'Can this be so?'
> Yes, dear lord, at Porchester
> Is a ship prepared
> Which will bring them with a great company.'
> The king sent straightaway,
> They found the ship ready.
> They took harness and rigging,
> They put the men in prison.
> They came back to tell the tidings to the king.
> When he heard all, he was full of wrath.
> Then he had his writs sealed,
> And sent beyond the sea
> To his two sons, who were there
> And held Denmark.
> He bade them, and his barons
> To take the lads
> And maim them secretly
> So they could not be cured.[3]

Emma's counterfeit restoration attempt appears to have goaded Canute into action. However, although she might have served as a catalyst, Canute was reacting to a potential threat to his throne within a much wider context. Having conquered England and secured it as a base for his empire building venture, in the late 1020s he was concerned with asserting his authority in Scandinavia.

In the autumn of 1027, he sailed to Denmark and wintered there with a big army in preparation for his campaign to subdue Norway and Sweden. His presence in Denmark provided a natural opportunity, in the light of Emma's claim of a pro-aetheling plot in England, to remove this small thorn in his flesh.

The order to have the aethelings maimed secretly fitted the mature Canute's character. There was a world of a difference between the youthful king of 1017, who cautiously sent potential rivals abroad with a letter of death, and the seasoned warrior-king of 1028 possessed of a dream of a Nordic empire, ordering the destruction of some minor irritants.

As Canute's giant dragon ship, propelled by 60 banks of rowers, was sailing at the head of an awe-inspiring battle fleet composed, in the words of Saxo, of 'huge ships remarkably well fitted out and grand', along the Danish islands towards Norway, the lives of Edmund and Edward hung in the balance for the second time in twelve years. This time the killers sent after the aethelings had the advantage of secrecy and surprise. With Canute's dragon ships instilling mortal terror along the rim of the North Sea, escape seemed impossible.

But help came from the most unexpected quarter – Canute's own war council. According to Gaimar's version of events, the order to have the aethelings murdered was very much against the liking of one of the Danish barons 'who would, if he could, turn it another way'. Whether his stand was the result of religious qualms, revulsion at child-murder, or secret symphathies for the English, is not possible to establish. Whatever his reasons, he helped to thwart Canute's plan and changed the course of English history.

He tipped off Earl Walgar, the aethelings' guardian and tutor in Denmark, urging him that, 'if he held them dear at all, he should send them away' out of Canute's reach. Thus the survival of the ancient Anglo-Saxon line hinged upon Walgar, a vassal of proven loyalty to Canute.

Walgar reacted to the dilemma posed by Canute's secret orders with compassion and common humanity in a supposedly ruthless age motivated by Viking virtues. He had sufficient moral strength to brush aside alleged interests of state and binding allegiance to his suzerain, and follow his conscience. He left without hesitation or delay his home, wealth and high office and 'put to sea in three ships' to save the lives of Edmund and Edward.

The extant documents of the period offer no conclusive proof whether the aethelings were saved from the daggers of the executioners by a conspiracy of hearts, as claimed by Gaimar's somewhat stylized history, or other, more down-to-earth political interests in Scandinavia. What can be said with certainty is that the removal of the Anglo-Saxon princes from Denmark in 1028 or 1029 tied in with the eastward flood of refugees from Norway seeking safety in Sweden. Under the onslaught of Canute's huge invasion force the Norsemen were facing defeat and King Olaf, together with his son Magnus, was forced to leave his country and shelter at the hospitable court of his ally, King Onund Jacob of Sweden.

The Norsemen were given a dose of their own medicine by Canute, compelling Sighvat the bard to explain the conquest of Norway with the words 'Our men are few, our ships are small, while England's king is strong in all.'

This is how the Norse scald recorded the terrifying spectacle of Canute and his ships descending upon Scandinavia:

> Canute is out beneath the sky
> Canute of the clear blue eye!
> The King is out on the ocean's breast

Leading his grand fleet West.
On to the East the ship-masts glide,
Glancing and bright each longship's side.
The conqueror of Aethelred,
Canute, is there, his foeman's dread:
His dragon with her sails of blue,
All bright and brilliant to the view,
High hoisted on the yard-arms wide,
Carries great Canute o'er the tide.
Brave is the royal progress – fast
The proud ship's keel obeys the mast,
Raising a surge on Lymfjord's strand.[4]

With Norway conquered and Canute's battle fleet in the neighbourhood, Sweden was hardly a safe place for the royal refugees. Nevertheless both King Olaf and Earl Walgar (with the aethelings) sought temporary refuge there. The aethelings' Swedish sojourn was recorded by ten out of fourteen near-contemporary Anglo-Norman chroniclers, and was also mentioned by Johan Messenius, the Bishop of Lund, in his *Scondia Illustrata*.

Even though the drama of Walgar's attempts to save the aethelings greatly exercised the Anglo-Norman chroniclers, their accounts of the princes' movements are contradictory and unreliable.

The paucity of reliable facts could be the natural result of the confusion sown by the work method of Anglo-Norman chroniclers. Another contributing factor was the monastic scribes' tradition of unquestioningly copying the materials of earlier accounts, thus compounding the errors of their predecessors. The honest mistakes of the chroniclers further hardened in the retelling of later generations, who never questioned the veracity of the original sources.

But there is a possibility that the confusion reigning in the near-contemporary accounts was, in part, due to Walgar's deliberate attempts to cover up his tracks and mislead everyone about the aethelings' escape route from Sweden. This would explain why the anonymous biographer of Edward the Confessor, who was not given to uncritical copying of old records, confidently asserted in about 1245 that no one knew what had happened to them ('mes nevuz, le fiz Aedmund ne seit nuls ke devenuz sunt'), even though the aethelings were the nephews of his eponymous hero.

Although it was not strictly true that historians of the thirteenth century had no knowledge of what had become of Edmund and Edward after their Swedish sojourn, the sum total of reliable facts is close to nil. In fact, the Continental odyssey of the two princes has remained shrouded in mystery to this day, despite a periodic interest in their fate.

This interest was fired by the realisation among the historians of the immediate post-Norman Conquest period that Edward Aetheling came to play a key role in Edward the Confessor's last minute attempt to keep the crown of England in Anglo-Saxon hands and thus forestall a Norman take-over. And this lent an extra dimension to the aethelings' story, at least as far as the Anglo-Norman writers were concerned, because, given the rapid integration of the Norman conquerors into the fabric of British society, delving into the Anglo-Saxon past became a respectable pastime.

But for a tragic stroke of fate the Norman Conquest might not have taken place and the oracles of the prophets of doom not come true. This crucial 'might-have-been' of British history alone would have justified this present endeavour to piece together the aethelings' 'missing' exile years and establish Edward's and his son's role in the turbulent events preceding 1066.

There are, however, other, equally compelling reasons: thanks to Edward Aetheling's marriage in exile the Anglo-Saxon royal house survived and, through the children born abroad, eventually expiated the curse placed on Aethelred's house.

6. *Twenty-nine false leads and a cold trail*

In 1029 the world must have looked a dangerous and inhospitable place to Walgar as he took stock of the situation and prepared to move on from Sweden with his charges. Edmund and Edward, still very vulnerable at the ages of 13 and 12 respectively, were being hunted by the assassins of the most powerful ruler of Northern Europe, while Walgar himself, having broken his fealty to his lord, was a marked man with no standing among Norsemen. It was not a combination to recommend them to any king or prince of the region.

There were other complicating factors that had to be taken into consideration. The repeated English attempts to get the heirs of the true English line back into the country had altered both the aethelings' international position and the terms of reference of Walgar's mercy mission. Instead of merely trying to save the children's lives, he now had to find a conveniently situated refuge where they could be in touch with developments in England and await the country's call. And that meant that he had to find a king not only sympathetic to the aethelings' cause but strong enough to face Canute's wrath.

The immediate needs for a safe haven and the exigences of the fight for the crown of England required diametrically-opposed solutions, deepening Walgar's dilemma. In order to shake off Canute's assassins, he had to take the children well outside the Norseman's traditional places of refuge, but a move away from north-west Europe would have made an active exile well-nigh impossible. Thus the first imperative ruled out the countries of the North Sea and the Baltic across which now stretched Canute's brash new empire, while the second militated for just such a choice.

The answer to be found in near-contemporary chronicles to Walgar's dilemma is bewildering: he took the rightful heirs to the Anglo-Saxon court to the court of the Hungarian king in south-east Europe. The north of Europe was the world of Walgar and the aethelings, a world made familiar by ties of kinship, and shared traditions, similarity of customs and social norms. A move to Hungary would have been so radical and the choice so extreme that it cannot be taken on trust. Nor can the testimony of these sources be completely ignored, however.

Since eighteen chroniclers nearest in time recorded the aethelings' flight to Hungary, there must be a kernel of truth in the hotchpotch of facts, hearsay and distorted events filling their annals. But to establish the truth, the chroniclers' common source of information must be traced and subjected to a diligent scrutiny. So must be their work methods.

Historical detective work is rarely hampered by deliberate deception on the part of medieval chroniclers, but it is made that much more difficult by their lack of a critical approach to evidence. Twelfth-century readers, for whom the majority of the chroniclers under scrutiny wrote, liked to have a rapid succession of bright incidents and adventures well seasoned with supernatural prognostications, but the reliability of facts did not concern them unduly. Chroniclers therefore paid more attention to amplifying their stories with anecdotes and strange occurrences than to the veracity of their sources. Events were not presented in terms of cause and effect nor the correct geo-political context because historiography was dominated by the aesthetic standards of contemporary vernacular fiction. Closely reasoned argument, well-grounded facts and chronological cohesion did not suit the prevailing episodic style of narrative, and so today's historical sleuth is confronted with a welter of unsubstantial information.

Even if the mode of the writing of history in twelfth-century England led to uncritical reporting, the chroniclers' honesty cannot be questioned. They wrote their annals to provide their readers with news of current events and posterity with a record of the past. There is a quaint aesthetic harmony between the form and content of the chronicles recording the aethelings' flight from Sweden, and if one wants to extract the actual truth from them, one has to use the tools of a paleographer and a crime investigator.

A first step towards gleaning the truth from the works of a handful of early twelfth-century chroniclers who were personally acquainted with members of Edward Aetheling's family circle or could draw on now lost primary sources was to gauge the effect of their work method. The uncritical copying of earlier works circulating in the channels of Europe's monastic network was a serious source of errors. This was compounded by garbled chronology, mispelled names, wrongly copied-out geographical placenames and misunderstood source materials.

In reading these chronicles, the total unreliability of geographic terms used by them was the most striking first impression. They used the words 'Souabi', 'Swevi' and 'Suavi' indiscriminately to describe the Swedes; Denmark was quite frequently referred to as 'Dacia'; and the Norwegians as 'Norici'. Even such a reliable historian as Orderic Vitalis erroneously called Denmark 'Dacia' and the ruler of Hungary 'the king of the Huns'.

An even greater source of error was the uncertainty of dating. Some monasteries used the Dionysian tables for recording events, others preferred the Dominical date. The confusion was deepened by the fact that the annalists did not have a fixed time for the start of their historical year and by the misreading of Roman numerals in copying. A further cause of garbled chronology was that so many events took place in the course of one year that the allotted space did not suffice, so that some of the transactions were entered in the space of preceding or following years.

To avoid these pitfalls and establish the truth about the aethelings' Continental odyssey it was necessary to catalogue all extant works mentioning Edmund and Edward and, with the aid of textual comparison and stylistic analysis, trace their common sources.

A textual comparison soon indicated who had cribbed or borrowed from whom, and so it became possible to reduce the twenty major works listed in Table 1 to six chronicles with varying degrees of original information. The details of the textual analysis, though the work itself was full of excitement, had to be left out of this present account because of the repetitive nature of the basic information running through the chronicles.

The closest account in time containing a reference to the Hungarian sojourn is to be found in the *Anglo-Saxon Chronicle* but the entry was dated 1057, the year of Edward Aetheling's return to England from Hungary. His return from that country could well have inspired the assumption pervading the entry that he had spent all his exile years there:

> Here came Edward Aetheling
> To Engla-land;
> He was King Edward's
> Brother's son,
> Edmund King,
> Who Ironside was called
> For his valour.
> This aetheling Cnut king
> Had sent away
> To Unger-land
> To be betrayed.
> But he grew up
> To a good man,
> As God him granted,
> And him well became.[1]

The *Anglo-Saxon Chronicle* confirms Canute's attempted murder-by-proxy but gives no facts on the exile route, on where Edward had grown up, or the time when he actually reached Hungary.

All the other works mention the Swedish first leg of their Continental peregrinations, and with the aid of stylistic comparison it is not too difficult to trace back the origin of this seemingly vital information to Florence of Worcester's *Chronicon ex Chronicis*. If later works are added to this list (see Table 2), the ruinous effect of the unquestioning copying of original information becomes more apparent.

Table 1.

No.	Date	Chronicler	Work	Aethelings' exile route
1.	1057	Anon.	*Anglo-Saxon Chronicle*	Direct to Hungary
2.	1100–18	Florence of Worcester	*Chronicon ex Chronicis*	King of Sweden; then court of King Salamon of Hungary
2a.	1100–18	Florence of Worcester	*Regalis Prosapia Anglorum*	King of Sweden; then Hungary
3.	1130	Simeon of Durham	*Hist. de Gestis Regum Angl.*	King of Sweden; court of King Salamon of Hungary
4.	1135–47	Henry of Huntingdon	*Historia Anglorum*	Taken to Sweden; then on to court of Hungarian king
5.	1172	Radulph de Diceto of London	*Abbreviationes Chronicorum*	King of Sweden; court of King Salamon of Hungary
6.	1160–80s	Roger of Hoveden	*Chronicon*	Swedish court; then Salamon's court in Hungary
7.	1154	Abbot Ailred of Rievaulx	*De Genealogia Regum Anglorum*	Sweden; then king of Hungary
7a.	1154	Abbot Ailred of Rievaulx	*Vita Sancti Edwardi Regis et Conf.*	Sweden; then king of Hungary
8.	Early 14th c.	Ranulph of Higden (monk of Chester)	*Polychronicon*	King of Sweden; then court of King Salamon of Hungary
9.	Early 12th c.	Orderic Vitalis (monk of Evroult)	*Historia Ecclesiastica*	Court of Danish king; sent on as 'hostages to King of Huns'
10.	First half of 12th c.	William of Malmesbury	*De Gestis Regum Anglorum*	Swedish court; on to king of Hungary
11.	12th c.	John of Brompton	*Chronicon*	Taken to Denmark; then to Sweden; on to court of King Salamon of Hungary
12.	1220s–30s	Roger of Wendover	*Flores Historiarum*	Court of Swedish king; then on to King Salamon of Hungary
13.	1220s–40s	Albericus Trium Fontium	*Chronicon*	To Swedish court; then on to Hungary
14.	1230s–50s	Matthew Paris	*Chronica Major*	To King of Sweden; then to court of King Salamon of Hungary
15.	1245	Anon.	*La Estoire de St Aedward le Rei*	'Not known what had become of them'
16.	Ends in 13th c.	Chronicle of Croyland Abbey	*Historia*	To Sweden; then to Hungary
17.	1280–90s	Anon.	*Chronica canonicorum Beate Mariae Huntingdoniensis*	Taken to Sweden; then to Hungary
18.	13th c.	Anon.	*Chronicle of Melrose Abbey*	To Swedish court; then to King Salamon of Hungary

Table 2.

No.	Date	Chronicler	Work	Aethelings' exile route
19.	14th c.	Henry Knyghton	*Chronica de Eventibus Angliae*	Swedish court; then king of Hungary's court
20.	14th c.	Capgrave	*Chronicle*	to Hungary
21.	14th c.	John Fordun	*Chronica Gentis Scotorum*	to Hungary
22.	1526	Hector Boethius	*Chronicles of Scotland*	First to Sweden, then King Salamon's court in Hungary
23.	1578	Bishop Leslie	*De Rebus Gestis Scotorum*	Straight to Hungary
24.	1580–1615	John Stow	*Annales*	Sweden; then King Salamon's court in Hungary
25.	1560s	George Buchanan	*History of Scotland*	Sweden; then court of Hungary's King Salamon
26.	1570	Johan Messenius (Bishop of Lund)	*Scandia Illustrata*	To king of Sweden; then court of St Stephen of Hungary
27.	1631	Johanus Pontanus	*Rerum Danicarum Historia*	Court of King Salamon of Hungary
28.	1661	Anon. (signed J.R.)	*Perfect Princesse*	Taken to court of king of Sweden; then Hungary
29.	17th c.	Laurentius Surius	*Vita Margaretae*	Sweden; then court of King Salamon of Hungary

Florence, whose life straddled the eleventh and twelfth centuries, relied on the same unknown primary source as the anonymous annalist of the *Anglo-Saxon Chronicle*; in addition he lifted material from the work of Marianus Scotus of Fulda. He also inserted a flawed piece of information from an unknown source and, because of the chronological error contained in it, made it possible to establish the chain of borrowing right through the centuries. More importantly, it gave this author the first tangible indication that the aethelings reached Hungary not in the first decade or so of their exile but towards the end of it.

His claim that the King of Sweden had sent the small Edmund and Edward to 'Salamon, King of Hungary, to spare their lives, and have them brought up at his court' – a theme that is repeated in virtually every work included in Table 1 – was an invaluable piece of evidence to date the information and establish its source.

In around 1029, Hungary was ruled by King Stephen: Salamon did not ascend the throne until 1063, when both Edmund and Edward were long since in their graves. Therefore the generous Hungarian king who, according to all these chroniclers, so kindly brought them up at his court, was not even born.

The original source from whom Florence purloined this alleged fact must have been Bishop Ealdred, who headed the embassy sent by Edward the Confessor to bring back Edward Aetheling from Hungary in

1054, or someone from his entourage. In 1058, when the good bishop once again travelled to the Continent and passed through Hungary on his way to the Holy Land, King Andrew I of Hungary had his infant son, Salamon, crowned king as a formality aimed to assure his succession.

Young Salamon was simultaneously engaged to the daughter of the Holy Roman Emperor in a move designed to heal the rift between Hungary and the Holy Roman Empire through a marriage of convenience. These two events were noted by most Continental chroniclers. Misled by the news of coronation and engagement, Florence's informant took the child for a grown-up and laid the foundations of a serious error that was to bedevil and confuse generations of British historians.

The third chronicler to have added his mite of original information to the aethelings' story was Orderic Vitalis, the English-born monk of Evroult. He was the first to affirm the princes' Danish sojourn, contained also in Gaimar's account, but he slipped up on his dates, confused Canute's contemporaries in Sweden and Denmark and had the Danish king send Edmund and Edward as 'hostages to the king of the Huns'.

The context of Gaimar's and Orderic's work does not suggest a common source on the Danish sojourn. Orderic could have gleaned it from the veterans who had fought with Edgar Aetheling, Edward's son, in the crusade or his Italian campaign, as Evroult was a well-known hospice for old crusaders and pilgrims. He could also have learnt it from Edgar's close Norman friends, made during his long stay in Normandy, who would still be alive when Orderic began gathering material for his great work.

He intimated that, in the course of his research, he visited Worcester monastery and read the original of Marianus Scotus's gesta. This would explain the similarity of part of his story with Florence's version but provides no clue as to the source of his astonishing assertion that 'Edward, with God's permission, obtained the crown of Hungary with the hand of the king's daughter'.

Since Hungarian historiography does not encourage one to accept this as a fact, Orderic must have recorded a distorted third- or fourth-hand account of certain historical events in Hungary in which Edward Aetheling was in some way involved. In so doing, Orderic adduced circumstantial evidence that, at some stage during their exile, the aethelings had indeed stayed in Hungary but offered no proof of the direct move from Sweden to Hungary.[2]

William of Malmesbury, the fourth in the chain of chroniclers with possible access to primary sources, lent respectability to the common Anglo-Norman version of the aethelings' exile by including it in his massive *History of the Kings of England*. Though well acquainted with Canute's murder-by-proxy plan, he had no reliable information on the exile route and even got the name of the older boy wrong, calling

Edmund 'Edwy'. But he had a new angle on Edward's marriage offering a promising fresh lead.

Ailred of Rievaulx, the Yorkshire abbot, at first sight appeared to speak with the greatest authority on the aethelings in his *Genealogia*. But an analysis of his work soon revealed that he derived his facts from Florence, Malmesbury and Huntingdon. A stylistic comparison between his and Florence's version of the story shows clearly that Ailred did not even bother to change the borrowed facts of the aethelings' exile.[3]

However, he gleaned valuable information on Edward Aetheling's marriage from King David, the aetheling's grandson, whom he knew well. Indeed, he made a special reference – 'rege referente' – to his royal informant and included many anecdotes emanating from the aetheling's grandchildren in his work. As for clues, or some hints, of the haven chosen by Walgar for his charges after Sweden, there is none in Ailred's account.

The last of the chroniclers included in Table 1 with access to primary sources was Bishop Turgotus, the father-confessor of Edward's daughter, Margaret, in Scotland. He wrote an account of her life but, to judge by a surviving Latin copy of the original, he chose to relate all her pious deeds for the benefit of wavering contemporaries and a more devout posterity, rather than waste time on recounting the then well-known details of her Continental childhood.[4]

Turgotus, 'Quhilk was aftir Bischop of Sanctandrois and wraitt the life of Sanct Margarette and King Malcolm in his wlgar langaige', affirmed that the aethelings were sent to Hungary in order to save their lives, but left no further useful pointers to help unravel the royal family's exile years.

Having checked the value and traced the sources of the works upon which later British historians based their knowledge of the aethelings' exile, it can be confidently asserted that there is no shred of evidence of the aethelings' move from Sweden straight to Hungary. Amidst all the uncritical copying, the trail of the two princes went cold in the Anglo-Norman chronicles.

7.   The Russian connection: the flight eastward along the Norsemen's route

The great detectives of the historical whodunit genre would never accept defeat after a setback so early in their investigations. They would fortify themselves with their favourite drink, toss another log in the fire and, taxing their little grey cells to the limit, turn the case upside down. The change of perspective would lead them to revise commonly-held attitudes to certain underrated material evidence, reject the testimony of star witnesses and so snatch victory from the jaws of defeat.

A change of perspective in the search for the aethelings' trail can only be attained by discarding the hallowed value judgments of medieval historians on Anglo-Norman chronicles. This fresh approach to the actual value of the surviving evidence, however challenging to traditional orthodoxy on the face of it, is hardly a revolutionary departure, considering that most of the official twelfth-century chronicles ascribed to learned monks investigated proved to be compilations put together from unchecked earlier sources.

The most underrated source on the attempted murder of the aethelings in the eyes of medieval British scholars was Geoffroi Gaimar, as previously noted, the early twelfth-century Norman author of the rhyming chronicle L'Estoire des Engleis. Because of the prejudices with which the news value of such versified chronicles and the sagas of minstrels were viewed by successive generations of scholars, Gaimar's account has not been accorded the attention it deserves. With so many solid, scholarly works of the Anglo-Norman period still extant, there is little point – so the traditionalist argument ran – in searching for hidden nuggets of information in a popular work like Gaimar's because he was, by inclination and force of circumstances, as it were, a 'gossip-columnist' rather than a historian.

Strange as it may seem, not one of the scholarly monastic chroniclers of the period knew so much about the aethelings' fate as Gaimar, yet they all devoted considerable time and energy to the story.

The many colourful details and surprising adventures contained in Gaimar's amusing narrative give a fuller, more rounded account of the aethelings' life and times on the Continent than the works of the contemporary establishment writers, who recorded their versions with an eye to posterity. Indeed, most of the information presented by Gaimar was completely unknown to the Anglo-Norman chroniclers who form the backbone of the official history.

The age-old prejudice against those who prefer to entertain rather than to edify must not be allowed to blind one to the true historical value of Gaimar's rhyming chronicle. Among the many incidents adduced by him, Emma's role in the children's attempted murder and the Danish first-leg of their exile have been proved correct.

Far from allowing himself wild poetic licence, Gaimar appears – in the light of textual analysis – to have relied heavily on Northumbrian and Scandinavian traditions and other now lost sources. Among his sources he specifically mentioned the English *Washingborough Chronicle* ('De Wassingburc un livere Engleis u il trouad escrit des reis') which has, regrettably, not survived. And his knowledge of English was so good that he could translate the *Anglo-Saxon Chronicle.*

Because of his avowed interest in society gossip and the goings-on in the bedrooms of the high and mighty of the Norman élite, he was personally acquainted with most of the important personages of his time. Among his informants were King Henry I, the son-in-law of Edward's daughter, Margaret; Robert, Count of Gloucester, Henry's bastard son; and the families of Edward's children.

With so much of the events of the royal family's exile years still fresh in the minds of the children of Edward Aetheling, their families and their old retainers, a writer of Gaimar's inquisitiveness and interest in royal scandals could easily have pieced together the aethelings' story. Some of the colourful details of Edmund Aetheling's sexual excapades and the descritions of the hot tears of a pretty Continental princess made pregnant by him, would not be out of place in the dossier of any twentieth-century, muck-raking Fleet Street journalist, but were not the meat of the monastic chroniclers of the period. Gaimar's story deserves, therefore, much greater attention.

His version provides an invaluable clue, the missing link, that none of the other Anglo-Norman chroniclers had: Walgar took the two Anglo-Saxon princes from Sweden to Russia.

Sa terre a ses treis fiz leissa.	He left his land to his three sons.
Od sul treis nefs se mist en mer;	With only three ships he put to sea;
Si espleita son errer	He so well accomplished his journey
Ken sul cinc iurs passat Russie	That in only five days he passed Russia
E vint en terre de Hongrie.	And came to the land of Hungary [1]

Even though the chronology of the eastward journey is much compressed to suit Gaimar's continuous narrative, the route is the same that was taken by the Norsemen fleeing from Canute in 1029. And this well-established escape route is of the greatest significance for this investigation.

Saxo Grammaticus, drawing on contemporary Scandinavian sources, confirmed that Norsemen in trouble looked to Russia as a safe refuge still within the Nordic orbit. King Olaf of Norway fled there too in 1029:

> It is related of King Olaf's [exile] journey that he went first from Norway eastward through Eyda forest to Vermeland, then to Vatsbo ... and when summer came he made ready for a journey, procured a ship for himself, and without stopping went to Russia to King Jarisleif [Yaroslav the Great] and his Queen Ingegerd. But his own queen, Astrid, and his daughter, Ulfhild, remained behind in Sweden, and the king took his son, Magnus, eastward with him.

King Olaf's brief Swedish stay and subsequent flight across the Baltic to Russia provides the natural pattern that Walgar himself chose to follow: a quick dash across the Baltic to the Bay of Finland, up the river Neva and thence the waterway south. It was the Norsemen's traditional route to Kiev, and there are very persuasive reasons why Walgar would have wanted to take the two young Anglo-Saxon princes there.

To begin with, the social fabric and political traditions established in Russia by the conquering Norseman Rurik's dynasty were not so different from those prevailing in Denmark or the Danelaw in England. The links between the Scandinavian countries on the one hand, and the Russian states of Kiev and Novgorod, on the other, were very close indeed.

Warriors with a sword to hire, enterprising seafarers and restless Vikings all travelled east in search of adventure along the bloody trail blazed by the Norse Varangians through Russia down to Byzantium. And the same people, when satiated with plunder, would go home with their booty linking the eastern and westermost extremities of the Nordic orbit in a constant two-way traffic.

This ease of communications assured that Walgar could be in regular touch with those circles in England which sought the restoration of the Wessex line to the throne. These channels of communications were supplemented by the frequent visits of English traders travelling along the ancient north-south trade route linking Byzantium with Northern Europe through Russia, the Baltic and the North Sea. Thus Kiev fulfilled all the requirements of an active exile without the drawbacks of isolation that a move outside the Nordic sphere would have entailed.

There was, however, an even weightier reason for the aethelings' eastward flight and this was the kinship between the ruling houses of Northern Europe and Kievan Russia. The Swedish royal house, that had sheltered the two Anglo-Saxon princes for a while, was through its women the dynastic link between Norway, Sweden and Russia. King Anund Jacob of Sweden, King Olaf of Norway and Grand Duke Yaroslav the Great of Kiev were brothers-in-law, and it would have been the most natural decision by a concerned Swedish host to send Edmund and

Edward to the safety of his brother-in-law's court in Kiev when King Olaf of Norway was forced to flee from Canute to Russia in 1029.

This Nordic network of polyp-like family ties also included the aethelings in one of its many tentacles. Queen Ingegerd, the wife of the mighty Kievan ruler, was a half-sister of Ealdgyth,[2] the aethelings' Swedish-born mother, and it was only natural that she should give a home to her persecuted nephews.

Kinship, customs, tradition and the clinging to a familiar Nordic way of life all justify Gaimar's suggestion that Walgar moved from Sweden to Russia with his royal charges. And these cogent reasons weigh more heavily than the apparent witness of the Anglo-Norman chronicles, justifying the conclusion that Edmund and Edward did not travel to distant Hungary from Sweden, but settled at their aunt's hospitable court.

There is, however, a world of a difference between a reasonable (indeed extremely plausible) working hypothesis and recorded facts. The commercial needs of Hanseatic city states to keep reliable accounts of events in their region have helped to bridge this gap by furnishing the clinching evidence of the aethelings' Kievan exile.

The new trade route from Italy, up the Rhine to the Hanseatic trade centres grew by leaps and bounds in the tenth century, and by the time the aethelings came to flee from Canute, monastic scribes conscientiously recorded all the important events that could have had a bearing upon their prosperous cities. Adam of Bremen, the Archbishop of Hamburg, had a further reason to keep a meticulous account of the political and church events in Northern Europe: a tenth-century papal bull made the archbishop of Hamburg (who resided in Bremen) the ecclesiastical ruler of the whole of the Scandinavian north.

Writing within a generation of the actual events, he recorded among the events of 1016 in his *Gesta Hammaburgensis Ecclesiae Pontificarum* the murder of Edmund Ironside and the flight of his children to Russia. 'Edmund, a warlike man, was removed by means of poison from the way of the victor [Canute], and his sons were condemned to banishment in Russia.'[3]

The care with which Adam approached his duty as keeper of the annals of Northern Europe is reflected in his remark that 'I have recounted these things in a truthful rendering of facts, although there were other events that would also have deserved to be written down.' And this care and selectivity stand him in good stead in the evaluation of his credit-worthiness.

Adam of Bremen's terse report confirming the aethelings' Kievan sojourn is, therefore, of the greatest importance. Unfortunately, the archbishop of Hamburg was more interested in the good works of English priests [4] in Norway and their support for King Olaf's fight against the country's many magicians, soothsayers, diviners, warlocks and 'other servants of the Antichrist', than in the details of the aethelings' Russian exile.

Apart from having pointed the investigation in the right easterly direction, Adam's report also helped to make sense of other seemingly doubtful pieces of evidence. The name, for instance, of the city where, according to Gaimar, the aethelings made their landfall after their flight across the Baltic and Russia, was rather baffling as there was no such place in Hungary as Gardimbre. But in the Kievan context it made perfect sense, offering a rare piece of linguistic proof of the aethelings' route.

Gaimar's unknown Scandinavian source was absolutely correct in giving Gardimbre as the spot where Walgar ended his sea journey. It was, however, Gaimar who, owing to his somewhat limited knowledge of geography or carelessness, misplaced that city and puzzled his readers:

> [Walgar] so well accomplished his journey [from Sweden]
> That in only five days he passed Russia
> And came to the land of Hungary.
> The sixth day he arrived
> Beneath the city of Gardimbre.
> The king was there and the queen,
> To whom Hungary was subject . . .[5]

The Norse *Heimskringlasaga* repeatedly refers to Russia as 'Gardar rike' or 'Gardar'. The name is derived from 'gardar' ('grad' or 'gorod' in Common Slavonic) and 'Rurike', the defensive settlement founded on Lake Ladoga by Rurik, the ninth-century Viking conqueror of Russia. The eleventh-century Russian chronicle *Nachalny Svod* clearly identifies the Ladoga town of Gardorika as Rurik's seat, and Gaimar's 'Gardimbre' is a philologically easily recognizable Norman corruption of it.

Its significance in tracing the aethelings' route is underlined by the intimation of the *Heimskringlasaga* that Ingegerd, the Swedish king's daughter, made conditional her marriage to Yaroslav the Great on the possession of this very town on Lake Ladoga: 'If I marry King Jaresleif, I must have as my bride gift the town and earldom of Ladoga', she told Yaroslav's envoys, and 'the Russian ambassadors agreed to this'.

Walgar therefore sailed across the Baltic from Sweden to the Gulf of Finland in five days, carried on up the river Neva and, on the sixth day of his journey, made his landfall at the Ladoga town of Gardorika (Gardimbre) which was owned by the aethelings' aunt. The 'Gardimbre' piece that would not fit Hungary slots into the Kievan end of the jigsaw with astonishing ease.

8. The 'Polish red herring': two vital pointers and a crucial discovery

Tradition of the historical whodunit genre demands that, just as the confusion surrounding the actions of the protagonist is about to be resolved in a satisfactory fashion, a red herring of considerable weight must be drawn across the stage threatening to undo all the good work of the master detective. Usually, however, the new evidence proves to be of little substance and the 'Polish exile' angle, dangled by J. Steenstrup and Laurence Larson, a couple of nineteenth-century Canute apologists, could also be eliminated without much further ado.[1]

They used the geographical confusion created by the Anglo-Norman chroniclers' references to the king of the 'Souabi', 'Suevi', 'Suebi' and 'Swavi' as the starting point of their attempt to whitewash Canute and reasoned that the king in question was the 'king of the Suebi', Canute's uncle.

The Suebi, a Slavonic people, occupied the lands stretching from the river Elbe to the Oder and the Baltic, and are better known as the Poles. Canute's connection with 'Slavia' and his descent from Gunhilde, a Polish princess, was noted by the Encomiast. When Sweyn 'divorced' his queen to marry Sigrid, Gunhilde returned to Poland to the court of Boleslaw Chobry and took her younger child, Canute, with her. He was fostered by Thorkill the Tall, the chief of the Jómburg Vikings at their fort on the Oder, and brought up among the Suebi.

This correct premise is used to advance the fallacious theory that Canute sent Edmund and Edward in 1017 not to the king of Sweden but to the Polish king of the Suebi, his maternal uncle, to have the children of his 'sworn brother' killed.[2] Duke Boleslaw, mindful of his sister's treatment at the hands of Canute's father, was not inclined to help his nephew and kept the Anglo-Saxon princes alive. His son, Mieczyslav, ascended the Polish throne in 1025 and, since he had close family ties with Gisela, wife of King Stephen of Hungary, he sent the aethelings there to be brought up at the Hungarian court, according to the Canute-apologists' version of events.

The 'Polish connection', however, can be dismissed not only because of its tenuous geographic (Suebi) argument, but also because it requires, on behalf of its propounders, further linguistic sleight-of-hand that would turn the documentary evidence of the Russian exile into Hungarian exile. In view of the Swedish family connections and Nordic ties linking Scandinavia with Rurik's Russia, the Kievan stay of the aethelings cannot simply be wished away.

A search in the archives of Poland, Germany and Hungary failed to turn up any additional documentary proof of the correctness of Adam of Bremen's and Gaimar's version of the aethelings' exile route and, for a while, the nineteenth-century Polish red herring came close to raising some actual doubts about the Kievan sojourn.

Astonishingly, corroborating evidence of the Russian exile was to be found not in Eastern Europe but – of all places – on the open shelves of the British Museum Library. A mildewed copy of a collection of Edward the Confessor's laws (*Leges Edovardi Confessoris*), compiled on the orders of William the Conqueror's son, contained – without rhyme or reason – a direct reference to Edward Aetheling's Kievan exile.[3]

This insertion of a reference to the exile years and the fate of Edward Aetheling's children in a dull collection of laws is so unusual that the reasons that prompted the anonymous compiler of the *Leges Edovardi Confessoris* must be examined with great circumspection, especially as the work also contains a vital pointer about Edward's wife.[4]

But the proof of Edward's Kievan sojourn is there for all to see: 'Edmund [Ironside] had a son called Edward who, upon the death of his father at the hands of King Canute, escaped to the land of the Rugos, whom we call Russians. The king of that country, by the name of Malesclodus, on having found out who he was, received him well.'[5]

Russia, then, was the refuge chosen by Earl Walgar for his charges. He could not have made a better choice. Queen Ingegerd gave her nephews a welcoming home in that easternmost outpost of the Nordic commonwealth and Yaroslav the Great showed kindness towards the Anglo-Saxon princes, whom he 'received well'. It offered safety, continuity and familiarity, and the great prestige and solid power base of Yaroslav held out the promise of an eventual return to England to reclaim the crown of Wessex.

But in trying to trace the aethelings' footsteps in Kievan Russia through the Old Russian chronicles, as well as the annals of the West, the most surprising realisation was that not one named Yaroslav the Great as their host.

Nestor's Old Russian *Nachalny Svod* (c. 1095) makes no mention of the aethelings' Kievan sojourn, nor do the three subsequent, and still extant codices based in part on Nestor's work. A careful reading of the *Ipatyevskaya Letopis* (c. 1420) giving a detailed history of Kiev up to 1292; the *Lavrentevskaya Letopis* (c. 1377) which covers the history of North Russia as far as 1305; and the *Novgorodskaya Letopis* (c. mid-thirteenth century) shows that the Anglo-Saxon princes' exile years went totally unrecorded.

Later Russian chronicles do actually show an awareness of Edmund and Edward's refuge at the Kievan court, but a closer examination reveals that their source of information was none other than Adam of Bremen's *Gesta*.

Karamzin, Russia's outstanding late eighteenth-century historian, drawing on Adam of Bremen, made the following entry in his comprehensive *Istoriya Gosudarstva Rossiyskogo*:

> The court of Yaroslav, famed by the reflected glory of his greatness, has served as a refuge for unfortunate kings and princes... Edward and Edwyn [*sic*], the children of the courageous English king Edmund [Ironside], as well as Andrew, Prince of Hungary, together with his brother Levente, had sought asylum in our country.[6]

Adam of Bremen's account, as retold by Karamzin, was made great use of by generations of Russian historians without further research or actual checking its original source.[7] The vital reference to King Malesclodus of Russia, contained in the Anglo-Norman *Leges Edovardi Confessoris*, remained totally unknown to Russian historians. The quest for corroborative sources in Russia drew a blank (see Table 3).

But Academician Mikhail Pavlovich Alekseyev, Russia's foremost authority on medieval Anglo-Russian historical links, helped to resolve the identity of Malesclodus in response to my request. In a lengthy linguistic analysis he pointed out that Yaroslav the Great was well-known to the contemporary Western chroniclers because he was the father-in-law of Henry I of France. Guillaume of Jumièges, the eleventh-century French historian, referred to the Kievan ruler in his *Gesta Normannorum Ducum* as 'Julius Clodius', while Orderic Vitalis called him 'Julius Claudius' in an apparent attempt to render a strange Slavonic name, using a distorted version of Yaroslav's Christian name – Jurius (from Georgius) Sclavus.

Drawing on further research by his Leningrad colleagues Academician Alekseyev proved that the name 'Julius Claudius' was the result of a traditional device used by medieval Western historians to substitute an unpronounceable, obscure foreign name with a sufficiently close Roman or ancient Greek name. Attempts made by some philologists to explain the name with the Latin 'claudus', a reference to Yaroslav's limp were misguided. The Jumièges version of 'Julius Clodius' was so very close to the Bullesclot variant used by the anonymous monk of St Dennis, that the 'Malesclodus' name mentioned by the Norman compiler of the *Leges* can be positively identified as a French corruption of Yaroslav.

Table 3. Chronicles recording the aethelings' Russian exile.

No.	Date	Chronicler	Work	Exile route	Marriage
1.	1050	Adam of Bremen	*Gesta Hammab.*	Banished to Russia	Edward married in Russia Agatha, of noble origins
2.	1134	Anon.	*Leges Edovardi Confessoris*	Direct to Russia, court of Malesclotus	Elder aetheling (erroneously called Edgar) married Hungarian king's daughter
3.	c.1155	Geffroi Gaimar	*L'Estoire des Engleis*	Denmark, 12 years later to Russia, then Hungary	
4.	1706	Erpold Lindenbrog	*Rerum Germanicarum Septentrionalium*	'Filiique (Edmundi) in Ruzziam exilio sunt damanati'	Both reflect Adam of Bremen
5.	1815	Karamzin	*Istoriya Gos. Rossiyskogo*	To court of Yaroslav the Great in Russia	

PART III: COUNTERS IN A EUROPEAN POWER GAME

9. At Yaroslav the Great's hospitable court: Nordic ethos and Byzantine statecraft on the steppes of Russia

The identifiable historical facts and chronological evidence contained in Gaimar's chronicle help to remove the last vestiges of doubt about the aethelings' flight to Russia.

The fascinating conversation that took place between Walgar and the Grand Duke Yaroslav upon the aethelings' arrival in his kingdom simply makes no sense in a Hungarian context. But removing Gaimar's erroneous information that Gardimbre was in Hungary, and restoring the town to its rightful place on the shores of Lake Ladoga, the intelligence imparted by the Norman chronicler falls into place almost miraculously.

According to Gaimar, Walgar knew the ruler, and his queen, who welcomed his party 'beneath the city of Gardimbre'. Now Walgar might well have met Ingegerd before – either in Sweden or in Denmark – to discuss the upbringing of her nephews, and an earlier encounter between the Dane and Yaroslav could not be ruled out either.

But he could *not* have been acquainted with King Stephen of the far-away land of Hungary. Nor could the Hungarian ruler have 'known well', either personally or by hearsay, the two Anglo-Saxon princes, not to mention Walgar's role in their rescue or their being 'the rightful heirs of England'. Yaroslav, however, would have followed as a matter of course the tribulations of his wife's nephews, and there were enough channels of communications between Sweden and Kievan Russia to keep him posted about developments.

Edmund and Edward were 'somewhat grown, and had passed twelve years' when they arrived at Gardorika-Gardimbre; and this was close enough since Edmund would have been over thirteen and Edmund about twelve at the end of their Scandinavian exile and the start of the second leg of their Continental peregrinations. Walgar's plea for pity on behalf of the princes affirms that they were still minors, whereas the aethelings were grown men when they eventually reached Hungary; such pleas then would have been completely out of place.

Having dramatically sketched the six-day flight across the Baltic with the children, Gaimar aptly set the scene of their welcome to Russia at the town of Gardorika-Gardimbre:

> The king was there and the queen,
> To whom Hungary [*sic*] was subject.
> Walgar *was acquainted* with them.
> He adorned the two children.
> He came to the king and greeted him.
> The king rose up to meet him.
> He embraced Walgar, set him beside him,
> And made cheer and joy with him.
> He *knew well about the two boys,*
> How he [Walgar] had cared for them,
> And that they were *right heirs of England.*
> But he knew not what he wished to ask
> Until the master spoke.
> The king asked, so he showed him
> Of the two boys, how it was
> That men wished to destroy them.
> Then he told him how they had fled,
> And how they came to ask his pity.[1]

Walgar, having found a safe refuge for his charges, must have felt that the onerous task of saving Edmund and Edward's life had been accomplished and entrusted the boys to the care of their aunt and uncle. 'As you have trust in God, I entreat you, keep them well', he pleaded with the royal couple at Gardorika-Gardimbre.

Having compromised his own position and become an outlaw in order to save the little princes, Walgar now stepped aside to let the boys' uncle help them recover the crown of England. It was a move reflecting the conclusions of an astute politician who saw that the means at the disposal of the ruler of Kiev were more suited to the task ahead than those a Danish baron on the run could avail himself of.

The sacrifices that he had had to make were not allowed to becloud his judgement at this crucial point in the Anglo-Saxon princes' life. Whether he stayed on at Yaroslav's court or attempted to right his position with Canute and return home to his estates, cannot be gauged from Gaimar's chronicle with any certainty. But the phrase 'the children remained there' would indicate that their guardian left Russia.

The last, tenuous tie linking Edmund and Edward with him was cut. Exile began in earnest, and not even the friendliest welcome to Russia could mask the fact that the boys were now on their own. But never having had a home or known the country they were supposed to recover, they might not have felt the rootlessness of exile as an intolerable burden.

Somewhat surprisingly, Edmund and Edward began their sojourn in

Kievan Russia not in the eponymous capital but in Novgorod. This north-ern, and most Nordic, of the Russian city-states, was on the shores of Lake Ilmen, a day's journey by swift horse from Gardorika-Gardimbre, Queen Ingegerd's Ladoga estate, where the aethelings had made their landfall.

Novgorod controlled the northern end of the flow of goods from the Baltic southwards through the Dniepr riverways to Constantinople and thence to the Araby of the Caliphs, to India and to China. This key posi-tion assured it great prosperity and considerable political influence. Nevertheless, it was not the centre of Russia's power and civilization: that position was occupied by Kiev.

Yet the aethelings' trail, picked up after many dead ends and false leads of the Anglo-Norman chronicles, was clearly pointing in the direc-tion of Kiev. The pointers provided by the Archbishop of Hamburg and the anonymous Norman expert on the law of Edward the Confessor's reign increased the expectation that the princes would be entertained not in the provinces, but at the Kievan court. This natural expectation took no account of the exigences of a long-drawn-out power struggle in Kievan Russia.

Although in 1029 Yaroslav the Great was already the undisputed ruler of the whole of Russia, he had his seat in Novgorod and therefore that was where he must have housed his wife's nephews. The situation obtain-ing in Russia at the time of the aethelings' arrival was the awkward heritage of the decision of Yaroslav's father, Vladimir, to divide the realm among his eleven sons, a decision that had fuelled round upon round of internecine wars among the princes of Russia.

From his allotted fief of Novgorod, Yaroslav had waged a bitter war against his elder brother, Svyatopolk, installed by their father in Kiev. The fighting had raged from 1014 to 1019, when Yaroslav's Varangian merce-naries recruited in Sweden defeated Svyatopolk's mercenary Pecheneg steppe horsemen. Upon this decisive victory, most of the other princes of Kievan Russia acknowledged Yaroslav's supremacy. There were, how-ever, further challenges to his rule from his brothers now with the aid of the Poles, now with the Lithuanians, or more often with the support of some or other nomadic steppe nation.

Wisely, Yaroslav decided to stay on in Novgorod and make it the *de facto* capital of the country. With this temporary arrangement he repaid the invaluable support of the mighty Veche, the city council, and of the people of Novgorod in his fight against his brothers and so succeeded in retaining his power base intact. He also avoided the dangers inherent in a move to take his defeated brother's seat, and simply bided his time.

A golden opportunity to move to Kiev was provided by an attack of the Pechenegs, Svyatopolk's erstwhile allies, on Kiev in 1036. The fierce steppe warriors had succeeded in penetrating the city's outskirts before Yaroslav's arrival, but subsequently he won a signal victory over the nomadic raiders. He used the indebtedness of the inhabitants towards their saviour to move his seat safely to Kiev and turn it into not simply the political, but also the ecclesiastical, artistic and intellectual capital of Russia.

The settling-in period of the aethelings coincided with the years of consolidation of Yaroslav's rule. It was a period of growth, conquest and rapid expansion in an unusual flowering of Nordic statecraft on the fringes of the great steppes of Asia.

The Varangian princes of Rurik's house had created a hybrid new civilization at the confluence of Byzantine culture, Nordic military tradition, Eastern-rite Christianity and pagan Asian despotism. The free political institutions of the Viking Varangians were coupled with good administration and Slavonic tolerance in Yaroslav the Great's rule, making it the envied golden age of democracy in Kievan Russia.[2]

In its tone it was a world more Byzantine than Nordic, but there was a sufficient number of reassuringly-familiar features to ensure the aethelings did not feel bewildered or lost. One of them was language. Most of the Varangian and Rus nobles understood the Norse tongue that the conquering Vikings had brought to Russia, and Queen Ingegerd used it as a *lingua franca* at court. The aethelings, brought up by a Dane, could of course communicate with them without difficulty.

A further frame of familiarity was provided by Yaroslav's army with its Nordic ethos, organization and mode of fighting. For royal princes in their teens the learning of martial arts was the single most important occupation, and since seasoned Norwegian and Swedish warriors formed the backbone of Yaroslav's *druzhina*, or housecarls, there can be little doubt that the aethelings' schooling in warfare and chivalry took place under Nordic guidance.

They must have earned their spurs in one of Yaroslav's campaigns well before their uncle's move to Kiev, for royal princes were expected to prove their mettle on the battle field in their mid-teens, not at twenty and nineteen, Edmund and Edward's respective ages in 1036. Whether they first tasted blood in one of Yaroslav's internecine wars or in his Western campaigns, the aethelings fought among the bravest and most enterprising Norsemen who sought gold and adventure in the east. The ideals that justified these wars counted for less in that company than the chance of pillage, rape and plunder.

Life in the *druzhina*, which at one point could count among its members King Olaf of Norway and his son, Magnus, trained the aethelings for war, while their uncle, Grand Duke Yaroslav, drew them towards learning and books. Since growing boys always seek ideals and examples to measure up to or set themselves against, Yaroslav must have exercised exceptionally great influence over the aethelings on the threshold of manhood.

Nevertheless, the ruler who shaped Russia's destiny with a foresight and political acumen unusual for his time, puzzled most of his contemporaries, and must have struck the aethelings as the embodiment of the many baffling paradoxes of Russian life.

To begin with, there was an almost insuperable gap between his warrior reputation and his appearance. Yaroslav was, as far as his stature was concerned, far from great and he looked more Slavonic than Viking in spite of his direct descent from Rurik. Indeed, he was short, stocky and, as attested by a contemporary source, he walked with a heavy limp as a result of a childhood illness.[3]

In an age beholden to warrior virtues he proudly pursued his bookish interests. He was a voracious reader of books and a noted scholar, a most unusual accomplishment for a Varangian prince. Yet despite his physical handicap and scholarly bent, he displayed greater aptitude for the art of war than those who made fighting the sole purpose of their existence.

The monk Nestor of the Kievan Monastery of the Caves, who wrote *Nachalny Svod*, the first Russian chronicle, in 1095, recorded that:

Yaroslav applied himself to books and read them continually day and night. He assembled many scribes to translate [books] from Greek into Slavonic . . . He caused many books to be written and collected, through which true believers are instructed and enjoy religious education . . . Thus Yaroslav, as we have said, was a lover of books and, as he had many written, he deposited them in the church of St Sophia.

Nestor's simple statement about Yaroslav's piousness can hardly do justice to the proselytizing zeal with which he tried to convert his people to the true Orthodox faith. Yet when his state interests so required he did not hesitate to wage war on Byzantium, the cradle of Orthodox Christianity.

He must have puzzled even more the aethelings, who were trying as it were to learn the trade of kingship at his side, with his ambivalent attitude towards the Greek Orthodox Church, the carrier and fountainhead of Christianity in Kievan Russia. While making generous donations to the church, he isolated the alien clergymen in a move aimed at making the church more responsive to the needs of the state and appointed Hilarion, a Russian, as Metropolitan. Having recognized early on the advantages of the subordination of the church to the exigencies of state, he laid the foundations of a new type of relationship that was to endure to the present day.

Under his direction, Metropolitan Hilarion wrote a highly sophisticated moral guide that was designed to supplement, within the correct political framework, the religious education of the people of Russia. The title alone, written in the traditional form of a ceremonial sermon, can give a fair inkling of the Kievan ruler's intellectual approach to church, state and religion:

On the law of Moses, given to him, and on the grace and truth which was Jesus Christ, and how the law departed, whereas grace and truth filled the whole Earth, and the faith reached unto all peoples even unto our Russian people; and a eulogy to our Khan Vladimir, through whom we were christened; and a prayer to God from all our land.

The aethelings could hardly have been exempted from the religious education their new guardian was so intent on spreading across his land, and their schooling must have duly reflected this all-consuming concern of Yaroslav's. Their reaction to this sudden and massive exposure to Orthodox Christianity can be gauged, to a certain extent, by their role in a pagan, anti-Christian rebellion in Central Europe some years later.

Though Yaroslav had rightly won the sobriquet 'Wise' (*mudry*) from his people, it is not likely that he would have allowed Edmund and Edward to register their reservations about the Byzantine nature of Kievan Christianity, or have tolerated any dissent. But even if the religious side of Yaroslav's guidance jarred upon the boys' sensibilities, there were other facets of his statecraft that could not but win the aethelings' full admiration.

He established new standards of justice more suited to the needs of his centralized power, while retaining the best features of Scandinavian jurisdiction imported by his forebears. The country's first law codex, the *Koronchaya Kniga*, was revised under his guidance, and a new set of laws, the *Russkaya Pravda*, was issued.

Though based on a Byzantine secular model, the new code of justice reflected the emergent Russian Orthodox Church's views on all aspects of life. It covered every detail of domestic life, including regulations of relations between husband and wife, adultery, desertion and the rights of women to property. But its novel feature was that it included the notion of sin, as distinct from the notion of crime, among the punishable offences.

Yet Yaroslav's set of laws was basically humane, replacing the barbarity of capital punishment with a complex system of fines and tempered the harsher features of both Varangian and Greek justice. Instead of the punishment of a murderer by execution, for instance, it laid down the scale and stipulated the method of the collection of *bloodwite* [fine for murder]. It also assured that all – both the ruling Varangian élite and the ruled Slavs – were equal in the eye of the law, and retained the Scandinavian jury system of twelve men for trials.

He turned the huddle of log cabins that was Kiev into a great capital city. Soon the magnificence of its public buildings and the grandeur of its many beautiful wooden churches were unrivalled anywhere north of Byzantium. It was perhaps the ring of its churches' seventy-five golden cupolas silhouetted against the flat expanse of the steppes that inspired

Adam of Bremen to describe Yaroslav's capital city as 'the glory of Greece' in a presumably Nordic incarnation.

In direct emulation of Byzantium, he had a passage built to the church of St Sophia which was decorated with colourful scenes of hunting, musical entertainment and dancing, reflecting Yaroslav's personal tastes. This blend of Viking values and Byzantine traditions, perfected by Yaroslav, permeated the aethelings' perception and determined their outlook.

10. *Anglo-Saxon counters in a Continental battle for dominance*

Edmund and Edward spent their most impressionable and formative years under Yaroslav's tutelage and reached manhood in his capital. His ideas of statecraft, religion, justice, honour and duty shaped the aethelings' intellectual horizon, and it would have been surprising if the sheer weight of Yaroslav's personality had not radically influenced their outlook. Without undue surmise it can be conjectured that the two fatherless boys grew up more Kievan Varangians than Englishmen in their tastes and manners at Yaroslav's court.

But the outward trappings and attributes of Kievan life that dominated the aethelings' waking hours did not eclipse the notions of duty towards their distant country instilled in them by Walgar. There is persuasive evidence that Yaroslav, while initiating his wards into the Byzantine complexities of the art of government, did his best to nurture in them this sense of duty towards England.

Although originally Yaroslav might have given the aethelings asylum at his court because they were relations of his wife, or out of pity, his subsequent interest in the Anglo-Saxon princes had more cogent reasons. The presence of the heirs to the English throne at his court gave his Western-orientated foreign policy a very useful negotiating counter.

His concern with the westward expansion of Russia's sphere of influence was reflected in his conquest of Galicia and his successive campaigns against Lithuania, the Polish Mazovians and the Finnish tribe of Iam. The latter three were in a north-westerly arc around the eastern finger of the Baltic, and were aimed at securing a firm foothold for Russia in the Gulf of Finland.

Such a foothold, let alone the cherished dream of supremacy, could not be achieved without the smashing of the stranglehold of Canute's empire on the Baltic.

The broader strategy of Yaroslav's Baltic plans foresaw, as a first step, the containment of Canute and his eventual destruction through a grand Continental alliance. In both phases the aethelings appear to have been allotted a crucial role.

Canute's empire was most vulnerable in England where, upon the king's death, the sorely-tried English could be expected to turn against the alien usurper's heir and restore the house of Wessex to the throne. In such a contingency, the aethelings could either be used as pawns in the negotiations on the future of the North Sea-Baltic region or, if one of them were to ascend the throne, as allies against anyone trying to resurrect Canute's empire.

From subsequent moves it can be inferred that Yaroslav banked on the aethelings' restoration and sought to neutralize Nordic expansionism through a Russo-German-English alliance. Such a triple coalition would have helped Yaroslav to isolate Denmark and restore Continental balance, while at the same time open up the Baltic to Russia. Such a development would not have been unattractive to King Henry of Germany (who was destined to become the Holy Roman Emperor), and it held out the hope of an important role in European power politics for one of the aethelings once he attained the throne of England.

This focal interest of Yaroslav's foreign policy can help to explain the meaning of a later part of the quoted conversation between Yaroslav and Walgar. Without this interest Walgar's offer that the aethelings 'will hold [the crown of England] of you and they will become thy men' in exchange for help in the fight for the throne, would have been meaningless.

That this offer was made in a strictly Nordic context is borne out by the similarity of means employed by King Magnus of Norway some years later to secure the north-western flank of the anti-Danish alliance. In order to make himself master of Denmark and thus the entrance to the Baltic, he took Edward the Confessor, freshly-elected king of England, as his 'father', bound himself to him by oaths of fealty, and accepted vassal status in return for support for his anti-Danish enterprise.

It goes without saying that Walgar would not have sought the advice of a south-east European king on ways the aethelings might recover their land. Furthermore, no permutation of alliances could justify the offer of vassal status in exchange for military help to a monarch so far removed from the Nordic orbit.

But to the ruler of Kievan Russia actively engaged in the construction of an anti-Danish coalition, the pledge of vassal status on behalf of a future king of England would have been of the greatest significance. It would also have justified his promise that 'all my power and my strength I will put forth to help them. I will exert myself to raise them. To my power I will make war on those who have taken their land.'

The dogged tenacity with which Yaroslav pursued the planned triple alliance can be gauged from the fact that, after Canute's death, the Kievan ruler sent a high-powered embassy to King Henry of Germany with a renewed offer of friendship and the evident intention of galvanizing the alliance into action. The visit of the Russian embassy at Henry's court at Altstadt was recorded by Saxo.[1]

Moves to cement the anti-Danish alliance continued apace after

Harthacanut's unexpected death and the ascent of Edward the Confessor, the aethelings' uncle, to the English throne. Henry at once offered friendship and established the closest ties with Edward, and Yaroslav sent posthaste a further embassy in 1043 to Henry to discuss the new situation and the steps needed to salvage the Russo-German-English alliance.[2]

Far from dismissing the aethelings from his plans, Yaroslav appears to have proposed that one or other of the Anglo-Saxon princes should be linked through a dynastic marriage to one of Henry's relations, and thus secure the central and western flanks of the anti-Danish alliance.

Marriage as an instrument of foreign policy was a familiar tactic for Yaroslav. Indeed, he employed it with consummate skill, when other means were unsuited or insufficient. He married his daughter Yelisaveta to Harald of Norway as a reasonable reassurance for the success of his Baltic plans; he married his sister, Maria, to King Kazimir of Poland and influenced through this tie Poland's internal power struggle to his own advantage; he made his son, Vsevolod, marry a daughter of Emperor Constantine Monomachos in a shrewd gesture of appeasement towards Byzantium; in a further westward opening he married his daughter, Anastasia, to Prince Andrew of Hungary whose country was rent by a war of succession; and he gave his daughter, Anne, in marriage to King Henry I of France, scoring his biggest triumph in the field of dynastic marriages in eleventh-century Europe.

Whatever contribution the political marriage planned by Yaroslav for the aethelings came to make to the strengthening of the triple alliance, his inspired Continental policy provided the gilded framework that determined the aethelings' future.

11. Hungarian princes join refugee colony: friendship among the exiles

In 1036, two new arrivals swelled the ranks of the colony of royal exiles at Yaroslav's court and brought fresh interests and pleasurable excitement into their cloistered lives. Prince Andrew and Prince Levente of Hungary, offspring of a branch of the ruling Árpád dynasty, fled to Kiev after the murder of their father threatened their own lives in Hungary's bloody struggle for a successor to King Stephen.

Though the newcomers were younger than the aethelings – contemporary chroniclers describing them in 1031 with the Latin word 'parvuli', or young boys – there was a great deal of similarity between their experiences and conditions. Owing to a curious coincidence both sets of princes were the victims of ambitious queens championing alien factions; both were defenceless children in a struggle for power that brought out the worst in the contestants and both had traditional right on their side; and both had been forced to flee for their lives across several countries before finding refuge at Yaroslav's court. Despite their different backgrounds, they appear to have become close friends. This friendship came to play a fateful role in the aethelings' subsequent Central European venture.

The aethelings, like most people of western and northern Europe, could have had little knowledge of Hungarians. The latter were feared horsemen and deadly archers. Their many raids across the Continent as far south as Rome and the Rhine in the west in the preceding century had caused priests to urge their congregations to end their prayers with the plea: 'From the arrows of the Hungarians save us, O Lord.'

Adam of Bremen considered the Hungarians and the Danes the scourge of Europe, their bloody wars a threat to the very existence of Christian civilization. In his chronicle he noted with grudging respect that 'the barbarous people of Hungary and Denmark, as well as the Slavs and the Norsemen, have overcome the [Holy Roman] Emperor more often through clever stratagem than war . . .'

Bishop Hartvik, who compiled the life story of St Stephen from near-contemporary legends in the twelfth century, mercilessly attacked his people's heathen past. His description, circulated widely still in Renaissance times[1] retains the unimpaired flavour of medieval Europe's approach to the warrior nation that fought its way into the heart of the Continent at the end of the ninth century:

> Of all the barbarous nations, which at divers tymes, have through divine iustice, concurred to the ruine of the Roman greatness, were (as it is well knowne) the Huns: who having left the inmost parts of Scythia, or Tartary rather, have more than once gone forth, and finally entred into Pannonia, and thence driving out the Lombards (for what occasion, it is not certaynly knowne) have been called by the new name of Hungars. From which tyme, with a native fierceness and rapacity, they have not ceased to molest the Church of God; being given wholly to the impure worship of Idols, and rather guiding themselves, with unbridled wills, then with lawes or decrees under the heads which successively they made choice of.

Stephen, who ascended the throne in 997, turned Hungary into a Christian country, gave it new laws and a feudal organization better suited to the circumstances prevailing in Central Europe. With the help of his wife, Gisela, the sister of the Holy Roman Emperor, and the German clergy, called in by her, he reoriented the country from East to West and firmly anchored it to Rome. The death of his son and heir, Emeric, in 1031, however, created an uncertain situation in the country with the various contenders and factions jockeying for position.

The more conservative elements, hankering after the old traditional lifestyle of the steppes, looked to Vazul (Basil) for leadership. He was the son of the king's uncle, Michael, and under the rule of seniority that had governed the succession of the princely houses in the past, he was the rightful heir to the throne. But in the eyes of Queen Gisela, who spoke only German and never learnt the Magyar tongue, Vazul was unsuited for the post not only because he stood for the old steppe traditions and heathen culture, but because he had undergone a *pro forma* conversion to Christianity in accordance with the Orthodox rite as his Greek given-name indicates. And a pro-Byzantine orientation would not be suffered by the Catholic Queen, who handled the succession in the name of the sick king. She began championing the succession of Peter Orseolo, the son of the Doge of Venice and Stephen's sister, with a zeal not unlike Canute's wife, Emma, believing that the youth's Italian upbringing would be a guarantee for keeping Hungary Christian and in the Roman orbit.

Stephen was prevailed upon to set aside the time-honoured law of seniority and nominate Peter as his heir. This flagrant break with tradition appears to have sparked off two attempts on the ailing king's life, one in 1031 and the second in 1037, the latter resulting in Vazul's execution and the exiling of his three sons – Andrew, Levente and Béla.

The events of 1037 were completely rewritten in the following century in order to whitewash the sainted King Stephen and place all the blame

72

3. Prince Andrew of Hungary and his brothers, Béla and Levente, advised by their uncle, King St Stephen, from his sickbed to go into exile. Andrew sought refuge in Kiev where he befriended the two exiled Anglo-Saxon princes (from the *Óbudai Képes Krónika*, Széchényi Könyvtár Budapest).

for the cruel execution of Vazul on his foreign wife, Gisela. In an attempt to erase any hint of pagan backsliding in the family of the aethelings' exile friend Andrew, whose descendants ruled the Magyar state for 255 years, the monastic scribes went as far as to change the paternity of Vazul's three sons implying that they were the offspring of the more pious László the Bald, Vazul's younger brother.[2]

Simon de Kéza, the thirteenth-century royal scribe, recounts this edited version in his chronicle:

After the death of Emeric, King Stephen fell ill from the great suffering and sadness and also suffered from shooting pains in his leg. He was worried in particular by the fact that there was no one of his blood to be raised to the crown of the realm, nor was there anyone

73

who could keep, after his death, the freshly-converted nation true to its Catholic faith.

He began suddenly to lose his bodily strength and was, furthermore, suffering from great weakness. He therefore sent with great urgency messengers to have his paternal uncle, Vazul, freed from Nyitra prison as he wished him to succeed him on the throne. On hearing this, Queen Gisela held council with the faithless and sent the Palatin's [son] Sebeok with the strict order to overtake the king's envoys, gouge out Vazul's eyes, pour molten lead into his ears and then escape to the Czech Lands.

When Vazul was taken [in this condition] by the king's envoy to Stephen, he cried bitterly over what had been done to his kin. He therefore called to his bed Andrew, Bela and Levente, the sons of Laszlo the Bald [sic], counselling them to escape abroad.[3]

Since the aethelings came to tie their future to Andrew and his brothers and fight for their cause, the true reasons behind the exiling of the Hungarian princes are not indifferent for the purposes of this investigation.

There seems to be persuasive evidence that Vazul, though no 'knight in shining armour', was not involved in a conventional attempt on the king's life. He was a prince imbued with the steppe traditions of the ancient Magyars, and in 1037 he acted to enforce an archaic relic of the Khazar custom to which the Hungarian tribes had adhered before their advent into Central Europe: that in the fortieth year of his reign the king must die. Stephen had begun his reign in 997, and in 1037 the traditionalist Vazul entered his chamber to strangle him in the time-honoured ritual of their forefathers. But the king cried out and Vazul was arrested as a common, suspected murderer by the Queen's foreign courtiers not conversant with the traditions of the heathen steppemen.

The near-contemporary *Annales Altahenses maiores* kept by the German monks of Alteich monastery provide sufficient evidence to piece together the true outline of the events of 1037: Vazul, enraged by the breach of the law of succession decided to kill, with the aid of several other magnates, the king either out of pique or out of tradition. The king, probably on Gisela's advice, had the plotters tried and blinded. So the Queen, who not only caused Vazul's death but did everything to disinherit and have his sons murdered abroad, had fully earned the undying enmity of Andrew, Béla, and Levente.

Near-contemporary Hungarian chronicles seem agreed that the tribulations of the three princes began soon after the first (1031) attempt on King Stephen's life. In order to thwart the murder plans of Queen Gisela's faction, they were first sent to the court of the Czech king, Udalrik, but were soon forced 'by their niggardly, poverty-stricken condition' to seek asylum in Poland.[4] There the teenage boy Béla showed such great valour

in the fight against the heathen Pomeranians that King Mieczyslav showered favours on him and eventually gave him his daughter in marriage.

Andrew and Levente, completely overshadowed by their brother, must
have found exile in Poland somewhat trying and, leaving Béla behind,
moved on to the court of Yaroslav the Great, where they were well received. The exact date of the arrival of Andrew and Levente at Yaroslav's
court cannot be established with any certainty from the contradictory
facts furnished by the Hungarian chronicles, but the claim that the princes
acquitted themselves in Yaroslav's campaign against the Pechenegs
would indicate that they had participated in the 1036 battle for Kiev. The
Russian chronicler Karamzin merely noted that 'the Hungarian princes
Andrew and Levente, children of Ladislas [sic], lived for a long time in
our country.'

The way the Russian chronicler passed over the other 'unfortunate
kings and princes' sheltering at Yaroslav's court without mentioning their
names, while referring to the Kievan sojourn of Edmund and Edward and
Andrew and Levente specifically and together, seems to emphasize the
closeness between the English and Hungarian princes. The analogy of
their predicament and similarity of their endeavours would readily explain this closeness. But occasionally there develops an elective affinity
between young people which, coupled with identity of condition, can
become a lifelong friendship. Only the combination of these two emotions
could explain (certain objective considerations notwithstanding) the
eventual teaming-up of the Anglo-Saxon and Hungarian princes in a
military adventure in Hungary.

One of these objective considerations was Yaroslav's decision to marry
his daughter, Anastasia, to Andrew towards the end of the 1030s, when
Anastasia was about 15 and Andrew in his late teens. Whether Yaroslav
granted this signal honour to the refugee prince as an acknowledgement
of his valour in the fight against the Pechenegs, or as a long-term dynastic
stratagem, is difficult to gauge. But the marriage between the cousin of the
aethelings and Andrew established firm family links between the Anglo-
Saxon and Hungarian princes.

Another consideration was that the rapid political changes affecting
the shape of the Continent in the 1040s, though seemingly full of oppor-
tunities, offered little real scope for the aethelings to shape actively their
future. Although now well into their twenties, their quest for the recovery
of their patrimony was no closer to success than at the outset. After
Canute's death in 1035, the Danish dynasty had succeeded in retaining
power in England, and although after Harthacanute's death in 1042, the
English finally managed to rid themselves of their Danish masters, they
did not recall the aethelings.[5] And this was a serious setback both for the
aethelings' restoration hopes and for Yaroslav's grandiose anti-Danish
alliance.

After the ascent of Edward the Confessor on the throne of England both Yaroslav and Henry III, the Holy Roman Emperor, sought to breathe new life into the Continental coalition through hastily-despatched embassies. But, in parallel, Yaroslav began to put into effect his alternative plan that foresaw the shoring-up of the western flank of the anti-Danish alliance through a dynastic marriage.

But in view of the *fait accompli* in England's succession the Kievan ruler dropped the aethelings from the forefront of his plans and proposed a marriage between Henry III and his daughter Anne.

The outline of this new East-West alliance through marriage, and the subsequent setback to the plan, can be clearly seen from an entry in Adam of Bremen's chronicle for the year 1043, when Henry III held court at Goslar. 'Among the envoys of different countries leaving [Goslar] for home were the ambassadors of the Russians. They were returning home sadly because they had to report back a definite hesitance in regard to the position of their king's daughter, whose engagement to Henry III they had hoped to arrange.'

Thwarted but not disheartened, Yaroslav soon married his daughter Anne to King Henry I of France. But Edward the Aetheling found himself at the age of 26 relegated from his original key position in the anti-Danish alliance to a candidate for a second-rank political marriage to a relation of the Emperor, and with no other tangible prospects.

Edmund, who in 1043, at 27, was becoming a bit old for the role of eternal aetheling, was in an even less enviable situation. Because of some political *faux pas* or possible moral lapse, he was left out completely from Yaroslav's various Continental schemes. Being the elder brother, it must have been a bitter pill for him to see Edward elevated to a position of sole responsibility where England's crown or dynastic alliances were concerned.

The hopes of a triumphant return to England, implanted by Earl Walgar and nurtured by Yaroslav, retreated like a mirage under the onslaught of chilling political reality obtaining in the 1040s. The temporary condition of exile suddenly stretched endlessly ahead of the aethelings, like the steppes of Russia. And Kiev, the welcoming haven and homely refuge of their youth, began to seem in the cold light of approaching middle-age nothing so much as a place of banishment.

It is therefore not very surprising that the disappointed and disillusioned aethelings transferred their own hopes to their friends' cause and began to watch the events in Hungary with the interest they used to devote once upon a time to news from England. Hungary was, admittedly, a strange land outside the Nordic orbit, but at least it was closer to home.

76

4. King St Stephen of Hungary (as portrayed on the embroidered Coronation Cloak, c.1031, on display at the Holy Crown Exhibition, Budapest) erroneously presented as the benefactor of the two Anglo-Saxon princes and father-in-law of Edward.

12. A call from Hungary: the aethelings leave the Nordic orbit to participate in Prince Andrew's military adventure

Hungary gave the impression of being a heartbroken nation upon the death of King Stephen in 1038. The signs of popular grief were so widespread, and the manifestations of pain so genuine, that the view of indigenous chroniclers that a great calamity had befallen the country seemed no exaggeration. Hungary, bereft of the founder of its first Christian state, was in the depths of despair. As a later Hungarian chronicler put it:

> All Hungary's minstrels turned to mourning, and all the people of the country, nobles and lowborn, the rich and the poor, cried with copious tears and much wailing for a most saintly king, the most pious father of waifs. The virgins and the young men of the country took to wearing sackcloth in their grief and gave up dancing for three years. All gentle and sweet music fell silent as the people wept for the king with the pain of the purest of heart; great and disconsolate was their sorrow.

Admittedly, the country was mourning the passing of Stephen with a zeal more appropriate to a nation steeped in Christian tradition than one newly-converted. But behind the keening and wearing of sackcloth there was a great deal of self-pity and fear for the future. After Stephen's long and stable government the future seemed uncertain and the portents menacing. Under the shadow of internal strife and foreign intervention, the people were crying out in fear.

Those who feared the worst were soon proved right. Peter Orseolo, the Doge's son, who ascended the throne with the support of Queen Gisela's pro-German faction, quickly forgot the knightly virtues for which he was so praised by his benefactress and degenerated overnight into a full-blooded tyrant. He ignored the advice of the Royal Council, dismissed Stephen's bishops, pillaged, raped and terrorized the people, and launched senseless wars abroad. He also wanted the dowager queen out of the way and, though he had sworn to Stephen to be her protector, soon had her locked up and her estates confiscated. According to the *Chronica Hungarorum*:

> After becoming king, Peter shed the piousness befitting royalty, huffed and puffed with German anger, paid no attention to the nobles of Hungary, devoured the goods of this land with arrogant eyes and insatiable heart in the company of his Germans, who roar like wild beasts, and his Italians, who twitter like swallows. And he entrusted the forts, castles and fortifications to his Germans for the purpose of guarding the country.
>
> Peter himself was excessively licentious, and during his rule no one could be sure of the purity of his wife and the virginity of his daughter owing to the insolence of the king's retainers, who could rape them with impunity. The leading men of Hungary, seeing the many sufferings of our people that went against the will of God, petitioned the king as a result of a joint decision to order his men to cease their pernicious activities.
>
> But the king, disdainful in his arrogance, and spreading the stench of the poison that had taken hold of him, replied: 'Should my health hold, I will replace every councillor, the highest as well as the lowliest, village elder and town magistrate, with Germans throughout Hungary; I will also people its land with [alien] newcomers and subject them completely to the rule of Germans'. This then, was the hotbed of the strife between King Peter and the Hungarians.[1]

Since all the Catholic priests in the country were either Germans or Italians, the mounting resentment against the rule of Peter's alien administration soon turned into indiscriminate xenophobia and cast a grave shadow over the Church. Some of those who decided to fight the foreign oppressors reverted to the old Magyar customs and heathen religion. The shamans again began sacrificing white horses under oak trees in sacred groves, and the people flocked to the heathen rituals. With no clear distinction between national politics and Christianity in the state founded by Stephen, the new religion and its priests became the first victims of the popular discontent.

This instinctive reversion to the old religion was hardly surprising in a country where Christianity had been imposed with the sword by Stephen's father, Géysa, and where even the princes retained their links with outlawed shamans. 'I am rich enough to afford two gods' was the haughty reply of one magnate when reproached for sacrificing to the old pagan gods, though duly baptized and received into the Catholic Church. Inevitably, therefore, the rising against Peter was accompanied by unchecked anti-Christian outbursts. And this bode ill for the aethelings' eventual intervention there.

In 1041, Peter was forced to flee to Germany, where Henry III promised him armed support. 'The Hungarians have illegally persecuted my follo-wers, and they will be made to feel what I am prepared to do [about this] and how far I am prepared to go', the emperor raged and sent his army against Samuel Aba, who was elected king by the Hungarians.

Aba's rule proved hardly better than Peter's, and as the fight with the emperor's army ebbed and flowed, the growing frustration drove many people to the pagan revivalists, who claimed to represent the old Hungarian warrior virtues, fair government and national independence. As the popular anger mounted the national opposition became openly pagan and the Catholic Church was facing annihilation.

In the event, the insensitive manner of Peter's restoration to the throne proved to be the last straw. After the battle of Ménfö in 1044 Aba was murdered and Henry personally attended Peter's coronation at the cathedral of Székesfehérvár. As an act of abject submission, Peter prof-fered the crown of Hungary to the Emperor to receive it back as the life-tenant of an imperial fief.[2] With this single act of humiliation he united all the factions of Hungary, and pushed the country to the verge of national revolt.

In their hour of need, the magnates and barons of Hungary looked to the exiled Andrew and Levente for delivery.

At this time, some magnates of Hungary, grieving over the corrup-tion of the country, wanted to deliver Hungary from Peter's tyranny. Towards Andrew, Béla and Levente, offspring of St Stephen's dynasty, they nurtured absolute loyalty and, through their messengers, they kept sending them all the goods they pos-sessed and served them honourably.

These magnates were Viska, Bua and Buhna and their relations, and with great sadness and many sighs they waited for an appropri-ate moment to bring Andrew, Béla and Levente back into the country. With all their might, they were trying to restore the king-dom to the rule [of the kin] of St Stephen, who used to love and esteem them. But Peter, trusting in the power of the German king, did no longer rule, but rather chose to oppress Hungary with tyranny.[3]

Having got wind of the magnates' restoration plot, Peter had them and their families murdered at a wedding. The popular anger over his gratui-tous act of cruelty ignited the pagan revolt throughout the country, with consequences for Andrew's cause. For the first act of the rebels was to turn on all Germans and Italians, priests and laymen alike, and massacre them.

Amid the wholesale murder of foreigners and burning of churches the nobles of the country met at Csanád and decided to send an urgent embassy to Andrew and Levente in Kiev to seek their return. The call to lead the country against Peter and his Germans, for which the exiled princes had been waiting for so long, came amid very inauspicious circumstances. They were invited to lead the country at such a late hour that they hardly could have hoped to check, let alone control, the forces of pagan reaction unleashed by the alien Peter's tyranny.

In stark terms, the choice facing Andrew and Levente was to head the pagan, nationalist rebels against Peter's foreign Christian army, or to forget their patrimony. Levente, to judge by his unconcealed sympathy for the pagans upon his return to Hungary, cannot have had many qualms or reservations. But Andrew, the son-in-law of the pious Yaroslav and the proud bearer of the sobriquet 'Catholic', could not have found it very easy to side with the pagans against a king anointed by the Catholic Church and backed by the Holy Roman Emperor, the twin pillars of Christian Europe. Furthermore, he could not very well judge from Kiev the extent of support for the pagan leaders of the rebellion in general and his role in particular.

The envoys of the rebellious magnates arrived in Kiev in 1045. They were empowered to assure the princes that:

> the whole country was loyally awaiting, and that the whole country was pledging obedience to them if they were to come to Hungary to defend the people against the fury of the Germans. And reinforced with oaths they futher asserted that as soon as Andrew and Levente were to enter Hungary every Hungarian, as if of one heart and one soul, would join their flag and submit themselves to their rule.

In spite of the pledges of loyalty and the fulsomeness of the promises brought by the envoys, the princes hesitated. They feared, in the words of contemporary chroniclers, 'a disguised ruse'. To make sure that they were not being lured into a trap, they sent their own secret emissaries to Hungary to report on the true situation.

Meanwhile, they began recruiting a mercenary army of Varangians and Russian warriors with the money the murdered magnates Viska, Bua and Buhna had sent to them. As Andrew and Levente awaited the return of their secret envoys to Kiev, the situation in Hungary deteriorated with every passing day. But Andrew's misgivings in particular were such that he was not prepared to take the plunge before he had had his envoys' eyewitness report.

Yet it was precisely during this period of vacillation that Edmund and Edward eventually decided to join their friends in their planned military intervention in Hungary. It could not have been an easy decision to take. Everything must have militated against such a venture: Nordic ties, religious convictions, a life devoted to their duty to England. But for some reason, the forces that propelled them from the safety of Kiev into the uncertainties of a bloody civil war in south Central Europe must have been even more compelling.

In spite of diligent searching, no documentary evidence could be unearthed among the records of the countries concerned to explain the aethelings' decision to leave the Nordic orbit for good. But since it actually meant the virtual abandonment of their *raison d'être* as aethelings, the promptings of friendship and new loyalties alone could not quite justify the move.

Even the disappointment over being bypassed by England after Harthacanute's death and the subsequent downgrading of Edward's role in Yaroslav's Continental schemes could not on their own have tipped the scales in favour of such a radical departure. To judge by their upbringing and later dutiful conduct in response to England's call, it must have been some wounding slight or affront to their pride that finally precipitated their departure from Kiev.

The aethelings' reaction to the scandal or clash involving Edmund in the Kievan court, and Yaroslav's exclusion of the elder Anglo-Saxon prince from any position of responsibility would seem to have been the motive force behind the move. Personal factors can, in emotionally-charged circumstances, outweigh other considerations and provide justification for extreme actions. The symbiotic link between individuals' response and historical circumstances offers the solution to the aethelings' move to Hungary, leaving a rich field of speculation for determinists and kindred disciplines.

In 1046, the secret emissaries returned from Hungary with unequivocal confirmation that the whole nation wanted Andrew on the throne. Soon Andrew and Levente set out at the head of a strong Kievan force for Hungary, and the aethelings went with them.

Even if Paris was deemed, by a hardpressed monarch, a few centuries later, worth a Mass, there must have been some lingering reservations in the minds of the aethelings about Andrew's decision to ride to power on the backs of pagan rebels. Nevertheless, they were prepared to give it a try.

13. In the rebel camp: riding to power on the backs of pagan Magyars

Russia was still in the grip of winter when, at the beginning of 1046, Andrew and Levente led their Kievan mercenary army across the snow-bound Carpathians and entered Hungary through the Uzhok pass. Spring had come very early that year to the Hungarian plains, and the country was basking in unseasonally-warm sunshine as the Varangian swords-men, Novgorod spearmen and Kievan axemen advanced along lush river meadows into the country's interior.

The seers and diviners accompanying the Norse Varangians reported exceptionally favourable omens, and the foreign soldiery, cheered by the fine weather and wildly enthusiastic welcome by the population, made good speed along the river Tisza. The gods, it seemed, were favouring the Hungarian princes' enterprise.

Edmund and Edward Aetheling, witnessing the triumphal entry of their exile friends into Hungary, must have felt elated at being part of such a daring venture. Although their joining forces with Andrew and Levente must have been as much due to the frustration of their position in Kiev as a sincere desire to help friends in their hour of need, they were to all intents and purposes knights errant in search of adventure. There was, indeed, very little to differentiate between the position of the Anglo-Saxon princes and the Varangian soldiers-of-fortune who made up the bulk of Andrew's army. If there was some actual difference between the princes and the rest of the mercenaries, it was that the Varangians were profes-sionals with a sword to hire, while the aethelings were amateurs.

The Varangians, like the Jómvikings, were disciplined, well-trained soldiers whose lifestyle embodied the warrior ethos of the Middle Ages. Fighting was their way of life, and war their true element. They were mercenaries in an era when no pejorative meaning attached to the word, and when the hiring of one's sword was an honourable occupation.

There were no truly national wars and there was little real fighting anywhere on the Continent without the Vikings' or some of the more fierce warrior nations' participation. The prince who hired them could be assured of their loyalty so long as he could pay their wages. The rights or wrongs of a dispute were of no consequence to them, and since they could be relied upon while the native forces with an axe to grind could not, mercenaries were much sought after in every war.

Knights errant were of the same ilk, but were the scions of noble families. They too were adventurers in search of gold and glory, but owing to the social responsibility imposed by their high birth, they were not indifferent to the justness of the cause they had elected to fight for. And this introduced an element of moral obligation into their code of conduct. The aethelings, knights errant *par excellence*, were hired swords in Andrew's war against King Peter without a say in the way the war was being fought. But because of their illustrious birth they could not escape responsibility for its excesses.

As Andrew's forces approached the new fort of Abaujvár 'the whole of Hungary converged [on the fort] and they joined up in droves'. But not even the proof of ecstatic, popular support for their side could have dispelled the aethelings' misgivings over what was being perpetrated in the name of their friends.

Villages and towns were burning everywhere and amid their charred ruins the murdered officials of King Peter lay unburied awaiting disposal by wild beasts and birds-of-prey. Bands of rebels roamed the countryside in search of tithe-collectors and priests. Churches were set on fire with their foreign priests and laymen locked inside them, as the fury of anti-German rebels degenerated into a general massacre of all foreigners.

A nobleman called Vata was in the vanguard of the Christian pogroms. His followers called themselves 'the reborn people' and they shaved their heads and plaited the hair on top of their heads in the old pagan manner. Vata's rebels wanted not only to exterminate every foreigner in the land, but to eradicate their soft, Western way of life and to revert to the old traditions of the warrior Magyars of the East. The constraints of Christian attitudes, introduced a few decades earlier, melted away like snow in the glare of the spring sun, and the leadership of the anti-German revolt slipped completely from the hands of Andrew's supporters to Vata.

Indeed, the multitudes gathered at Abaujvár made their joining Andrew's flag conditional upon being allowed to live in accordance with the pagan religion:

> Egged on by the devil's incitement, they also stubbornly demanded that the bishops and priests be killed, the churches razed to the ground, Christianity cast out and the idols worshipped.
>
> And since otherwise they were not prepared to fight against King Peter and for Andrew and Levente, they were allowed to live in accordance with their forefathers' belief and head for perdition that their hearts so desired.

In the face of this massive pagan revival Andrew behaved as befitted a true politician, and simply exploited the advantages of the pagans' anti-

German drive to his own ends. As for his much-avowed Christian faith, it was not even mentioned during the months of fighting. So his zealous monastic apologists could not point out his qualms, or note any extenuating circumstances, in their chronicles; they were forced to place the blame for the Christian massacres at the door of others and so exonerate him by default.

Levente was an enthusiastic and unashamed supporter of the country's reversion to paganism. According to the chronicler Thuróczy, he openly championed the pagan way of life and, had he lived, he would have been prepared to assume the leadership of the 'reborn' Magyars and secure paganism's victory over Christianity in the country.

The divided council of their friends could not have made it any easier for the aethelings to make a stand or dissociate themselves from the massacre of Christians. Owing to linguistic difficulties they might not even have been aware of the differences between Peter's overbearing and tyrannical German officials and the gentle Catholic priests of German and Italian extraction murdered with equal zeal by the rebels. But had they been able to understand Andrew's proclamation, read at night by his men infiltrated into the towns controlled by the king, they could hardly have maintained their uncritical posture.

> By order of [the pagan] god, Andrew and Levente, the bishops together with their clergy must be killed, the collectors of tenths put to death, the old pagan traditions restored, all food and war tax abolished, and the memory of Peter, and his Germans and Italians, damned for ever and even beyond that.

As Andrew and his army 'of innumerable mercenaries' moved across central Hungary this order was fulfilled in an orgy of gruesome blood-letting. The princes reached the Danube ford of Pest early in April and four out of the country's seven Catholic bishops – Gellert, Bestrik, Budli and Beneta – hastened to welcome them to the country and enter with them the capital of Székesfehérvár.

In one of the nastiest incidents of the civil war, three of the four bishops met their end at the Danube. The Venetian-born Gellert, travelling in a cart owing to his advanced age, was attacked and stoned by the rebels at the ford. As they struck him with rocks, according to legend that grew up around his martyrdom, he kept blessing his tormentors with the sign of the cross. Eventually he was dragged from his cart by his impatient murderers and rolled into the river from the top of a nearby hill.[1]

Bishop Budli too was stoned to death, while the other two bishops crossed the river to Andrew's camp, where Bestrik was mortally wounded. All the murders were blamed by the monastic chroniclers on 'Vata and his accomplices of diabolical souls', while Prince Andrew was personally credited with saving the life of Bishop Beneta.

But as the chroniclers noted in a more objective vein, 'the number of priests and laymen who suffered martyrdom for the faith of Christ on this day was so great that only God and his angels could count them'.

King Peter himself for a while fought vigorously against Andrew's forces, and in one of the engagements Levente was seriously injured, and died within a year of his wounds. Peter tried to enter the capital with his German mercenaries to make a final stand against Andrew's forces, but the townspeople locked the gates and refused to let him in.

In the face of the hostility of the entire country he tried to flee to Austria with his Germans, but Andrew's troops had succeeded in blocking the frontiers and prevented the king's escape. Peter's fate was sealed.

An envoy of Prince Andrew called him back under the pretext of peace negotiations, assuring him of due respect and honour for his person. He accepted the [safe conduct] pledge, as it is being said, but he returned more likely out of necessity because he knew that he had been cut off from his troops, and wanted to return to [Székes] Fehérvár.

When he entered the village of Zámoly, Andrew's envoy wanted to have him arrested in order to take him bound and gagged to his prince. Peter, sensing the envoy's intention, betook himself into a manor house and fought and defended himself bravely for three days. In the end, after all his soldiers had been killed by Andrew's archers, he was taken prisoner. His eyes were then gouged out by his captors and he was taken to the capital, where he soon died in agony.

His death on 15 April 1046 signalled the end of the anti-German rising that had brought the two Anglo-Saxon princes so fortuitously to Hungary. It also brought to an abrupt end the alliance of anti-German factions and pagan nationalist forces. The aethelings could now part company with the many warlocks, witches, magicians, seers and shamans who were used to strengthen Andrew's army on Levente's insistence, without giving offence to their hosts.

Andrew ascended the throne and was crowned by the four surviving bishops of the country the following year with all the pomp and circumstance of a Christian king even though, as the Alteich *Chronicle* remarked, 'earlier he had raged with great fury against the host of the Holy Church'.

Once securely in the saddle, Andrew outlawed the heathen religion and ordered his countrymen to return, on pain of death, to the Catholic Church. The lapsed laws of King Stephen were zealously enforced and Hungary once again took its place among the devoutly Christian states of Europe. The expediency of the power struggle was over and to distance himself from its excesses, Andrew called himself 'the White'. Loyal

ono dur augens a pturbaco
mbz hostum fciuus effectus
mtugia cuutate alba regalem
coronam e accpms. A tmbus
tautum epis qui mulla maj
sitage ypianoz auseram co
ronatus e Anno comm. O.
xl'vii precepit itap unucse

5. The coronation of Andrew I of Hungary in 1047 after his return from
Kiev accompanied by his Anglo-Saxon comrades-in-arms, Edmund and
Edward Aetheling. (From *Kézai Simon Krónikája* 1283).

chroniclers also appended the epithet 'Catholic' to his name in a further
act of symbolic absolution.

The aethelings, without having moved or changed sides, were once
again within the pale of the Catholic Church and fortune began to smile
on them. Their friend, the king, was handsomely rewarding all those who

had stood by him in his years of exile. The message Andrew sent to his brother Béla in Poland encapsulates his desire to show generosity to those who were kind to him in his hour of need: 'Once', he wrote, 'we were comrades in need and suffering. Therefore, I beg you, my beloved brother, do not delay your return so that we could be comrades in happiness as well, and, enjoying the goods of the country, we should share them out together in your personal presence . . .'

There are indications that Andrew showered the aethelings with estates and offered them an honoured place at his court. Since the lavishness of royal favours would indicate that they were in response to services rendered, not mere affection for exile friends, the conclusion is inevitable that they were in recognition of the aethelings' bravery in the fight for Andrew's throne.

Regrettably, there is now no documentary evidence of Edmund and Edward's role in the fighting against King Peter's German followers. But Henry III's seemingly inexplicable hostility towards Edward appears to have had its origins in the aetheling's part in the driving out of Hungary of the Emperor's protégé and his armies (see Chapter 19, p. 132).

The Emperor's animosity, however, did not worry the aethelings unduly just then. After so much helpless drifting, their ship was firmly anchored in a safe and friendly haven. Life was good in Hungary and the future promising. Fortune, at last, was giving them with both hands all that she had so cruelly withheld in the past.

PART IV: HOME FROM HOME IN SOUTH-EASTERN EUROPE

14. Signs of royal favour: In search of the aethelings' footsteps at Mecseknádasd, 'The Lands of Britons'

The year of Grace 1048 found Edmund and Edward happily settled in Hungary. They were not the wards of the pious King Stephen nor the recipients of charity at the court of King Salomon, as claimed by the Anglo-Norman chroniclers. But they *were* actually living in Hungary, even if they had arrived there under different circumstances and at a much later date than the jumbled accounts of the British chroniclers would have us believe.

They were living not as refugees but as comrades-in-arms of King Andrew the Catholic, favoured and cherished for services rendered to the throne. And this difference in their condition opens up fresh sources of material evidence in the reconstruction of their years of Continental exile.

Youthful refugees eating crumbs from the table of a benevolent king can hardly be expected to make their mark on their adoptive country. But foreign princes who had fought for the establishment of the regime enjoy equal rights with the indigenous supporters of the crown and are, as a result, integrated into the system by a grateful sovereign. Traces of the aethelings' life as feudatories of Andrew the Catholic could not have vanished completely, and the search for some evidence of it must begin with an examination of accounts of royal recognition of vassalage.

The traditional form of royal favour in eleventh-century Hungary, like in the rest of Central and Western Europe, was the granting of démesne lands for feudal tenure, which at once established the recipient's position in and obligation to society. Andrew is known to have granted large estates from crown lands to Hungarian barons in exchange for frontier defence service, and to foreign courtiers for a nominal scutage.

Some of these grants were recorded by the scribes of the royal chancellery, but other, especially before 1056, were verbal and so cannot be traced.

A Domesday Book-type compilation of all households, ordered by Judge Sarchas, an influential official at Andrew's court, in 1056, is most likely to have contained an account of the aethelings' possessions, but

6. Crucial evidence of the Anglo-Saxon princes' sojourn in south Hungary near Nádasd: a 1404 copy of a 1235 land deed believed to have been faked in the 15th century, which mentions 'the land of Britons' (Terra Britanorum de Nádasd) as a well-known landmark. The use of centuries-old local landmarks in a 15th century land dispute was supposed to have lent verisimilitude to the rights of one of the claimants. (Ms. Somogyvári transsumptum 76/1404, originally from the Archives of the

unfortunately it was destroyed in the Mongol invasion of the thirteenth century.[1] Those wishing to prove ownership in land disputes were forced thereafter either to have their title reaffirmed by the sovereign or to sift through thirteenth-century or later deeds and church property registers for clues about their lands in the missing period between the middle of the eleventh and the middle of the thirteenth century.

A deed of gift issued in 1235, but surviving in a 1404 copy, contains a tantalizing reference to lands in south Hungary that might have been part of the aethelings' estates. The land of Máza was presented by Andrew II to Bishop Bartholomew of Pécs for important services rendered. The Latin-language deed,[2] describing the boundaries of the bishop's lands, makes a passing reference to 'the Lands of Britons as Nádasd'. At any rate, this was the reading of the first firm medieval reference to lands owned by the aethelings in Hungary in the full transcript of the deed included in György Fejér's authoritative *Codex Diplomaticus* published in 1829.[3]

The excitement engendered by this possibly crucial piece of evidence in the 1235 deed is heightened by the fact that the scribe not only included the 'Lands of Britons' among the best-known landmarks near the bishop's estates, but referred to them twice. The other landmarks mentioned by the scribe were an oaktree, a pine tree (described quite unusually with the Hungarian word *fenyeufa* in the Latin text, perhaps because the scribe did not know the Latin equivalent) and the church of St Ladislas. All four were in the village of Nádasd (now Mecseknádasd) in the Pécs district of the county of Baranya, right next to the medieval properties of the bishopric of Pécs.

The church still stands but has subsequently been renamed St Stephen's church and serves as a chapel in the village cemetery. The oaktree is gone but the minutes of a 1777 *Visitatio Canonica* record that Father Vizer, the village priest of Mecseknádasd, had measured a giant oaktree then still standing on the rim of the village boundary and found its circumference to be six *öl* (one *öl* equals 1.83 metres, making it about 33 feet) and its height 13 *öl*, about 80 feet. The extraordinary girth and height of the oaktree, noted in 1777, would date it to the eleventh century, therefore one of the best-known landmarks together with the 'Lands of Britons' which the 1235 deed could have used in describing the territorial boundaries of Bishop Bartholomew's lands.

There is a fiercely-contested controversy among Hungarian medievalists whether the extant deed is a straightforward copy made in 1404 of the 1235 original, or a forgery prepared for use in a fifteenth-century land dispute. Jozsef Holub, a Pécs medievalist, seems to provide the last word in this long-running controversy, claiming it to be a 1404 copy of the now missing thirteenth-century original, but even if it were to prove a fifteenth-century forgery, it would not diminish its importance for the purpose of this inquiry.[4]

For a start, the document is not purporting to establish the aethelings' actual ownership of the 'Lands of Britons'. The aethelings' land is used only as a landmark. And a fifteenth-century forger determined to lend verisimilitude to a land claim, would have gone out of his way to use only very well-known landmarks along the boundaries of the disputed estates. For unless these landmarks were locally well established and went back several centuries, their inclusion would be counterproductive. And this indicates the 'Lands of Britons' was still the local place-name in the Pécs district of Nádasd in the fifteenth century.

Though the intrinsic value of this land deed rests on its emphasis of the existence of a local tradition about the aethelings' presence at Nádasd at some stage, a palaeographic examination of the text is necessary in view of a further controversy among philologists regarding the reference to 'Lands of Britons'.

Fejér's authoritative 1829 transcription of the deed gives in the preface its date as 1235 and establishes that the crucial landmark refers unequivocally to 'the Lands of Britons of Nádasd'.[5] The relevant passage of the deed is as follows in the nineteenth-century orthography of the transcriber:

> ...Transit ad dictum fluvium a parte orientali ad plagam meridionalem procedendo vadit ad quandem arborem *Fenyeufa* dictum; ubi est arbor illicis, cruce signata meta terrae circumfusa, et ibi incipit vicinitatem tenere *cum terris Brittannorum de Nadasth*, adhuc de parte meridionali procedendo versus occidentem iuxta terras memoratorum Brittannorum in via magna, que est in vertice montis, per quam venitur ad Ecclesiam Sancti Ladislai Regis cum continuis metis, et continuantur metis Monasterii Varadiensis...
>
> (Past the said river, the boundaries [of Máza] stretched in the east proceeding in a southerly direction to the tree called pine tree; where stood at the southerly end of the eastern boundary an oak, marked with the cross, and at which point the lands of the Britons of Nadasth began: and then proceeding from the south due west along the mentioned lands of Britons on the great road, which is on a mountain top and runs along continuously marked boundary marks, we come to the church of St Ladislas and then continue with the boundary marks of the Várad monastery...[6])

Fejér's change of the original script of 'terris Britanorum de Nadasd', to the nineteenth-century orthography of the word (Brittannorum) made no difference to the actual reading of this crucial passage. But Dr Dezsö Csánki, who published an exhaustive study of the region in 1897,[7] questioned Fejér's transcript of the deed insisting that it referred to 'terris Bisanorum de Nadasd', the land of Pecheneg frontiersmen, not Britons.

Szabolcs de Vajay, a noted medievalist now living in Switzerland, also

7. The key sentence referring to the 'Terra Britanorum de Nádasd' in the 1404 land deed. There has been a long-running dispute among Hungarian philologists as to the significance – and correct reading – of the words.

construed this crucial passage to be a reference to the Pechenegs who were settled in the region to defend the Buda-Osiek-Nándorfehérvár military road, alluded to in the deed as the 'great road'.

The opposite view, insisting on the absolute correctness of the 'terris Britanorum de Nadasd' was taken by Dr József Rézbányai who joined battle with the challengers in a learned article in the Budapest *Katholikus Szemle (Catholic Review)* of 1896. He and a succession of others have argued with equal conviction that the deed reads 'terris Britanorum' and that there can be no philological doubts about the correctness of this view.[8] The latest recruit to this camp is Dr Maria Sándor, the offical archaeologist in charge of the restoration of the ancient St Stephen's Church at Mecseknádasd. In her account of the work, carried out under the auspices of the Institute of Archaeology of the Academy of Sciences, she quotes the 'terris Britanorum' among the landmarks leading to the church. Far from challenging the reading of the passage as the 'lands of Britons', she extends recognition to the erudition of the medieval Latin script expert who confirmed the correctness of her rendering of the words.

Professor György Györffy, the foremost Hungarian authority on the period appears to settle the linguistic argument by pointing out that the mass migration of Pechenegs only began after 1071; therefore they could not have been named *after* the Pechenegs places in the 1040s. Besides, Pecheneg locality names do *not* accord with Nádasd.[9]

In view of the controversy over the reading of this key reference to the aethelings' reputed estate, it seemed absolutely necessary to form a personal, dispassionate opinion by analysing the script of the deed *in situ*. However, a research trip to Mecseknádasd, within the framework of the British Council's cultural exchange programme with Hungary, was blocked without explanation in the last minute by the Hungarian authorities revealing unsuspected twentieth-century political dimensions to the Hungarian sojourn of the two Anglo-Saxon princes.

The best alternative solution in the circumstances was to obtain, through intermediaries, a photographic enlargement of the deed from the Hungarian National Archives. An analysis of the script indicated a Renaissance hand using traditional letters and abbreviations. In the first of the two references to 'Britons' the capital 'B' is followed by a clearly-recognizable 'r' and 'i' but the crucial next letter poses some problems. It appears not unlike the 't's in the rest of the text, though somewhat smaller than those immediately preceding and following it. A statistical measurement of a set number of identifiable 't's and 's's would place this key fourth letter in the word closer to a 't' than an 's' and, together with the following 'a', 'n', 'o' and 'r' would add up to 'Britanor', rounded off with a traditional abbreviation reasonably construed as standing for 'um'.

The second reputed reference to 'Britons' in the same sentence was not sufficiently legible in the photographic copy to allow identification, let alone analysis, making this present, somewhat handicapped, attempt at coming to a definitive conclusion in the 'terris Britanorum' / 'terris Bisanorum' controversy indecisive.

This does not obviate the recognition that old documents can shed unexpected light on stubbornly-held local beliefs, like the Anglo-Saxon princes' association with Nádasd, not through their intended meaning but their vocabulary, grammar or the use of certain expressions.

The use of the word 'Britons' in the Máza deed is a case in point. What prompted the monastic scribe to use the term 'Britons' – if that be the correct interpretation – when the traditional reference to the island races in Western and Central Europe was 'English', and what could this surprising local usage reveal?

Most French and German chroniclers of the tenth and eleventh centuries refer in their Latin-language writings to the people of England as 'Angli'. The English chronicles and legal documents of the period also preferred to describe the indigenous population as 'English' and the newcomers as 'French'.

Scribes writing in the first century of the new millennium generally used the term 'British' to describe the Celtic peoples of the islands, while the anonymous author who compiled the *Leges Edovardi Confessoris* around 1130 in Coventry used the term 'British' more than once in a brief historical passage on the last Anglo-Saxon kings in order to claim the lordship of 'Britain', including the Celtic kingdoms.

But parallel with this fairly clear-cut usage, there appears to have been an older, monastic tradition which applied the etymon 'British' both to these islands and all their people. The *Anglo-Saxon Chronicle* begins with the significant description: 'Brittene izland is ehta hund nula lang', while another Saxon scribe of the *Chronicle* referred to the country as 'Britannia insula'.[10]

Owing to the laxity of the use of nation names in Latin, the reference to the island race became more ambiguous especially in South and Southeast Europe. Prokopius, for instance, used the word 'Brittia' when writing about the British Isles between the Saxcn conquest and the advent of Christianity.[11] He was apparently well aware that 'Bretannia' was an island, as well as a country. When offering 'Bretannia' to the Goths, Belisarios is quoted by him as saying that it was an island much bigger than Sicily.

Prosper, in his *Chronicon* also referred to these islands as 'Britannia' ('Britannia usque ad hoc tempus variis cladibus eventibusque laceratae, in ditionem Saxonum rediguntur') emphasizing that the reference to the island races as 'Britons' went back to the Dark Ages in the Mediterranean region.

The use of the term 'terris Britanorum' in a land deed penned by a medieval Hungarian scribe could well have been the reflection of established local reference to the aethelings employing the accepted Southern European usage of the word Britons. The diocese of Pécs's extremely close links with Byzantium in the preceding centuries could well be behind the scribe's choice of Britons instead of English. To the Byzantines, with their classical education, the barbarian Saxon invasion was merely a hiccup, and they continued to refer to the British Isles by their classical names.

But the usage may also contain a hidden indication of how the aethelings used to refer to the island race and themselves. Having been removed from England while still babies, they could hardly have known the current word used by their compatriots to describe themselves. Indeed, they could only have seen their homeland with and through the eyes of foreigners, and since the cultural environment of Kiev where they had grown up was dominated by the Byzantine Orthodox Church, the traditional South-European reference to the island race would have seemed the natural one to them.

This view is reinforced by the eleventh-century Polish monastic chronicler, Dlugosz, who, in writing about the 1066 invasion of Britain, used the word 'English' as a voguish synonym of the established 'British', indicating that in Eastern Europe the two words were coextensive.[12]

This reference to Britons at Nádasd surfaced a few centuries later in the most unexpected and at the same time significant form of the middle-name 'Britanicus' in the family of Count Nádasdy whose forebears came from the region. Indeed, the family name derives from reedy water (nádas in Hungarian) and the forebears of the Nádasdys had in their coat-of-arms a wild duck standing in reedy water. The link between this unusual middle-name in a family that still owned the territory in the thirteenth century and the original tenure of the Mecseknádasd estates by the aethelings would seem to be too great a coincidence to be dismissed as of no significance from a thorough-going investigation, raising the possibility that the Nádasdy forebears were perhaps retainers left in charge of the estates after Edward's return to Britain.

On the strength of documentary evidence it can be established that towards the end of the thirteenth century the Mecseknádasd lands and a castle that stood there were owned by a Count Cletus, and in 1296 there was a reference to 'possessio et castrum Nadasd', then still in the county of Tolna; subsequently Count Cletus's three sons, then his three grandsons, shared the Nádasd lands;[13] in 1330, the priory of Tolna took possession of the estates, when the uninhabited castle was already in ruins; the next owners were the Darabos family who were closely related to the Nádasdys; in 1433, it belonged to Philip Korogyi, and in 1454, the estates were ceded to the county of Baranya; in 1465, there was a reference to the 'oppidum Nadasd' then owned by the Marothi family; in 1473, it went to Miklos Csupor. Such are the ascertainable facts about the owners of the lands at Nádasd.

But in order to gain true insight into the vanished world of the aethelings one has to look beyond the recorded facts of the period, for the chronicles and annals were written in response to the interests of the powers temporal and spiritual and this implies a certain selectivity.

The aethelings' arrival in Hungary in the course of the pagan rebellion could have elicited an unfortunate bias in the attitude of monastic scribes who recorded the events, both local and national, after the restoration of Christianity.

Local myths, on the other hand, contain sometimes the vestiges of events uncensored by official interests, and the oral tradition of Nádasd seems to encapsulate the memory of the aethelings' stay. Not unlike the unintentional intelligence included in land deeds, the oral tradition harbours hidden but useful pointers in the quest for Edmund and Edward's sojourn in south Hungary.

The deeply-incised marks of the aethelings' presence at Nádasd can be discerned from local place-names, for popular memory can go back a surprisingly long way and the names that were handed from generation to generation are the monuments of events and people that stood out amid the trivial preoccupations of ordinary villagers.

Mecseknádasd, like so many other villages and towns in Hungary, had a ruined castle, memento of the many invading armies that left their mark on the countryside. The remains indicate a once impressive building which used to crown a hillock in the eastern, so-called lower end of the village. It is called 'Castle Mound' to this day.

Documentary references to the 'Castle Mound' edifice go back to the sixteenth century but not further. The Turks occupied it in 1543 during their drive to Vienna and the Turkish traveller, Chelebi Evlia, noted its

8. View of the mountain at Nádasd, south Hungary, where the ruins of
Rékavár castle, reputed to have belonged to Edward the Exile in the early
1050s, have been uncovered. Preliminary excavations were carried out by
the Museum of Pécs in 1963.

existence in his book: 'The castle stands on an almond-shaped hillock
surrounded by a strong, double palisade. . . Inside the castle stands a
church now converted into a *dzhami*.'

The records of the canonical visits after the explusion of the Turks refer
from 1721 until the Napoleonic wars to the castle and a map of the village
drawn by German colonists settled there as a replacement for the destroyed local population in about 1720 duly marks the castle on the
Schlossberg (Castle Mound).

In spite of the presence of romantic ruins of historic distinction atop
Castle Mound, local tradition has always associated a mound west of the
village with the stay of the Anglo-Saxon princes. Since the wooded slopes
are now singularly lacking in ruins, this association is rather significant.

In its many layers, the local lore has retained a jumble of odd references
and thrilling (but unverifiable) information about Edward and Edmund's
sojourn. Like traces of gold in an abandoned mine, the information is too
patchy and, in part, contradictory, to be taken at face value, yet certain
facts ingrained in the oral tradition have a quaint sense of plausibility
about them.

The mound, west of the village overlooks the stream Réka, and is
locally known as 'Rékavár' (Réka Castle), even though there are no visible
remains of any castle. The odd thing about this association of the aethelings with 'Rékavár' is that Réka was the reputed – though historically

99

never proved – daughter of King Stephen, whose death had started the civil war that eventually brought the aethelings to Hungary.

According to the villagers, not only the aethelings but eventually Edward's wife and three children had lived in the 'Rékavár' castle and they cite as evidence of popular memory the unexpected local place name of 'The English Virgin's Hill' allegedly so called after Edward's daughter, Margaret. A bridge, between Mecseknádasd and the nearby village of Hidas, is still known as 'the Bridge of the Three Princes', after Edward's three children, and is locally seen as further evidence of the Anglo-Saxon princes' association with the village.

As far as historical facts are concerned, however, these local names are of no provable value even if, like the rest of this stubbornly maintained local belief, they might contain hidden pointers to events that took place over 900 years ago in the life of the village.

In the quest for tangible proof of the aethelings' stay at Mecseknádasd, the topographical features and landmarks described in the 1235 Máza land deed provide a more profitable opening and, quite astonishingly, the recorded position of the 'lands of Britons' appears to fit Réka Castle.

In 1937, exploratory excavations were begun by János Dombai, a Pécs archaeologist, on the Réka Castle mound. They uncovered the remains of unusually solid walls under the surface but the outbreak of the Second World War brought the work to a halt. Malcomes gave the following description of the finds:

> On one side, Réka Castle looked down on the quaint valley of the Réka stream, dotted with water-mills, on the other side on the valley of Óbánya, through which flows a smaller brook. Outside the castle walls, the shape of a deep moat is clearly visible along the wall's far side. The walls emerging from the debris were virtually level with the ground when the excavations began. . .
>
> The ruins stretch from the north-west in a south-westerly direction. Since the mound is covered by undergrowth and is strewn with rubble, and furthermore the ground is very uneven, only a rough sketch of the castle area could be made. The outer wall is 105 by 30 metres, and the walls on the longer side have circular arches. At the south-west and north-east corners of the castle, ruins of several buildings can be discerned. What remains of the walls shows that the castle gate must have been between the two towers in the north-east side.[14]

The uncovering of foundation walls on the site seems to have filled Malcomes with uncontrollable enthusiasm and his subsequent approach to the possible tenants of Réka Castle lost all historical perspective.

His categorical assertion, on the strength of a preliminary dig, that Réka Castle was the home of the aethelings and their family members ignored the possibility that the uncovered buildings might date from the days of the Frankish empire or even Roman times.

Not until 1963 was work resumed once again on the Réka Castle site. Lászlo Papp, who headed the excavations, confirmed the presence of foundation walls surprisingly massive even by the scale of medieval masonry.[15] But his exploratory dig soon ground to a halt in some confusion because, in the opinion of Pécs archaeologists, he mistook the Castle Mound site for Réka Castle and tried to use the historical documentation of the former to map out the work on the latter.

After this setback, the question whether the controversy about the medieval tenant of Réka Castle could be settled with the aid of further excavations was left in abeyance. A recently-begun excavation, led by Dr Mária Sándor who restored the nearby St Stephen's Church, may yet throw up some material evidence that could, conceivably, settle the vexed issue of the Anglo-Saxon princes' sojourn at Nádasd. But the work, carried out more circumspectly, will take a long time to complete and, as she informed me in a letter, 'the evaluation of the uncovered material has not yet begun'.

Like the 1235 Máza land deed, the tantalizing clues ingrained in the local lore seem to substantiate the aethelings' stay at Nádasd but the provable facts are inconclusive.

15. Scandal at court: the fiery love of a Hungarian princess and its consequences

The lifestyle of Andrew the Catholic's court provided the framework for Edmund and Edward's existence during their sojourn in Hungary. Life centred round royal castles and manor houses, overlaid by a social superstructure borrowed from the Frankish empire.

But the tone remained distinctly Hungarian, despite the Western trappings. The aethelings, brought up on Nordic ideals and Kievan orthodoxy, must have found this tone somewhat trying. The heady mixture of ornate Carlovingian elegance, German fervour and Eastern warrior ethics that characterized Andrew's court could hardly have appealed to them in the massive doses that their friendship with the king would have made inevitable.

The court moved from one manor house to another in order to spread the burden of feeding the king's huge retinue among the royal estates. But this peripatetic existence also fulfilled a deeper, psychological need rooted in the free-roving past of these newly settled steppe warriors. The movement of the court from manor to manor followed the Magyars' age-old rhythm of life, the natural cycle of horsemen and animal husbandmen moving from pasture to pasture.

Though the pagan rebels had systematically burned down the properties of Peter's German and Italian courtiers, the network of castles and manor houses created by Stephen to cover the whole country remained essentially intact. Their density was greatest on the central plains, where the estates of the ruling Árpád clan lay. In the fertile central reaches of the Danube, there was a royal manor every 25 to 30 kilometers so that the king's cortège could move to the next house without effort, with plenty of time for hunting, drinking and resting along the route.

Since the aethelings' estates were on crown lands, whether at Nádasd or elsewhere, they were included organizationally in the year-long social whirl of the itinerant court. This moveable feast required that each manor house on the royal roster should have considerable food surpluses and amenities, and in order to assure these they needed lots of land and manpower. An eleventh-century register of the estates of the Pécsvárad abbey, the next-door neighbours of the tenants of Réka Castle at Nádasd, gives a fair inkling of the size and organization of the aethelings' own démesne.

The estates, settled on the abbey by King Stephen, comprised 40 villages and 1116 souls. The lands were contiguous and the manor house, built in a quadrangle, was well fortified and surrounded by earthworks. The manor owned 120 horses, 84 cows, 137 pigs, 92 goats and 1464 sheep.

But its real source of wealth was the skill of its villeins, composed of freemen, semi-tied farmers and artisans, and slaves.

The manor had twelve beekeepers, six coopers, twelve platemakers, three millers, three potters, nine bakers, ten cooks, ten blacksmiths and farriers, five goldsmiths, eight carpenters and six tanners. Its lands were tilled by slave ploughmen, but the bulk of the manor's food supplies came from villeins farming on their own who had to surrender a fixed percentage of their produce.

The semi-free vintners, fishermen and fowlers provided specialized services and mounted serfs, with flocks of their own, contributed a set amount of field labour with their animals and carts. The herds and flocks were tended by sixteen shepherds, and the safety of the entire manor and its inhabitants was entrusted to free warriors, who made up 18 per cent of the Pécsvárad population.

The wealth they produced assured ample resources and a pleasing lifestyle for the lord of the manor. The aethelings, like the other magnates of the realm, could devote their time to enjoyable pursuits. The court's arrival at a manor house signalled the start of a round of masculine entertainment that would sometimes go on for twenty days or longer.

Hunting was the chief diversion and the employment of falconers, dogkeepers and netmakers, apart from huntsmen proper, gives some idea of the wide variety of game pursued by the king and his retainers. After a day's sport they would eat, drink and make merry in the new style befitting a Christian king's court, although minstrels still sang in praise of the joys of the pagan forefathers' plundering raids on Western Europe.

Not surprisingly, in view of the Frankish example, great attention was paid at court to dressing, and the material for the costly apparel of the magnates and the king were imported from Italy and Byzantium. Tailors and furriers in the royal train were kept just as busy as the swordsmiths, arrow-makers and saddlers, giving a fair impression of the Magyar court's horizon of interests.

The attention devoted to horses was the one sphere of courtly life where the traditions of a nation of steppe horsemen differed greatly from the Western European nobles' attitude to their charges. The king had scores of studs to provide the court, the royal messengers, and bailiffs with mounts, but the money spent on horse-breeding at the main royal stables on the Danube island of Csepel reveals something of an obsessional preoccupation with horses.

Surviving documents of the time show the existence of post stations at points where military roads intersected county (comitatus) boundaries. There the king, his court, his messengers and the royal princes could have a change of horses to take them as far, but no further, than the nearest station in the next county. (A similar organization inside Genghis Khan's empire, governed by almost identical privileges and prerogatives, was revealed when the Mongols invaded Europe in the thirteenth century.)

As a woman, Queen Anastasia, the aethelings' cousin, was left out of the masculine sports of the king and his barons. While the men roistered, Anastasia and her ladies-in-waiting did needlework and embroidered vestments for presentation to churches on the royal lands.

But Anastasia made her presence felt in many other ways and ushered in stricter, Christian *mœurs* in court life. Although to some sceptical courtiers it might have seemed paradoxical that the Russian Orthodox wife of a sovereign swept to power by a pagan rebellion should be trying to instil the moral teachings of the Roman Catholic Church in Hungary, her sincerity could not be questioned. The Christian fervour of her father, Yaroslav the Great, was too well known to allow that.

There were other forces at work too which helped to change the Eastern attitude to women and their position in society. Together with the ideals of chivalry, the romantic adoration of gracious ladies was imported from Western Europe. Hungarian knights began exalting, like their German and French comrades-in-arms, the divine creatures whose service reputedly lent strength to their arms in battle. The cult of chivalrous love began to influence the nobles at Andrew's court.

But while knights in shining armour placed the ethereal object of their desire on a pedestal, the yearnings of the flesh forced them to seek the favours of more down-to-earth ladies not given to the new-fangled rigmarole of verbal love-making. Being worshipped like a goddess with ecstatic love poems might have amused some aristocratic maidens, but most highborn girls still preferred the steppe people's time-honoured ritual of courtship. And lower down the social scale the ancient ways of wooing, intertwined with pagan beliefs and customs, remained unaltered.

In this changing world, the old traditions of courtship and imported Western courtly morals lived side-by-side in uneasy coexistence. Even Andrew the Catholic kept concubines in the pagan style, in spite of the Church's and his wife's vocal disapproval.

The old Magyar ways were being discouraged but the new, Western sexual *mœurs* still seemed too alien to many, and not even the Church's ruthless intervention could alter this. Though the singing of the ancient 'flower songs', the traditional means of wooing, had been declared a mortal sin by the Church, determined to extirpate all vestiges of the pagan past, the old ways persisted.

Edmund was 30 and Edward 29 when they moved to Hungary in 1046, men in their prime, not indifferent to the charms of the opposite sex. Their friend's court, full of intriguing, ambitious women, must have offered

104

plenty of temptation and even more opportunity for adventures. Amid the conflicting – and for a foreigner, probably incomprehensible – sexual attitudes, Edmund appears to have followed his male instincts. It led him into the bed of a high-born lady and, quite naturally, a scandal ensued.

Gaimar's chronicle has preserved for posterity the outline of Edmund's *faux pas* that compromised a princess's honour and endangered his own position. But the time of the romance, the girl involved and the actual resolution of the crisis cannot now be gauged with certainty from the confusion of facts included in the second half of the chronicle.

Nevertheless, the account rings basically true, and since Gaimer could not have had any political reason to include an apocryphal sexual escapade, his story must have a kernel of truth worth disentangling.

Gaimar places the beginning of the love affair three years after the aethelings' arrival in Hungary. But since he left out of his calculations the 17 years the princes had spent in Russia (for reasons explained in Part II, Chapter 7), Edmund was not in his teens but at least thirty when he made a royal princess pregnant and set the tongues of court gossips wagging.

There are other discrepancies too in Gaimar's version of the scandal. The elder English prince in the eye of the storm was not Edgar but Edmund; and his high-born mistress could not have been the king's eldest daughter because Andrew's oldest child, the princess Adelheid, was born in Kiev around 1040, or 1041, which would have made her barely eight at the start of the torrid love affair. Furthermore, Margaret, the future queen of Malcolm of Scotland, and Edgar the Aetheling, her brother, were not born out of this romantic union as claimed; they were the children of Edward, Edmund's younger brother, though admittedly they were born in Hungary.

The strands of at least two, but possibly three, sets of events can be discerned here which Gaimar spun, with the knack of a born story-teller, into one racy yarn. Whether he did this out of carelessness, confusion, or in order to lend his story consistency, is difficult to say. Certainly, his geographical confusion over Russia and Hungary and the resulting chronological discrepancy required a bit of blurring of known subsequent events, otherwise these would not have fitted into the general drift of his chronicle.

To an extent, therefore, Gaimar could be suspected of having dovetailed certain facts in the interest of the chronological continuity of the narrative, although he is much more likely to have misunderstood the fading recollections of ageing informants upon whose account the greater part of his chronicle is based.

A careful reading of the account of the escapade leaves one with the clear impression that Gaimar must have heard about a scandal involving Edmund and a Continental princess, although his informant could not be sure anymore about the names of people involved, or the place and exact time of the recounted incident. But because of the underlying factual thread, it is worth examining further Gaimar's garbled version.

> The children remained there [Hungary];
> Three years later they were grown up.
> The younger was fifteen years old.
> But the eldest was the taller.
> He had passed nineteen years.
> Edgar [*sic*] was his name. He was well favoured.
> The king's daughter took him for her lover.
> And he loved her, this was known.
> Before a whole year had passed,
> The lady became pregnant.
> What shall I say? It went so far
> That the matter could not be concealed.
> The king heard it, it was related to him.
> He was but little wroth.
> He even said he would agree to [a marriage].
> If he would take her, he would give her to him.
> The youth kissed the king's foot.
> And he summoned his folk.
> The next day was the meeting;
> The king gave his daughter to Edgar.
> Before his people he married her,
> And the king gave all to know
> That Edgar should be his heir after his days.
> As he had no son, he made him his heir,
> Because of his eldest daughter whom he took.
> Therefore have I told you, I would have you know,
> Marvel not at it.
> From this Edgar and his wife
> Issued the precious gem,
> Margaret they called her.
> King Malcolm made her his queen.
> She had an elder brother,
> Edgar the Aetheling was he named.
> The English sent for the children,
> For their father was no longer alive.
> The two children were the right heirs,
> To those who would acknowledge them as true.[1]

Leaving aside the problems posed by the many confusing errors of fact, the most interesting information to emerge is that Edmund did not actually seduce his princess; the tall, handsome English prince was coolly chosen as a lover by an aristocratic lady in accordance with the customs of the old Magyar traditions. And this would fit the ambivalent *mœurs* of Andrew's court, wavering between Eastern and Western ways.

The freedom enjoyed by women, especially aristocratic women, in the clan system of pagan Magyars would have made the more usual Western scenario of seduction, pregnancy and a 'shotgun wedding' quite implausible in the Hungary of the late 1040s. Gaimar, a product of Anglo-Norman court *mœurs*, could not have known this, which underlines that he did not invent Edmund's escapade. He must have heard about it from one of his family sources.

But who was Edmund's concupiscent lady, since age ruled out Andrew's daughter? A process of elimination would also rule out a daughter of King Stephen – if one were to try and move the incident back to 1031, the year indicated by Gaimar for the love affair – because his children would have been far too old. Nor could this sexual transgression have taken place in Gardorika-Gardimbre, assuming that Gaimar's faulty knowledge of geography had made him place a Russian court scandal into Hungary, because Yaroslav's daughters were the aethelings' cousins and the Orthodox Church considered love-making between cousins as incest. In the face of such an illicit relationship, the royal father in question would most certainly have been more than 'but a little wroth'.

This leaves one of the several branches of the ruling Árpád dynasty in Hungary, whose daughters would be styled, in the transcription of Western chroniclers, as royal princesses. A sister of Samuel Aba, who ruled briefly between 1041 and 1044, could fit the bill, or any other royal princess from the huge Árpád clan.

The chronicles of Anglo-Norman historians offer no help either in identifying Edmund's royal paramour. Ailred, the Yorkshire abbot of Rievaulx, recorded that Edmund married the daughter of the Hungarian king but omitted to include the name of the king or his daughter.[2]

The chronological logic of Ailred's account would place the event in the reign of King Stephen – a possibility already discounted. Even more baffling is the remark of the near-contemporary Bishop Guy of Amiens about Edmund that 'the boy was raised to the rank of king'.

This wild claim seems to be reflected in Gaimar's confident assertion that the Hungarian king gave his court to understand that his son-in-law 'should be made his heir after his days. . . because of his eldest daughter whom he took'. The laws of succession under the Árpád dynasty, strictly observed even in the strained circumstances of civil war, would rule out completely the idea of a foreign heir to the Hungarian throne. Only a descendant of the Árpád clan, or at least a blood relation, had the right to succession and Edmund, of course, could not fulfil this basic requirement.

Somewhere, someone, along the long chain of tale-bearers, misunderstood or misconstrued the facts of Edmund's escapade, allowing the Anglo-Norman chroniclers, hungry for royal scandal, to interpret its consequences in accordance with the expectations of their readers. The colourful accounts of Gaimar and Ailred were avidly copied by generations of writers – as disparate as John of Brompton, Ranulph of Higden and Henry Knyghton – until the true events at Andrew the Catholic's court could not be disentangled.

Yet behind this almost impenetrable 'edited version' of Edmund's *faux pas*, two crucial facts can be discerned: first, that Edmund lived as a grown man at the Hungarian court for a while; and second, that he was attractive to women and the waves of the scandal surrounding his affair with a high-born lady eventually reached England.

He died not long after his enforced marriage, inviting speculation that the two events might have been connected in some way. The chroniclers offer no clue as to whether he died from the stab of a rival lover's dagger or from sudden sickness. But they all agreed that he died prematurely.

The stock phrase used by the Anglo-Norman historians – 'Edmund died young in Hungary' – leaves the issue wide open. Only local legend, still current at Nádasd at the beginning of this century, claims to know that it was the pox that carried off the handsome English prince. His untimely death on the shores of the Danube made the struggles of a lifetime of exile seem very futile.

He left no children, no good works to be remembered by, and died an exile in an alien land, forsaken and forgotten by his own people. The conspiracy of hearts that saved the life of Edmund Ironside's first-born son had been in vain.

16. Edward's marriage to a 'lady of royal descent': the riddle of Agatha's origin resolved.

Edward the Exile was just 31 when his brother died in Hungary. Although life, as a rule, was short and brutish and death sudden in the eleventh century, the demise of Edmund must have affected him greatly. Owing to the shared misfortunes of their exile years, the death of Edmund was more than an ordinary bereavement. It had removed the final link with home and family, and made their wanderings from court to court across Europe appear like a life sentence.

Life, however, had to go on and, perhaps ironically, Edward had little cause for complaint. He was rich, owned great démesne lands, and enjoyed the friendship of the king. Furthermore, he was part of the system and held his position at court in his own right, not out of charity. And for a lifelong exile this was, perhaps, of greater importance than the material side of royal favour.

Though alone now, deprived of the moral support of Edmund or the guidance of Walgar, he was not lonely. According to the sights of the times, he must have been an unusually appealing and polished man. With so many adventures behind him he could hardly have been a dullard, and if the tribulations of his youth had made him somewhat cynical, a measure of insouciance could only have increased his attraction for women. The testimony of his recorded actions suggests behind the worldly mask of a professional exile the workings of a cautious intelligence, and his choice of a wife bears out the correctness of this impression. His marriage was dictated by higher political considerations, and there was certainly no hint in the annals of tempestuous affairs, pregnant princesses or irate fathers insisting on instant marriage, as in the case of Edmund.

Close on two score chroniclers reported Edward's marriage and named his bride as Agatha. But this unusual uniformity of a part of the records was marred by a jumble of contradictory information about her descent and country of origin. The confusion sown by the Anglo-Norman historians has not been clarified satisfactorily in the intervening centuries. Since it was through a descendant of Edward and Agatha that Aethelred's house regained the crown of England – linking, incidentally, the present royal family with the ancient house of Wessex – the riddle of Agatha's origins must be resolved conclusively.

According to the *Chronicle of Melrose Abbey*, Edward married 'the daughter of the German Emperor Henry'; Simeon of Durham attested that she was 'the daughter of Emperor Henry's kinsman'; Orderic Vitalis claimed to know that Agatha was 'the daughter of the King of Hungary'; William of Malmesbury insisted that she was 'the sister of the Hungarian queen'; while Abbot Ailred repeatedly referred to her as the daughter of 'the Holy Roman Emperor's kinsman'.

To deepen the confusion, later medieval chroniclers used variations on these themes since in keeping with the monastic work methods of the period they had copied unquestioningly the account of Edward's marriage from their predecessors' annals (see Table 3, p.58). Amid the welter of information, the ascertainable facts about Agatha became elusive.

Since the tradition of copying would rule out the later chroniclers' versions of events, those nearest in time deserve especial attention. The 1057 entry in the *Anglo-Saxon Chronicle* said of Edward that he grew into a good man in exile, 'as God him granted, and him well became; so that he obtained the Emperor's kinswoman to wife and by her fair offspring he begot: She was called Agatha.'

Florence of Worcester, who began collecting material for his great chronicle while Edward's children were still alive, also provides a similar account: '. . . Edward married Agatha, a daughter of the Emperor Henry's kinsman, by whom he had Margaret, queen of the Scots, Christina, a nun, and Edgar the Aetheling'. As if wishing to emphasize the illustrious birth of Edward's wife and the reflected glory of the family ties with the Holy Roman Emperor, he laid great stress on Emperor Henry III specifically being Agatha's kinsman in the appendix of his work, the *Regalis Prosapia Anglorum*.[1]

Although Florence's account has a convincing, authoritative ring, his flagrant mistake in naming King Salamon of Hungary as the aethelings' guardian-host in 1017, makes for caution and suggests the need for further checking. A process of elimination, using textual comparison and chronological verification in tracing the chain of borrowings among the chroniclers, can successfully reduce the field to five categories of candidates for Agatha's parentage: the King of Hungary; a sister of Queen Gisela of Hungary; the Holy Roman Emperor Henry II, the Saxon; Emperor Henry III, the Salian; and finally, a kinsman (*germanus*) of the last two.

This Latin word *germanus*, from Florence's key sentence 'Eadwardus Agatham, filiam *germani* Imperatoris Henrici in matrimonium accepit', was grievously mistranslated by later historians as 'German Emperor Henry' unintentionally introducing a further complication into the vexed question of Agatha's origins.

There were of course, only Holy Roman or Byzantine Greek emperors in Florence's time, Germany being ruled by a king, and he was not using it to denote nationality but the exact degree of relation. In medieval Latin *germanus* meant brother or cousin, even in the vaguest formulation a close blood relation but never a relation by marriage.[2] The historical context of the sentence makes it perfectly clear that this was the intended, quite precise sense of Florence's phrasing. And this narrows further the circle of candidates for Agatha's begetter.

Having verified the sources and checked the credibility ratings of the Anglo-Norman chroniclers in connection with the aethelings' exile route, the simplest yet most effective way of unravelling the mystery of Agatha is to set the dates of the mooted parental candidates against the known lifespan of Edward and his wife.

The two purported royal fathers of a Hungarian Agatha are named as Salamon and Stephen. Orderic, the propounder of Salamon, though generally well-informed and reliable, is demonstrably at error here.[3] Salamon was born in 1052 and did not ascend the throne of Hungary until 1063, when Edward was already dead. Since in 1057, when Edward returned from Hungary to England with Agatha and their three children, Salamon was aged five, he could hardly have been Agatha's father. Clearly, Orderic and his followers were misinformed.

A number of historians, especially Scottish and Hungarian, interested in the origins of St Margaret of Scotland, changed tack in view of the untenable Salamon theory and asserted that Agatha was the daughter of King St Stephen. Daniel Cornides, an eighteenth-century Hungarian historian, wrote a closely-argued Latin language critique of the Agatha question (*Regum Hungariae, qui seculo XI regnavere, genealogiam illustrat* 1778) and put forward the view that Agatha was St Stephen's daughter. He also named the king's five other children as Otto, Emericus, Bernardus, Hedvigis and Dobuka on the authority of Pelbartus, Johannes Tomcus, Arnulph and *Vita Eberhardi*.

However, the annals of Hungary and the many legends of the pious St Stephen make no mention of a daughter called Agatha. Indeed, they speak of all Stephen and Gisela's children as having died in infancy with the exception of Emeric, who was killed in a hunting accident in 1031.

But even if we were to accept, for argument's sake, that Stephen and Gisela had a nubile daughter, the age difference between this girl and Edward would have made a marriage almost impossible. Stephen and Gisela were married in 996 and their children were born between 997 and the early years of the eleventh century. This would have made Agatha at least 10 to 15 years older than Edward, born at the end of 1016, and an exceedingly old mother of 50 when she gave birth to Edgar Aetheling in 1055.

There are even weightier reasons why Agatha could not have been the daughter of Stephen. Had the king had a daughter and a resident son-in-law of royal descent, he would most certainly not have made Peter

Orseolo, the Italian-born son of his half-sister and the Doge of Venice, his heir, because Agatha and Edward would have had prior claim to the throne, owing to Agatha's direct descent. Furthermore, Queen Gisela, a possessive mother, would certainly not have championed an Italian for the throne against her own child and son-in-law.

And since it has been demonstrated (in Part II) that Edward and Edmund had never set foot in Stephen's court and only arrived in the country in 1046, after a long-drawn-out civil war caused precisely by a dearth of direct descendants of the saintly king to ascend the throne, the case for Agatha being the daughter of either Stephen or Salamon can be dismissed firmly.

Yet such is the attraction of a supposed direct relation between St Stephen of Hungary and St Margaret, Scotland's patron saint, that attempts at reviving this romantic theory continue. As recently as 1938, the 900th anniversary of the death of St Stephen, a number of Hungarian legitimists revived the story in order to win British royalist support for 'the homeland of St Margaret's mother' and have the Treaty of Trianon, which truncated Hungary after the First World War, rescinded.

They reasoned (and a handful of Scottish writers with especial interest in St Margaret unquestioningly accepted) that had Edward married the daughter of the Holy Roman Emperor, not a Hungarian royal princess, he would have made his home in Germany. That Edward was not a mere appendage of his wife obviously was not even deemed worth considering. And this preconceived idea prevented these – and many earlier – historians from investigating the possibility that Edward, Andrew the Catholic's comrade-in-arms, was living in Hungary in his own right.

Their 'clinching evidence' was claimed to be the well-documented decision of Edward's family to try to return to Hungary from England after the Norman Conquest. That they were heading for Hungary because they owned lands there, the children had been brought up there, and the king's friendship promised succour in their hour of need, were overlooked in favour of the simplistic view that the intended flight to Hungary was 'the final proof' of Agatha's Hungarian descent. But this faulty reasoning failed to take account of the blood-debt dividing the family of Vazul, blinded by Stephen, and the offspring of the late holy king. A supposed daughter of Stephen and Gisela would hardly have sought refuge at the court of Andrew, the son of her parents' victim.

The third version of Agatha's origins, propounded by William of Malmesbury, who claimed to know that she was the sister of Queen Gisela of Hungary, does not stand up to a chronological scrutiny either.[4]

Gisela was a sister of the Holy Roman Emperor Henry II, who reigned from 1014 to 1024. Her father had died on 28 August 995, and even if Gisela's younger sister were to have been born posthumously in 996 – the latest possible date for her birth – she would have been at least 20 or 21 when Edward was born, and over 50 when he reached Hungary in 1046.

9. The Holy Roman Emperor Henry: he tried to block Edward Aetheling's return from exile by delaying Edward the Confessor's envoys in Cologne for a year with endless theological debates and flattering entertainment (from his 'Sacramentarium', Staatsbibliothek, München).

However unlikely a match, the marriage of a sister of Emperor Henry and Queen Gisela would have been duly recorded as an important social event in Central Europe. Although all the family events of the emperor's house were meticulously documented by such outstanding annalists as Ekkehard, Sigebert, Saxo Grammaticus, and Thuroczy, there is no record anywhere of the existence of such a young sister of Gisela and Emperor Henry, or of her marriage.

This leaves Emperor Henry II, the Saxon, and Emperor Henry III, the Salian, and their elusive *germanus* as father candidates for Agatha. The family trees of both emperors will convince anyone at a glance that Agatha could not have been the daughter of either, making Florence's version of 'a daughter of Emperor Henry's kinsman' the sole working hypothesis. Even Ailred, who in his *Genealogia* introduced Agatha as the Emperor's daughter, corrected himself in a later work, *Vita Sancti Edwardi Regis*, where he described her as 'a kinswoman of Emperor Henry'.

Several eighteenth-century historians, among them István Katona, Georgio Pray and O. F. Suhm of Denmark, misread the source materials and named Bishop Bruno, a brother of Emperor Henry II and Gisela, as the father of Agatha. Though undoubtedly he was a 'germanus Henrici Imperatoris', he was ordained bishop of Augsburg in 1006, thus any acknowledged child of his must have been born before that date. And here again the age difference between Bruno's supposed daughter, born after the turn of the century and Edward, born at least 15 years later, would have been unacceptable.

There is always, of course, the possibility that, like other libertine princes of the medieval Church, he fathered a child after his consecration. But the Augsburg chronicles speak of him as of 'beatae memoriae', making his fatherhood distinctly unlikely. Furthermore, there would have been very little incentive for Edward the Exile to marry a woman who was not only much older than himself but illegitimate and without any social position. And this effectively rules out Henry II's brother Bruno.[5]

The process of elimation thus focuses attention on the mysterious 'germanus' of Emperor Henry III as Agatha's begetter, just as Florence of Worcester indicated in the appendix of his great chronicle. But there is invaluable evidence straight from the horse's mouth, as it were, that the investigation is on the right track: it came from Agatha's daughter, Christina, and was miraculously recorded by the compiler of a dry Norman law collection.

17. Two tell-tale insertions in a Norman law collection: the glossarist's account of a political marriage in Russia

Medieval chroniclers with a sense of perspective recorded the events of their days with an eye on posterity. They wrote for a select male readership about kings, political prelates and warriors who, for better or worse, shaped their countries' destiny. They paid little heed to the women behind the men of action. Women were named when they married a man of importance, or gave birth to an heir, for the legitimacy of the line, but were not deemed of further interest by the monastic annalists.

Even the highly professional contemporary chroniclers paid so little attention to Agatha, the wife of Edward, the rightful heir to the throne of England, that when the growing fame of her saintly daughter, Margaret, focused the interest of the Church on the family, the Anglo-Norman historians of the twelfth century could no longer answer with any certainty the basic questions that suddenly everybody wanted know: who was Agatha's father, where did she hail from, where and when did she marry Edward?

In view of the professionals' shamefaced resort to hearsay and guesswork about Agatha, it is quite astonishing to find an obscure Norman scribe, entrusted by Henry I to catalogue the laws of Edward the Confessor, providing clear-cut answers to these questions. He also sheds light on the fortunes of Edward's family and the fate of the lands of his second daughter, Christina, facts which could have had no link with the laws of Edward the Confessor. Furthermore, he provides corroborative evidence of Edward's Kievan sojourn and further clues to fill in the missing details of the aethelings' exile career.

Because of the significance of the information about Edward and Agatha, inserted for no apparent reason among ponderous laws, it is not looking a gift horse in the mouth to seek an explanation for the motives of the scribe's digression and establish his sources.

The anonymous author of the *Leges* was a Frenchman who lived near Coventry and wrote his work around 1130. His information was precise and from a source unknown to the Anglo-Norman chroniclers: Edward had sought refuge after his father's murder in Russia; he lived at the court of Malesclotus (Yaroslav the Great's French name) and there, that is, in Russia, he married a lady of noble descent who bore him Edgar Aetheling, Margaret and Christina.[1]

The only serious omission – the failure to mention Edmund's fate in exile – can be explained with the elder aetheling having left no descendants. As the author appears to have been preoccupied with the Anglo-Saxon line's right to succession, Edmund was of no interest to him.

The hard facts about Edward the Exile's marriage to Agatha in Kiev were inserted in a brief historical account of the rule of the last Anglo-Saxon kings which was intended to give the laws of Edward the Confessor a historical perspective. The author ended his interpolation in Chapter 35 with a further invaluable piece of intelligence. It concerned the fate of lands allegedly given by Edward the Confessor to Christina, Edward's second daughter ('Cui Cristinae Eadwardus dedit terram, quam habuit postea Radulphus de Limiseia'). That these lands, actually donated by William the Conqueror, not Edward the Confessor, went to Ralph de Limézy upon her having taken the veil in 1086 would seem to be local news of little interest for posterity. Yet the author of the *Leges* must have felt it important enough to interpolate it even though in so doing he disrupted the stylistic continuity and construction of the work.

A quick check in the Domesday Book shows these lands to be extensive but of little consequence to Ralph de Limézy, the son of a sister of William the Conqueror, who owned lands in ten counties and held forty manors in the south of England.[2] The inclusion of a reference to these lands, therefore, would seem to have been an attempt to reaffirm the legality of Limézy's inheritance in the face of some challenge. The most likely explanation is that the author, a Frenchman, hailed from the neighbourhood of Pavilly, the Limézy seat near Rouen, and the interpolation was the result of some personal indebtedness or simply a desire to do a good turn for an influential friend involved in litigation over the lands.

But this tenuous acquaintance with the fate of Christina the Nun's property alone does not quite explain the author's privileged information about Agatha's origins or Edward's Russian exile and marriage.

Since not one English chronicler, including the writers of the *Anglo-Saxon Chronicle*, knew of the Kievan sojourn nor the whereabouts of the aethelings between their banishment in 1017 and Edward's recall in 1054, the author of the *Leges* must have known personally a descendant of Edward's family or learnt of it from a local tradition still current in his time in the lands previously owned by Christina the Nun.

Either way, the information about Edward's Russian exile and marriage is so specific that a compilation from assorted sources, in the accepted monastic tradition of the time, is most unlikely. The use of some since lost contemporary documentary evidence can also be discounted, because it is unlikely that no other Anglo-Norman chronicler should have been acquainted with it, and this leaves the family tradition which the author of the *Leges* could draw on, owing to his friendship with a descendant of Edward and Agatha.

But this is not all the information that can be gleaned from the *Leges Edovardi Confessoris*, of which 41 copies are known to have been made in the century following its compilation. A further interpolation in a thirteenth-century hand adds the following astonishingly precise information about Agatha's origins immediately after the insertion about her Kievan marriage:

> Fuitque predicta Margareta [Agatha's daughter] generosa valde et optima, scilicet ex parte patris ex nobili genere et sanguine regum Anglorum-Britonum ex parte vero matris ex genere et sanguine regum Rugorum, sanctissimisque antecessoribus suis in bonis et laudabilis actibus consimilis praeclara effulsit.

This fulsime, and at first sight rather complex information about the origins of St Margaret's mother was interpolated by an English copier of the original between 1200 and 1210, according to Felix Liebermann, a learned nineteenth-century student of the laws of the Anglo-Saxon period. With typical German thoroughness he unravelled the intention behind the second interpolation and the sources used for it. Since his interest in the *Leges* was entirely due to his lifelong study of the Anglo-Saxon laws, and the inserted news about Edward's Russian exile and Agatha's origins only attracted his attention because of the resulting violence to the work's structure, his neutral analysis is a most welcome confirmation of the correctness of the line followed by this investigation on Agatha's descent.

The interest of the thirteenth-century glossarist in St Margaret's parents and her 'saintly forebears' was due to the legal problems of English succession. Harold and William the Conqueror had broken the Anglo-Saxon law of succession, and since Edgar Aetheling, Edward the Confessor's rightful heir, had died without formally-acknowledged issue, the descendants of St Margaret of Scotland were the lawful heirs to the crown of England in the copyist's view. To lend credence to this theory he interpolated powerful new evidence about Agatha's exalted origins, which he could only have learnt from the family of King David, St Margaret's son, about whom he was amazingly well informed.

This living family tradition and apparently shared dynastic allegiance can explain the glossarist's description of Agatha as a lady of royal blood related to the ruler of Russia. From the phrasing, however, it is clear that the English glossarist had no intention of presenting Agatha as a daughter of Yaroslav the Great. He was simply restating, for effect, in condensed form the facts already known to the author of the *Leges*, that Agatha was of royal blood and had married a royal relation of the ruler of Russia in Russia.

However compressed these events are, they contain a recognizable reference to Edward's kinship with Yaroslav (through Ingegerd) and a pointer to Emperor Henry III's *germanus* from whom Agatha inherited her royal blood.

This great emphasis on the Russian connection in the interpolations of the glossarists with inside family information, is the key to Edward and Agatha's marriage. The clarification of how the daughter of a *germanus* of Emperor Henry III came to Kiev also helps to pinpoint the actual date of the wedding. The idea of an alternative dynastic tie was, in all probability, mooted during the delicate Russo-German negotiations in Goslar in 1043, when Emperor Henry politely declined to marry Yaroslav's daughter, Anne. In an unexpected move, he upset the dynastic chessboard of Europe, set up with such loving care by Yaroslav, by marrying Gunhild, the daughter of the late Canute and Emma and a half-sister of the Confessor. This new constellation of relations must have seemed to Henry to offer a better chance of exerting a direct influence over Canute's Danish heirs and English successor than Yaroslav's outdated plan.

The great disappointment of the Russian envoys returning from Henry's court in 1043 was noted by Adam of Bremen, as we have seen. To sweeten the bitter pill the emperor sent Agatha back with the embassy to marry Edward and thus keep alive the triple alliance, although on a much lower level politically.

This dynastic marriage between the Emperor's niece and Yaroslav's English nephew could have taken place, at the earliest, upon the Russian embassy's return to Kiev at the end of 1043 or in the ensuing months in 1044. The clear statement of the author of the *Leges* that Edward married Agatha in Russia makes it obvious that when the aethelings moved to Hungary in 1046, Edward was already married. And this helps explain why his name was not romantically linked with some princess or other, as Edmund's was, in Hungary.

It is not very flattering to be married for the purposes of a moribund alliance, to be tied together for life for remote, political considerations, but Edward and Agatha made a success of their marriage and this commends them both. They stayed together during the political disappointments and slights of the final two years of Kievan exile, faced the hardships together of the move to Hungary, and when their friend, Andrew the Catholic, consolidated his power, settled down and raised a family.

Amid all the royal favours and licentiousness of the court, Agatha brought up Margaret and Christina strictly. She imbued them with strong, Catholic faith and instilled in them moral and ethical standards which came to be greatly admired in Britain. She also proved a worthy consort to Edward, and her steadfastness helped to keep the family together in the turbulent years ahead.

Where then did this remarkable woman come from? Having found further confirmation of her descent from a close blood relation of Emperor Henry III, the inner logic of all the investigated documentary evidence points to a half-brother of the emperor. Following the same line of investigation, but independently, Szabolcs de Vajay, the noted medievalist, came to a similar conclusion and successfully resolved, with genealogical proof, Agatha's descent.

In a paper published in the Pittsburgh University periodical *Duquesne Review*, he too demonstrated that the Anglo-Norman annalists' description of Agatha as 'filia germani Imperatoris Henrici' could only have referred for chronological reasons, to a half-brother of Henry III, the Salian, not Henry II, the Saxon. To prove it, he worked out the genealogical correlations:

> Henry III was the only son of the Emperor Conrad II and of Gisela of Swabia. Nevertheless, Conrad was the third husband of Gisela, who had been married before to Bruno of Brunswick and to Ernest of Swabia. Gisela had issue from each of her three marriages; thus the Emperor Henry III had three older uterine brothers. As we have noted above, *germanus* can perfectly well be taken to mean *half-brother*, this being a close blood relationship.
>
> Consequently, we put forward the proposal that Agatha's father was Gisela's eldest son, born of her first marriage with Bruno of Brunswick, around 1009. He was Liudolf Margrave of West-Friesland, who was in fact 'germanus imperatoris Henrici'.[3]

Thus the date of Agatha's birth can be taken to have been about 1025. She was therefore nine years younger than Edward, was aged 18 when she married and was about 29 – and not 50 – when she gave birth to Edgar the Aetheling. 'The chronology is thus perfectly reestablished', de Vajay added.

This correct genealogical correlation allows this present investigation to elucidate the reasons for the Anglo-Norman chroniclers' persistent attempt to link, in some form or another, Edward and King Salamon of Hungary. Although, as has been demonstrated, Agatha was not a Hungarian princess and in any case could not have been the daughter of Salamon for well-established chronological reasons, there was a kernel of truth in the relationship between Edward and Salamon. It was indeed Agatha who provided the link but it was forged only after Edward's death. In 1058, a year after Edward's demise, Salamon married Princess Sophie of Germany, Emperor Henry III's daughter, who was Agatha's first cousin. Thus Edward did become, even if posthumously, a relation of King Salamon of Hungary though not by marrying into Salamon's family but through the latter's marriage into Agatha's family.

The Anglo-Norman chroniclers writing several generations later were,

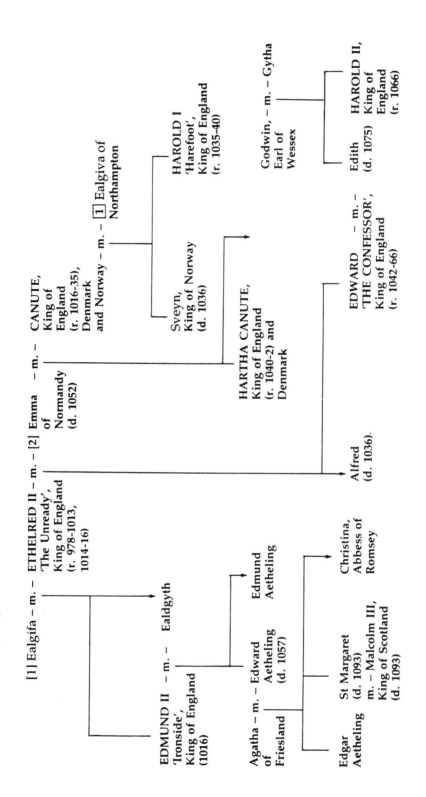

however, not to know this. Having heard second- or third-hand reports emanating from German sources of a relationship through marriage between Edward and Salamon, they tried their best to fit this into the framework of available information. The resulting confusion has bedevilled generations of historians and endured to this day.

PART V: HEEDING ENGLAND'S CALL: A TRAGIC HOMECOMING

18. The shadow of the Bastard of Normandy over England: The king sends for Edward the Exile

After the first seven years of his reign – a period redolent of great symbolic significance in medieval Britain – Edward had his reputation as a pious king firmly established. His otherworldliness was seen as a sign of heavenly favour, and his ceaseless prayers an indication of his intimate communion with the Lord's Host. Signs of the strength of his faith, and heavenly recognition of it, abounded. His dreams were accepted as prophetic revelations and were interpreted as oracles. And his reputation for healing the sick and the blind went a long way to deepen the belief in his miraculous powers. Regardless of his firm disavowal of any such powers, a legend was in the making.

In the process, his manifest weaknesses were turned into strength and his erratic government was made out as a proof of the ascendancy of the powers spiritual over the powers temporal. But the Confessor's chaste marriage, fasting and bouts of prayer had little immediate impact on the many problems besetting the country.

With the waning of the euphoria engendered by the restoration of the native kings and the ending of Danish rule, social problems multiplied. Factional interests reared their heads and divided loyalties among the rulers spiritual and temporal undermined the social fabric of the country. Although formal royal power in the weak hands of the Confessor was buttressed by the sanction of the Church, real power was rapidly slipping to Earl Godwin, England's premier baron, and his sons.

The king, owing to his Norman upbringing, surrounded himself with Norman courtiers and filled the highest ecclesiastical and state posts with them. The forts and castles were garrisoned by French-speaking soldiers, and the towns offered special privileges to the ever-growing flow of French and Flemish artisans. The king's preference for all things Norman was beginning to tell and affect the country at large.

With the backing of the Saxon party, Earl Godwin opposed the sway of the Normans, further polarizing factional interests. Whether he did so out of conviction or political opportunism can hardly be established, and from all accounts he was not given to introspection or bouts of doubt about the wisdom of his actions. But he certainly enjoyed the challenge.

Having defied the Danes in 1042 and organized the restoration of the Anglo-Saxon line in the Witan, Godwin's popularity was at its height. The political credentials of this one-time protégé of Canute were impeccable. Besides, he was immensely rich. His earldom stretched across southern England from Cornwall to Kent. His sons Sveyn and Harold held two other great earldoms and his nephew Bjorn a fourth. And his daughter Edith was the Confessor's wife, giving him a further not inconsiderable leverage of power.

However unintentional the division of power between them, the Confessor and Godwin together nevertheless assured a long peaceful spell for England. Their roles were differently assessed by the Anglo-Saxon and pro-Norman factions, and the attitudes of the Confessor's two biographers to Godwin clearly reflect this division.

The anonymous author of *Vita Aedwardi Regis*, who wrote his work between the Confessor's final illness and 1074, reveals an undisguised partisanship for the Anglo-Saxon faction in general and Godwin in particular.[1] He praises Godwin's prudence, constancy, and service to the state and claims that his great popularity in the country was a reflection of his merits as soldier and statesman. In a quaint little rhapsody in verse, he compares Godwin's four children with the four rivers of Paradise, but since the work is dedicated to Queen Edith, Godwin's daughter, the eulogy is understandable.

By contrast, the Norman author of *La Estoire de St Aedward le Rei*, who in turn dedicated his work to Queen Eleanor of Provence, the wife of Henry III, systematically vilified Earl Godwin and his sons.[2] Godwin, he claims, betrayed Aelfred, the Confessor's younger brother, and was responsible for his torture and terrible death at the hands of the Danes. This, of course, might well be true but, in his politically-motivated attempt to discredit the mainstay of the Anglo-Saxon faction, the author resurrected Edmund Ironside's murder and laid the blame at Godwin's door. And to underline Godwin's treacherous nature, his work abounds in heavy hints about the schemes and stratagems by which the premier baron of the realm engineered the union of the king and his own daughter with an eye on the political advantages of such a marriage for the Godwin family.

Inevitably, the Confessor and Godwin fell out, for the king, wishing to give ecclesiastical preferment to his Norman friends, came up against Godwin's hardline championing of indigenous priests for all the key posts, frustrating the Confessor even in the one field in which he wanted his own way. The ostensible reason for the public quarrel was a nasty brawl in Dover involving the burghers and Count Eustace of Boulogne, the king's brother-in-law. When the townfolk refused to give lodgings to his soldiers, the good count decided to teach the burghers a sharp lesson so that in future they should respect the wishes of a Norman gentlemanat-arms. The Normans conducted the tutorials somewhat harshly and in the ensuing rough-house twenty burghers and nineteen soldiers died.

The count demanded satisfaction, and the king ordered Godwin to punish Dover for offending his guest. Godwin, however, refused to move against the town, insisting that the burghers could not be punished before their case had been heard. This act of insubordination, coming on top of years of frustrations and rankling memory of Aelfred's murder, made the Confessor act; Godwin and his sons were banished from the country and Edith confined to a convent.

The king showed for the first, and probably the last, time in his life, the will to act. But he grossly misjudged the situation and his wrong-headed action brought the country to the brink of civil war. In spite of Godwin's attempts at a reconciliation, the Confessor, influenced by his Norman counsellors, refused to back down.

This battle of wills between the two most powerful men of England, favouring as they did diametrically-opposed political leanings, was lent an unexpected dimension by the surprise visit of William of Normandy to England in 1051. With the Godwins out of the country, William's presence on English soil appeared to reinforce the Confessor's commitment to the kingdom's Norman alignment.

Although a visit to a cousin was not so unusual, the splendour of William's retinue and the inclusion of so many high-ranking officials in his party indicated that there was more behind this social call than met the eye. The circumstances speak for themselves. The Confessor was of an advanced age and, having refused to consummate his marriage with Edith, he was without hope of heirs. William, on the other hand, was young, ambitious and a born leader. His warrior reputation, established in the fight for his patrimony, commended him to the pro-Norman faction in England, and the Confessor's thoughts too must have turned naturally to his young nephew while grappling with the problems of succession. In the power vacuum created by the exiling of the Godwins, the Bastard of Normandy cast a giant shadow over England.

Most Norman chroniclers imply, without offering actual proof, that it was not family affection but the promise of the crown of England that made William cross the Channel in 1051. There is no record of the long conversations between Edward and William, but from the Norman duke's later claim to the crown it can be deduced that, in his vague fashion, the Confessor must have made him some promise.

But any such promise was worth little without the sanction of the Witan and, especially, in the face of the continuing popularity of the Godwins.[3] Indeed, within a year Earl Godwin returned from Flanders with a strong fleet to a hero's welcome and sailed against London. His sons invaded England simultaneously and advanced along the Thames. The king wanted to fight but the Witan, headed by Bishop Stigand of Winchester, pleaded for peace talks. Bereft of support and deserted by his

French advisers, the Confessor had no option but to give in. He pardoned Godwin and his sons, restored to them their earldoms, took back his wife and sent into exile his favourite Norman courtiers.

Triumph of the Godwins was complete and the fortune of the Saxon faction was suddenly in the ascendancy. Not even the death of Earl Godwin within a year of his rehabilitation altered the situation. Harold was promoted to his father's earldom and, as the king's reign became more and more erratic, he took on the burden of practical government. Soon he became the most powerful man in the realm, styling himself 'Duke by the Grace of God', while the Confessor, tired of the wars with the Welsh and Scots and of the day-to-day affairs of the state, turned with even greater fervour to religion.

His appetite for prayer was only matched by his passion for hunting. These two pastimes filled his days. 'After divine service, which he gladly and devoutly attended every day, he took much pleasure in hawks and birds of that kind which were brought before him, and was delighted by the baying and scrambling of hounds,' his biographer wrote. But the country at large came to pay a heavy price for the king's sport.

The Confessor's abortive attempt to curb the power of his most influential earls rebounded and his bid to secure his Norman nephew's orderly succession actually played into the hands of the Saxon faction. It was as if everything he had planned to do misfired and all that Harold had hoped to achieve came true without a hitch. Nevertheless, though Harold might have succeeded in making his power-base unassailable, he failed to find a remedy for the country's all-pervading social malaise. England was at peace but divided against itself and enfeebled by moral decay.

William of Malmesbury saw the decadence and corruption of the nation as the root cause of the inevitability of the Norman takeover of 'our dear country'. His list of the sins of the English offers a *tour d'horizon* of the moral climate of the country in the decade preceding 1066.

He begins his sad catalogue with the nobility which 'was given up to luxury' and sexual gratification. The clergy, more interested in food than learning,

> . . . could scarcely stammer out the words of the sacraments, and a person who understood grammar was an object of wonder and astonishment. The commonalty, left unprotected, became the prey of the most powerful, who amassed fortunes by either seizing on their property, or by selling their persons into foreign countries; although it be an innate quality of this people to be more inclined to revelling than to the accumulation of wealth.

Malmesbury singled out the moral turpitude of the nobility as much for their lack of Christian standards as for the poor example they were giving to the rest of the people: 'They did not go to church in the morning as

Christians should, but merely, in a careless manner, heard matins and Masses from a hurrying priest in their chambers, amid the blandishments of their wives.'

In the view of the Anglo-Norman monk, their empty, soulless attitude to Christianity was only one of the many symptoms of their degeneracy. He found certain sexual proclivities of the rich and mighty particularly abhorrent, and his castigations came close to the fiery zeal of Bishop Wulfstan's homily to Aethelred: 'There was one custom, repugnant by nature, which they adopted, namely, to sell their female servants, when pregnant by them and after they had satisfied their lust, either to public prostitution or foreign slavery.'

The population at large was, he bewailed, much given to drinking in parties 'in which occupation they passed entire nights, as well as days . . . The vices attendant on drunkenness, which enervate the human mind, followed. They consumed their whole substance in mean and despicable houses, eating until they became surfeited and drinking until they grew sick.'

In contrast to this image of the English, the vices of the Normans, and those who championed their ways in England, seemed more moderate to Malmesbury and explained, in his view, the inevitable outcome of the fight for supremacy between the Anglo-Saxon and pro-Norman factions

> The Normans, that I may speak of them also, were at the time, and are even now, proudly apparelled, delicate in their food, but not excessive. They are a race inured to war, and can hardly live without it; fierce in rushing against the enemy; and where strength fails of success, ready to use stratagem, or to corrupt by bribery. As I have mentioned, they live in large edifices with economy; envy their equals; wish to excel their superiors; and plunder their subjects, though they defend them from others; they are faithful to their lords, though a slight offence renders them perfidious. They weigh treachery by its chance of success and change sentiments with money.

This stark contrast in lifestyles and values, even if seen through the eyes of an Anglo-Norman historian, gives a fair inkling of the depth of feelings dividing the Saxon and Norman factions. The former looked to Harold, the latter to William, and the issue of succession rent the country right down the middle.

Amid the extreme passions aroused by the two warring factions the Witan was trying to steer a middle course. Spurred on by the king's frail health, the Witan was casting about for a compromise candidate who could remove the threat of civil war and foreign intervention. The continuity of succession had been interrupted by Canute, and in spite of the restoration of Edward the Confessor to the throne, the line of Aethelred seemed to be dying out. The Witan, conscious that the people revered the blood of their ancient princes, considered for a while Ralph of Hereford, a grandson of Aethelred, as a possible neutral figurehead.

Although he was of the true Anglo-Saxon royal line, his mother tongue and outlook were French, and in view of the prevailing anti-Norman popular mood, he stood virtually no chance of election. Besides, by tradition the English elected their kings from those who were of royal blood by direct male descent, and being the son of Aethelred's daughter, Ralph was a non-starter even for a compromise candidate.

It was the Confessor who, having heard about his surviving nephew in Hungary from Emperor Henry III, suggested Edward the Exile as a compromise candidate. In the circumstances, the mooting of the recall from Hungary of Edward was a stroke of genius, regardless of whose idea it was. He was of English royal blood by direct male descent; his father, Edmund Ironside, was a much-loved national hero; and, more importantly, he had not been born in France or influenced by French culture in his exile. Hungary was a faraway country posing no threat to England, whereas Normandy and the pro-Norman faction were seen as the enemy at the door threatening the old ways.

The decision in 1054, to invite Edward home could only have been made on the joint authority of king and Witan, as the composition of the embassy sent to fetch him and its official status at the courts visited *en route* testify. This joint invitation was tantamount to declaring Edward the Exile the heir apparent, a virtual guarantee of succession which, under English law, was usually the prerogative of the son of a reigning monarch. But in the circumstances, the crown of England was offered to Edward on a silver salver.

Malmesbury,[4] Ailred and Florence of Worcester record both the recall of Edward and the intention to make him king of England. Drawing on their virtually identical versions of events, John of Fordun, the medieval historian, so interested in the origins of St Margaret of Scotland, wrote in his *Chronica Gentis Scotorum*:

> King Edward [the Confessor], bowed with age, and having no children himself, while he saw Godwin's sons growing in power, sent to the King of the Huns to send him over Edward, the son of his brother Edmund Ironside, and his family – for that either he was to succeed to the kingdom of England by hereditary right, or his sons would do so; because of his own [the Confessor's] childlessness ought to be made good by the help of his kindred.

After having lived the life of an outcast of England for 38 years, Edward's exile was suddenly drawing to an end. The dream of a triumphant homecoming that had made the tribulations of a lifetime in exile bearable, was coming true. In its hour of need England was reaching out for its long-forgotten son. Edward the Exile was once again Edward the Aetheling, the future King of England, and the wrongs and wounding neglects of the past were wiped away. It seemed all too good to be true.

Edward's recall from Hungary was an act of desperation, a gamble born out of the recognition that desperate situations need desperate remedies. The shadow of the superior Norman military might and culture was occluding England and members of the Witan recoiled in horror from the threatening *tableau* of change. In the search for measures to maintain the Anglo-Saxon ways, the recall of Edward must have seemed the simplest and most effective plan in 1054. But no one could predict then with any certainty whether Edward could fulfil the hopes pinned on him or what would be the reaction of the other contestants of power to an interloper on the tense English political scene.

19. An innocent abroad: the Emperor's double-cross foils Bishop Ealdred's mission

The Confessor's plan to recall his nephew from exile was approved by the Gemot (Great Council) at the 1054 Whitsun session. However heartening this broad support for the succession of Edmund Ironside's son must have been for the backers of a compromise candidate, it was soon realised that it was one thing to talk about Edward's recall and quite another to put it into effect.

The practical difficulties of such a mission were almost insurmountable. There could not have been many people in the Kingdom of Wessex who actually knew where Hungary was beyond a vague impression that it must be a very, very long way away. Furthermore, the country did not have envoys of the rank and experience that such a delicate mission certainly required. And to send messengers on a royal mission who were totally ignorant of the political realities obtaining in Central and Eastern Europe, was to court trouble on a massive scale.

The Confessor chose Bishop Ealdred of Worcester to head the embassy because he had already travelled to Rome for the king and had accomplished that foreign mission successfully. The *Anglo-Saxon Chronicle* recorded Ealdred's 1054 journey, but did not include the names of his companions. But a grant of land by the Confessor in Huntingdonshire to Abbot Aelfwine (Alwin) of Ramsey, in recognition of his ambassadorial services, suggests that he was the other senior member of the embassy.[1] Having represented the English Church at the Council of Rheims, he must have been considered a seasoned envoy, although his grasp of church dogma did not necessarily indicate a matching political perception. Although Bishop Ealdred seemed more competent to grapple with both ecclesiastical problems and the delicate issues of state, this eleventh-hour enterprise of the king did not have an auspicious start.

Perhaps it was because of the geographical remoteness of Hungary that it was decided to send Ealdred and Aelfwine to Emperor Henry III's court, instead of directly to Hungary, with the request that the Emperor should parley with Hungary and seek permission for Edward's return.

The Holy Roman Emperor was certainly bound to have direct contacts with the King of Hungary, the officials of the Confessor's chancellery must have reasoned, and they rightly argued that, owing to the close links between the King of England and the Emperor, Bishop Ealdred could count on a friendly reception at Cologne. Though Gunhild, the Confessor's half-sister was dead and Emperor Henry had remarried, it was felt he was bound to help his former brother-in-law and ally in this matter of such vital importance for England. Although the logic of the argument, as far as the Anglo-German side of it was concerned, was impeccable, the unknown eastern half of the equation had been left out of the reckoning, with grievous consequences.

With an uncharacteristic reserve bordering on deliberate obfuscation, the usually well-informed writers of the *Anglo-Saxon Chronicle* recorded Bishop Ealdred's mission to Germany, but omitted to explain its purpose. In his 1054 entry, the Abingdon monk hinted, with his emphasis on the great reception accorded to Ealdred, at the official business of the embassy at the imperial court.[2] But neither from this account, nor from the Peterborough or Worcester versions, could one deduce that Bishop Ealdred's mission and the recall of Edward the Exile were in any way connected.

Considering the Worcester monk's privileged position, it is rather surprising that he too should have concentrated on the splendid reception of his bishop by the emperor in Cologne and the value of the presents, but not given away what his actual business was beyond stating that it was 'on the king's errand'.[3]

The explanation for this dearth of information in the contemporary chronicles could be explained by the writers' preoccupation with the honours bestowed upon one of their number by the Holy Roman Emperor, but a more likely reason is that the embassy got bogged down in Cologne and for well over a year there was no news about it in England. So the chroniclers filled in the allotted space with details of the pomp and circumstance surrounding Ealdred's visit.

Even Malmesbury, who showed such interest in the fate of Edmund Ironside's exiled children, seemed to have been at a complete loss as to the true purpose of Bishop Ealdred's embassy. In his *Vita St Wulfstani* he wrote at length about the two Holy Service books, once so admired by Wulfstan, which were presented to Ealdred during his Cologne sojourn, but not a word about the purpose of the visit. And, owing to this general lack of information on the subject in the Anglo-Saxon sources, he mentioned in his *History* the Confessor's embassy to Hungary to find his nephew not knowing that it went to Cologne, not Hungary, nor that it was headed by Ealdred.

It was Florence of Worcester, drawing no doubt on his ecclesiastical predecessor's notes, who cleared up the confusion surrounding the Bishop of Worcester's mission and filled in some of the misssing details.[4] From him we learn that the embassy had spent a year in Cologne, while envoys, sent by the Emperor to Hungary at the Confessor's request, sought to arrange Edward's return to England. Considering, however, that Germany and Hungary shared a common frontier, the year Ealdred spent in Cologne awaiting word from Edward was clearly not due to the distances involved. Indeed, the English embassy's return home after a year without any contact with Hungary would indicate that something must have gone terribly wrong with the other half of the king's errand, the part that was entrusted to Emperor Henry.

As the months passed, the public fêting, the bestowing of gifts and honours should have aroused Ealdred's and Aelfwine's suspicions that all the pomp and circumstance served up were to disguise a lack of action by the Emperor. In the face of the endless evasions and excuses, the English envoys must have been very naive not to realise that the Emperor was stalling. But, it seems, in their innocence they did not perceive the political intent behind the delays and instead of trying to do something about it, they accepted the situation with good grace.

Time was, as it were, standing still to give England a last chance to avoid civil strife, but the Confessor's envoys, instead of trying to reach Hungary on their own, meekly acceded to Archbishop Hermann's invitation to study in depth the ecclesiastical organization of the German Church. Far from protesting against this blatant attempt at sidetracking the embassy, the churchmen sent on the king's errand piously contemplated the great spiritual values accruing from a long-overdue reform of the English Church along the German lines. After a whole year of waiting, they returned to England, greatly edified and reassured no doubt, that the emperor would continue to try and establish communications with Edward the Exile regardless of the difficulties.

The reasons for the delaying of the English embassy at Cologne were, of course, closely linked to Emperor Henry's bitter quarrel with Hungary, but Ealdred, completely untutored in Continental power politics, had no way of knowing this. Henry never forgot or forgave the defeat of his two military interventions in Hungary on behalf of Peter Orseolo and the subsequent murder of his puppet by the rebels. Andrew the Catholic on Hungary's throne was a constant reminder of this setback to his imperial design. And as if this were not enough, in the 1050s Andrew was aiding and abetting the rebellious Duke Conrad of Bavaria's struggle against the emperor in a further gesture of defiance of imperial rule in the heart of Europe.

Both the time and the person selected by the Confessor's chancellery for an intercession with the King of Hungary were singularly ill-chosen. But because of his kinship with the Confessor, the Emperor could not very well refuse outright the appeal for an imperial intervention.

Of course, had Henry really wanted to comply with the request of his English ally, he could easily have communicated directly with Edward, who was, after all, married to his niece. Apart from the family channels, there were intimately close contacts between the churchmen and the nobility of Germany and Hungary, and Andrew need not have known about a message passed to Edward through one of these contacts. But Henry preferred not to act.

The obstruction of such a high-powered embassy, travelling on the authority of the King of England and the Gemot, amounted to a hostile act which, among friendly nations, was quite out of place. As Henry's relations with his former brother-in-law had always been exceedingly cordial, this hostility could not have been directed against the Confessor but against Edward.

Since the Emperor and Edward had never met, only the aetheling's role in the fighting against the imperial army could explain this personal antipathy and justify Henry's stand. And this, coupled with his hatred of Andrew, could make comprehensible Henry's decision fo thwart Ealdred's mission and thus possibly precipitate a war of succession in England. Henry, it seems, was determined to prevent Edward ascending the throne of England.

His stand was the obsessional attitude of a stubborn man, but then the Emperor's policy towards Hungary showed marks of a similar pig-headed obduracy.[5] An unbending, intransigent ruler, Emperor Henry was prepared to forego the advantages of having the husband of his niece on the throne of England in order to punish the humiliation of his arms in a pagan uprising.

That Emperor Henry remained unyielding on this issue can be gauged from the fact that the first move to establish contact with Edward in Hungary was made only *after* his death in 1056. It was probably Agnes of Poitiers, the emperor's second wife, who smoothed the passage of Edward and his family and made the journey across Germany possible after a delay of three years.

'Eadward, having received these news', one of the near-contemporary chroniclers wrote, 'took journey with a fair train of Hungarian lords and gentlemen and arrived happily in London.' The year was 1057.

20. A tragic end to Edward's continental odyssey: a murder most foul with two suspects and a belated conviction

In the middle of August 1057, Edward Aetheling set foot on English soil after forty years in exile. The bitterness of a lifetime of banishment must have dissolved amid the emotional euphoria of homecoming. It was a triumphant return made the more memorable by the ecstatic welcome accorded by the English people to Edmund Ironside's son and his family.

The cheers for the aetheling and the royal acclaim were quite justified, for he was recalled, as everyone knew, and Florence of Worcester recorded, to be declared heir to the throne of England.[1] Yet there must have been something bizarre in that first encounter between England and the aetheling.

The officials of the welcoming party at the quayside were addressing themselves to the last direct male descendant of Aethelred's royal house, but they only saw a very foreign-looking, middle-aged man overcome by emotion. Like the posse of Hungarian retainers surrounding him, he was dressed in strange clothes and was unable to speak a word of English.

With the gap between hope and reality so wide, the aetheling's welcomers could hardly have suppressed some nagging doubts whether this alien prince, so utterly ignorant of the customs and way of life of the country, would be able to stand up to his powerful challengers in the struggle for the crown of England.

Edward, on his part, set eyes for the first time on the countryside and the people of a land completely unknown to him but which he had been taught to call his homeland. Yet he was of England, even if exile in East Europe shaped him and made him aware, and the very Anglo-Saxon name of his infant son Edgar demonstrated this affinity with his native land. However, the chords that connect a prince to his people were never knotted for Edward the Exile.

And, of course, there were the ghosts of the past that could not be wished away. Amid the quayside jubilation Edward could be forgiven for wondering whether the lords uttering honeyed words of welcome were perhaps tainted by collaboration, or worse, with his father's murder.

Thoughts of the past must have balanced the glittering prospect of a royal future in England on that sunny spring day.

However promising his first encounter with his future subjects, the memories of the murderous events of the fight for the crown forty years earlier must have warned him, as he set out for London with his train of attendants, that there might be powerful factions in the country that found his presence a danger to their own plans for the succession. If he was in any doubt, the strange events of the following days brought rapid confirmation.

His return to England was greeted with a poem by the Worcester writer of the *Anglo-Saxon Chronicle*. In his 1057 entry, he recorded Edward's homecoming but added a curious and, in its consequences, ominous incident:

> Here comes Edward Aetheling
> To Engla-land;
> He was King Edward's
> Brother's son,
> Edmund king,
> Who Ironside was called
> For his valour . . .
> Nor wist we
> For which cause
> That was done,
> That he could not
> His kinsman Edward
> King behold.

That there were sinister forces which were determined to prevent a meeting between the king and his intended heir can be seen from the carefully-phrased account of another contemporary annalist, the Abingdon writer of the *ASC*. Making his 1057 entry with a weary eye on these powerful people, he nevertheless felt impelled to remark: 'We do not know for whatever reason that was done that he [Edward the Exile] was not allowed to see his relation, Edward the King.'

The trustworthy testimony of these two accounts shows, without stating the obvious, that certain influential people in the king's retinue were prepared to go to any lengths to interpose themselves between the Confessor and his nephew, and deny the latter admittance to the royal presence. Such a meeting would have resulted in the king's formal approval of Edward Aetheling's succession, and this these mighty men were clearly not prepared to allow to pass.

And since the succession of the last descendant of the Anglo-Saxon royal house had a great popular support, more drastic action was required, and very quickly at that, if the interests of certain other contenders were not to be harmed irrevocably. Within days, certainly before an entry unusually dated 31 August in the *Anglo-Saxon Chronicle*, Edward the Exile was dead.

The chroniclers of the time – like the Peterborough writer of the *Anglo-Saxon Chronicle*, Abbot Ingulph of Croyland and Florence – duly record the unexpected demise of the aetheling but, significantly, they make no mention of illness.[2] They confine themselves to stating that he had died shortly after his arrival in London. But his totally unexpected death clearly shook the Kingdom of Wessex. The popular outburst of grief was spontaneous and heartfelt. 'Joy [over his arrival] turned into mourning, laughter into tears', one chronicler summed up the national mood.

The laments for the son of the legendary Edmund Ironside were not wholly sentimental. They reflected the fear of the silent majority of an uncertain future, their dread of a war of succession and foreign domination. The Worcester poet who had welcomed Edward in verse rewrote or supplemented his 1057 entry in the light of the events of 1066.

> Alas! that was a rueful occurrence
> And harmful
> For all this nation
> That he so prematurely
> His life did end
> After that he to Engle-land came,
> For the mishap
> Of this wretched nation.[3]

The remark that Edward the Exile's untimely death spelt tragedy for England is the more significant as it comes from one of the select annalists of the *Anglo-Saxon Chronicle*, keeping the official records of a country ruled by the aetheling's adversaries. He could not name names or be explicit without risking retribution. His linking, in a cause-and-effect relationship, of the aetheling's death and the Norman takeover appears, therefore, as an unmistakeable pointer that the death was *not* accidental. Taken in conjunction with the remarks of the other Anglo-Saxon writers who had found the blocking of Edward's meeting with the king so suspicious as to warrant its inclusion in their annals, it justifies a full murder inquiry.

There can be little doubt that the aetheling was not ill at the time of his arrival in England, for had he shown the least sign of failing health, the rhetorical questions about the reasons behind the thwarted family reunion would have been redundant and out of keeping with the chroniclers' terse style. But with sickness as the cause of death eliminated, they become deliberate comments on the machinations of factions hostile to Edward's recall. And this strengthens the impression, deliberately left by observant but politically hamstrung contemporaries, that not sudden illness but the poisoner's cup was the cause of Edward the Exile's death. For only poison could explain a death so sudden without an preceding signs of illness.

For if it was Harold who hired the assassin, then it would have been unpatriotic to accuse – under the Norman occupiers – the last champion of Anglo-Saxon rule with murder. If, however, William and his Normans were behind it, then the inclusion of an open accusation of murder would have been suicidal. So the wise keepers of England's records resorted to innuendo.

The charge that he was murdered by his own countrymen, not wild foreigners, is so serious that most students of the Norman takeover have shied away from investigating it. Only a handful of nineteenth-century historians dared to commit themselves and, after reading the chronicles, point an accusing finger rather tentatively at Earl Harold.

But they laboured under two debilitating handicaps. They had no knowledge of the aetheling's exile career and they judged, like everyone else, the fateful events that decided England's future either from William's or from Harold's point of view. They were not aware of the true position of the aetheling in the king's compromise plan to resolve the succession and therefore they did not approach Edward's murder from the crucial 'third man's' point of view. That was left to this present investigation.

Sir Francis Palgrave, that flamboyant exponent of Anglo-Saxon attitudes, found that the lamentations of the contemporary annalists implied that there was more behind the aetheling's death than met the eye and concluded that 'Harold gained exceedingly by this event'. C. H. Pearson came to an almost identical conclusion, while Edward Freeman tried to exonerate Harold and, by implication, accuse William of the crime. In the end, in a gesture of sham objectivity, he delivered a 'not proven' verdict, although admitting that the suspicions voiced by the contemporary writers showed the prevalent belief in murder at the time of Edward's death.

Johann Martin von Lappenberg, the most eminent Continental student of the Norman period, too joined the chorus of nineteenth-century accusers of Harold but fell silent before the finale. He accused Harold's supporters of having kept Edward from meeting the king but, perhaps because of a lack of actual proof, he backed away from the inescapable conclusion that whoever had prevented the meeting would in the end, of necessity, have also killed the heir to the throne, and left the issue open.

The only near-contemporary record of Harold's involvement which might have escaped Lappenberg's attention, is to be found in Saxo's chronicle. His chance remark that 'Harold murdered King Edward', might be the reflection of a popular tradition still extant in his day. However, the confusing reference to *King* Edward greatly reduces the value of the entry even though there has never been any suggestion of King

Edward the Confessor having been murdered. The most likely explanation is that Saxo, having misunderstood the meaning of the Witan's invitation, upped the rank of the heir apparent to king.

To get to the bottom of the mystery surrounding Edward the Exile's untimely death, the question that must be asked is who benefited most from his removal from the political scene? Since his recall was a compromise arrangement to keep the crown out of reach of both William and Harold, suspicion focuses on the faction which might have felt cheated out of victory by Edward and wanted to reopen the succession issue in more favourable circumstances.

The rapid ascendancy of Harold's star after the rehabilitation of the house of Godwin and the parallel eclipse of the Norman influence would point to Harold. With so much of the power and prerogatives of government already in his hands, zealous supporters of his cause might reasonably have felt that he was incomparably better suited to rule the kingdom than Edward the Exile. Harold had proved himself a brave warrior and able administrator, a man fit to ascend the throne of England, while the aetheling was an unknown quantity.

Indeed, in Malmesbury's harsh and questionable judgment, he was 'neither valiant, nor a man of abilities'. But he had one great advantage that Harold could not match – he was of royal blood, and with the traditionalist island-race that counted most. No one, who was not of the ancient royal house, had been able to stay on the Anglo-Saxon throne. Furthermore, the heroic Edmund Ironside's son was very popular and the Confessor's recommendation of Edward to the Witan as his successor made his election a foregone conclusion.

However, if Edward was to be removed in secrecy and without a scandal, the Saxon faction could turn naturally to the worthiest of Englishmen and make him their king even though he was not of royal blood. The tradition of electing a kind from Cerdic's royal house would have been of no consequence in ther new situation in which the stark choice was between the Norman William and the English Harold.

This scenario sounds the more convincing as Harold's supporters could not thwart the Confessor's succession plan until *after* Edward's arrival in England but *before* his formal approval as heir apparent by the king. With one heartbeat between Harold and the crown of England, someone acting with, or perhaps without, Harold's consent, might have decided to extinguish that life.

Harold, therefore, stood to gain a kingdom if Edward was to be cleverly disposed of. But the motive is not proof of guilt, the establishment of personal interest in the crime is not actual evidence. In spite of the weight of circumstantial evidence against him, he was not alone in profiting from the murder of Edward.

William of Normandy too had good reasons to wish Edward the Aetheling out of the way. Having been promised the crown by his cousin in 1051 while the Godwins were in exile, he found himself removed from the line of succession after the Godwins' return to favour and his supporters at court banished. Since the aetheling's right to the throne was beyond question and his nomination enjoyed the support of the king, the Witan and the country at large, he could hardly challenge it on the strength of a verbal promise.

To assert his claim against an outsider, like Harold, would be one thing; against the son of a heroic and popular English king, Ironside, quite another. And a formal approval of Edward's succession by the king during the planned family reunion would have further lengthened the odds against William.

He was not without influence at the Confessor's court even if the most powerful exponents of the Norman interests had been expelled. Bishop William of London, Robert the Deacon and Hugolin the Treasurer were Normans, and a precipitate attempt to prevent a ruinous damage to their cause could not be put past them. But admittedly, their chances of keeping Edward away from his uncle would be much smaller and, therefore their desperation arguably greater to stop Edward at any cost. The possibility therefore of their bribing a servant to poison the aetheling could not be ruled out.

On balance, however, the case against Harold's well-placed supporters is much stronger. Indeed, considering the commanding positions they held at court, in government and among the warriors, is overwhelming. They had the opportunity and the motivation to do away with the defenceless aetheling, and, if the unscrupulousness shown by the Godwin faction in their fight for supremacy is anything to go by, they had the will too.

Though only one chronicler linked, on the strength of hearsay, Harold directly with this dastardly act, the harsh streak revealed by him during his brief reign suggests that he himself would not have been above ordering the removal of a frustrating obstacle barring his way to the throne. His father in his time did not hesitate to betray and deliver Alfred Aetheling to his executioners when his interests so required, yet the prize for which he was prepared to pay with another man's blood was far more modest than the crown of England. This similarity of approach and lack of moral scruples can explain how Harold could rely, in spite of his proven probity as a warrior, on the black art of the secret poisoner to further his ascendancy in a difficult moment. Ruthlessness ran in the family.

Though this conclusion seems inescapable, no hard, documentary proof could be unearthed to prove it. But having approached all the available contemporary sources from the aetheling's point of view, and thus seen the actions of the protagonist and deuteragonist of this drama from a fresh angle, I became absolutely convinced of Harold's guilt. Nothing has come to light to shake this conviction.

Edward's murder was a setback to the Confessor's hopes for an orderly succession and for the country the starting point of a calamitous chain-reaction that, eventually, swept away Anglo-Saxon England. The wailing of the Anglo-Saxon chronicler who blamed all the miseries of the Norman occupation on the aetheling's untimely death gives a measure of the people's enduring grief.

But the grave national consequences cannot obscure the Greek dimensions of Edward Aetheling's personal tragedy. Saved as a baby to keep alive his countrymen's hopes of ridding themselves of a foreign invader, his death opened up the country to a far more formidable and lasting occupation. And in between there were forty years of tribulations in foreign parts which were deprived of any meaning by the murderous reception awaiting him on his home-coming.

Having come so close to the fulfilment of his exile dreams, he was struck down as Fortune seemed set to make good all the sufferings of his Continental odyssey. Condemned to live out his days in banishment, he was missed and lamented by his countrymen after his death.

The paradox of his death gives the measure of his unusual life. His was not a distinguished public career although given a chance, he might have served his country well. At least he had had the satisfaction that in their hour of need, his countrymen had turned to him for succour.

As he was laid to rest in St Paul's minster in London in 1057, the superstitious people of the city spoke in hushed whispers of the fulfilment of St Dunstan's awful augury. The sword of fate poised above Aethelred's doomed house had cut off his seed, for the second generation running, as predicted. And there was no one left to prevent, as the seer had prophesied, the passing of the kingdom into the hands of aliens whose customs and language the people did not know.

21. Edward's son groomed for the throne, but king's deathbed words secure crown for Harold

Soon after the aetheling's death, Ralph, the other Saxon prince of royal blood, died too and events began moving inexorably towards catastrophe. The horror and sadness over his miscarried succession plan proved too much for the ailing king. Never having got over the humiliation of the Godwins' forced return, he now abandoned all attempts to guide the affairs of the country. He left the day-to-day government entirely to Harold and his brothers, and contented himself with the discharge of the formal duties of a sovereign. Apart from this he spent all his time in prayer, as befitted a pious old man.

His only apparent interest in life was the welfare of his nephew's widow, Agatha, and her three children. He gave them a home at his court and brought up Edgar, aged about two in 1057, as his own son. According to several contemporary sources, including the *Leges Edovardi Confessoris*, he made Edgar an aetheling and considered naming him the heir to the crown, revealing his hoped for solution for the succession.[1]

While Edgar was groomed for the throne, Margaret and Christina, his nephew's two little daughters, were given an education fit for royal princesses. Although the differences in tone and style between the courts of Andrew the Catholic and the Confessor must have been considerable, the Benedictine monks in charge of religious life at both courts provided a sense of continuity for the children. They were taught to read the sacred manuscripts in Latin, introduced to the lives of the saints and the teachings of Gregory and Cassian and given a good grounding in the works of Augustine.

They were taught French, because the king preferred to speak it in private, and instructed in deportment and courtly customs. The girls were also trained in needlework, while Edgar was introduced early to the martial arts. But the accent of their education was on religion in keeping with the lifestyle of a court dominated by religious observances.

Before long, the extreme religious devotion of the king, coupled with the spiritual guidance of the Benedictine teachers and the firm hand of the Mistress of Maidens, made an indelible impression on the royal children.

Margaret, in particular, showed signs of deep, Christian devotion. As Bishop Turgotus wrote,

> While yet in the flower of youth, Margaret began to live a very strict life, to love God above all things, to employ herself in the study of the divine writings and therein with joy to exercise her mind. Her understanding was keen to comprehend any matter whatever it might be; to this was joined a great tenacity of memory, enabling to store it all up, along with a graceful flow of language to express it.

A youthful refugee prince brought unexpected excitement and fresh interests into the lives of the royal children. Malcolm Canmore, the son of King Duncan of Scotland, was sent to the Confessor's hospitable court for safety after his father's murder. He was received with great friendship by the king. He was seated at the Confessor's table, like Agatha's children, and encouraged 'to consort with the king's knights' and, together with Edgar, learn from them the art of warfare.

The adjustment to the more formal ways of the English court could not have been any easier for young Malcolm than it had been for the Confessor's relations when they first arrived from Hungary. This natural affinity, based on a similarity of exile experiences and conditions, created a bond between the royal children and the Scottish prince and brought them closer, with unexpected consequences for the history of the British isles.

While the fatherless children of Edward the Exile were being reintegrated into British society, with the help of the king, the country at large was beginning to show the strains of the uncertainty of succession. In spite of his affection for his own kindred, the Confessor could not ignore the fact that the Danes and the Norwegians were all set to recover Canute's patrimony and that the child Edgar would hardly be able to avert a new Viking onslaught. Indeed, King Magnus had claimed the crown of England immediately after Harthacanute's death, and only a challenge to his own throne had prevented him from sailing against England. Should the dragon ships of the Norsemen once again appear at the shores of these islands, who would defend the country?

The king's answer was a prudent compromise. Edgar Aetheling, with Harold behind him, he appears to have reasoned, offered a formidable combination of forces which would keep the country's enemies at bay. Harold was a seasoned warrior, while Edgar Aetheling had right and the support of the patriotic faction behind him.

That this lopsided tandem might not work never occurred to the king. Since he naively believed that the tradition of the Anglo-Saxons debarred a person of Harold's ancestry from ascending the throne, he was quite happy to see all the power of the realm concentrated in the hands of Harold and his brothers. But he took the precaution of recommending Edgar to the magnates as his choice for the throne, a choice sanctioned by precedent and custom because, as he told the Witan, the aetheling was the sole direct male-line descendant of the house of Cerdic. Such a royal recommendation carried very great weight with the Witan, in spite of the aetheling's slight technical handicap that he was not the son of a king. Even though this was a prerequisite of kingship among the Anglo-Saxons, the Confessor could rightly expect that, with the royal house on the verge of extinction, the grandson of the heroic King Edmund Ironside, should be acceptable to the country.

What he left out of his reckoning was that with so much power in the hands of Harold Godwin, the earl might look upon himself as the *de facto* ruler of the country and reach out for the crown.

The position of Harold, already exceedingly powerful at the time of Edward the Exile's murder, began to take on the aspect of semi-royalty – 'subregulus' in the words of Florence – in the years of his supposed partnership with Edgar Aetheling. In public documents his name appeared together with the king's in a most unusual combination, vassals pledged fealty to the king and Earl Harold linking them in shared authority, and foreign princes addressed him as 'the duke of the English', a title to which he was certainly not entitled by birth but which, in the eyes of foreign envoys, his position warranted.

However mighty Harold might have been, there is no evidence in the contemporary chronicles that his semi-royal position was formalized. This missing formal act, so important in an elective monarchy, did nothing to allay the growing concern of Duke William of Normandy over Harold's intentions. Indeed, the prevailing climate of uncertainty seems to have goaded him into action. His own claim to the Anglo-Saxon crown, based on a promise made by the king, could not be pressed against an English-born prince of Aethelred's house like Edward the Exile, but it could be asserted against a usurper and perjurer, as Harold was in the eyes of the Norman duke. Harold's 'illegal' candidature for the throne was in fact a veritable godsend for the duke. And for the first time, the threat of an armed intervention in England began to seem a distinct possibility.

With the two main contenders set for a showdown, England's hope of avoiding a bloody war of succession rested on whether the king would live long enough to allow Edgar to reach manhood and ascend the throne. But that hope was fading fast.

Duke William's accusation that Harold callously broke an oath of allegiance made over the relics of saints rested on a curious incident which, in conflicting versions, was recorded by Norman, Anglo-Norman and Scandinavian chroniclers. In that superstitious age it strengthened his hand against Harold and justified his insistence that the faithless perjurer must be punished for insulting holy relics. With the Pope's eventual backing, his moral case against Harold became unassailable.

According to William of Poitiers, Duke William's chaplain, and the main exponent of the Norman side, Harold sailed to Normandy on the king's errand in 1064 bearing the Confessor's formal promise of making William his heir. Caught by a storm, he put in at a harbour on the land of Count Guy of Ponthieu, a vassal of Duke William, who promptly imprisoned him at Beaurain but was forced to let him go on his lord's order.

Harold was entertained with great hospitality at Rouen, made a Norman knight and sworn, apparently over the hidden bones of saints, to become a liege-man of Duke William. He also agreed, the duke's chaplain claimed, to represent William's interests at the Confessor's court and to use all his power to secure the crown of England for his liege-lord when the king died. He further promised to hand over Dover and other castles to Duke William and, in exchange, the Duke of Normandy graciously agreed to bestow upon Harold the hand of his daughter and to confirm him in his earldom and public position.[2]

It seems most implausible that Harold should have voluntarily conceded all this, or that the Confessor should have entrusted to him a message confirming his rival's right to the throne, but unfortunately the *Anglo-Saxon Chronicle* has nothing to say about it. However, by collating all the extant versions, the factual basis of the story can be pieced together.

Harold sailed from Bosham harbour in Sussex in the summer of 1064 on an expedition to Bretland (Wales, perhaps), according to Saxo. But when his ship was at sea contrary winds drove him far out into the ocean and, eventually, he made a landfall in Normandy. While the virtual prisoner of William, Harold did swear fealty to his host and he admitted as much in a message to William, recorded by Malmesbury. But he reasonably argued that an obligation contracted under duress could not be deemed binding.

The Normans also put to good use medieval man's great reverence for holy relics and surreptitiously introduced a set of bones into the proceedings, with devastating effect.

The perjury committed over the relics, the most damning part of the accusation against Harold in contemporary eyes, was a ruse, and Norman chroniclers admitted this. In an apparent attempt to underline William's shrewdness and flatter his statesmanlike thinking, they described how the duke hid the bones of saints under a table at which Harold was made to swear him allegiance in order to make the oath more binding. The Bayeux Tapestry, which depicts Harold's swearing of fealty, shows the earl standing at a chiffonier with a mysteriously covered lower part, two raised fingers of his right hand touching a cross in an oath-taking gesture as Duke William, seated on his throne, looks on.[3]

Thus the claim to the throne by both William and Harold rested – unlike Edgar Aetheling's – on half-truths and distortions, and to lend them credibility they needed the old king's blessing. As he had made it patently clear that he wanted Edgar on the throne, they were unlikely to

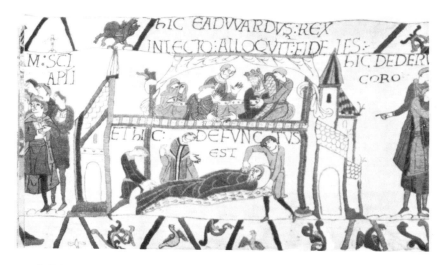

10. Edward the Confessor on his deathbed (as pictured in the Bayeux Tapestry). He sent a powerful embassy to the Continent to bring back his nephew, Edward the Exile, from Hungary to succeed him on the throne of England. But, as the *Anglo-Saxon Chronicle* noted, influential men at court prevented the heir apparent from meeting his uncle, the king, and within 48 hours of reaching England, Edward the Exile was dead.

get it and so their last hope was to seek, by hook or by crook, a recommendation in his will.

The pro-Norman partisans of William claimed, without adducing acceptable proof, that there were two wills in favour of William's succession. Even Orderic recorded that the Confessor had bequeathed the realm of England to William. According to the monk of Evroult, the king first made known his intention through Robert, the Archbishop of Canterbury, and later, after allegedly having obtained the consent of the nation, through Earl Harold. The claim that the king's wish to make his Norman kinsman his successor was not only made known to his nobles but actually received their approval, is totally unfounded and brings into question the Norman account of the two wills.

In a different form but with the same aim, Malmesbury, the doyen of the Anglo-Norman chroniclers, insisted too that William was formally declared heir to the throne: 'The king, in consequence of the death of his relation [Edward the Exile], losing his first hope of support, gave the succession of England to William, Duke of Normandy.' Though he does not say where or in what form the Confessor made his decision, by tracing it right back to the aetheling's murder, he involuntarily emphasises the historic significance of that tragic act. This he further stresses with the remark that Edward, not William or Harold, was his 'first hope'.

The supporters of Harold, with no will in his favour, were pinning

11. Harold presented with the crown of England in the presence of Archbishop Stigant (the Bayeux Tapestry). But the mysterious death of Edward the Exile overshadowed his coronation and led to the Norman invasion of 1066.

their hopes on an affirming, testamentary word from the king. This became the more urgent as the Confessor went into rapid decline after a dangerous conspiracy against Earl Tosti, who was closest to the king among the Godwins. The king once again proved too weak to protect a friend from being forced into exile and he never recovered from this humiliation. He was seized by a fever, and the alleged last words he uttered on his deathbed became the basis of Harold's claim to the crown of England.

On 5 January 1066, as the king lay dying, he was surrounded by Earl Harold, Archbishop Stigand of Canterbury, the queen and Robert FitzWimark, a friend of the Confessor, and of Norman extraction. The strongly pro-Godwin author of the *Vita Aedwardi Regis*, who knew the king personally and dedicated his work to his queen, Godwin's daughter, gives a very detailed account of the deathbed scene and the monarch's last words.

As he felt his death approaching, the king gave his hand to Harold and asked him to protect the queen and the country and gave him instructions for his funeral.

> I commend this woman and all the kingdom to your protection. Serve and honour her with faithful obedience as your lady and sister, which she is, and do not deprive her, as long as she lives, of any honour she has received from me. I also commend to you those men who have left their native country for love of me and served me

148

faithfully. Take an oath of fealty from them if they wish, and protect and retain them; or send them with your safe conduct across the Channel to their own homes, with all they have acquired in my service.

There is no word – as claimed by Harold's supporters – of Harold being made the successor to the throne, only the natural commendation of a dying king of his queen and country to the premier earl of England. The care with which the author seems to be quoting the actual words of the king leaves little doubt as to the meaning of his deathbed appeal, leaving Harold harldly better off than William.

Whether these crucial final words were deliberately phrased so vaguely because they were actually written down in the post-invasion years, or because this is what the dying king said, is open to debate. But Saxo, who gathered together the Danish and Norse traditions, gave the clear impression that Harold used the moment of the king's death to give him the desperately needed affirmation that he was his chosen heir by putting words into the dead man's mouth.

It is said that when the king was near his last hour, Harold and a few others were with him. Harold first leaned over the king and then said; 'I take you all to witness that the king has now given me the kingdom, and all the realm of England.' And then the king was taken *dead* out of bed.

What the witnesses actually heard was Harold demanding of them to attest that the king had given him the crown, not the king's words, because the king was dead already. By producing the witnesses in the Witan later in the day, Harold overcame the hesitancy of many, who wanted to follow the Confessor's behest and give the crown to Edgar Aetheling, and had himself elected King of England.

The alleged testamentary words of the pious old king, attested by perfidious or confused witnesses, carried the day in the Witan. But some magnates and thanes outside London, determined to resist the upstart Harold, wanted to elect Edgar king. However, they were forced to abandon the aetheling because of the bishops' opposition to his succession.

Malmesbury, whose impartiality derived from his mixed Anglo-Norman parentage, gives a vivid account of the confusion and divided council prevailing among the men who decided the fate of the Anglo-Saxon kingdom.

When King Edward the Confessor had yielded to fate, England, fluctuating with doubtful favour, was uncertain to which ruler she should submit herself; to Harold, William or Edgar. For the king had commended Edgar also to the nobility as nearest to the sovereignty in point of birth, concealing his better judgment from the tenderness of his disposition.

Wherefore, as I have said above, the English were *distracted* in their choice, although all of them openly wished well to Harold. He, indeed, once dignified with the crown, thought nothing of his covenant with William. He said that he was absolved because his [William's] daughter, to whom he had been betrothed, had died before she was marriageable. For this man, though possessing numberless good qualities, is reported to have been careless about abstaining from perfidy, so that he could, by any device, elude the reasoning of men on this matter.

One would be offending the intelligence of the hard-headed men of the Witan by believing that they had swallowed whole Harold's account of the Confessor's deathbed blessing. In the light of all the available evidence, it seems much more likely that, having been offered a time-honoured formula for Harold's succession, they opted for the devil they knew. Under the threat of foreign intervention and the noisy clamour of the powerful Godwin faction, the Witan bypassed the last scion of Cerdic's house and gave the crown to the one man they believed could defend England.

But in so doing they unwittingly ended the line of Anglo-Saxon kings which, but for the brief Danish interlude, continued unbroken for 571 years, and launched the brash new dynasty of the house of Godwin. In the eyes of the more traditionalist wing of the Saxon party, for whom the West Saxon kingdom was synonymous with the house of Cerdic, this was treason. In their despair they looked to Edgar Aetheling for leadership.

22. The comet of revolution over England; death of a kingdom

The Year of Grace 1066 began badly for the Anglo-Saxon kingdom. With their gentle and beloved king dead and Harold on the throne, the people looked to the months ahead with trepidation. The omens were the worst in living memory and, according to those who understood the language of heavenly signs, they presaged ceaseless woes, wholesale calamities and terrible upheavals.

King Harold's supporters who mocked the faint-hearted were silenced when a terrifying comet with a burning tail appeared above the country in the spring and remained stationary for a fortnight. It was observed throughout Europe and noted even in China. An English poet was inspired by the apparition to encapsulate the event in a rhyming couplet:

> In the year thousand and six and sixty more
> A comet's tresses streamed o'er England's shore.

The monastic writer of the *Rheims Chronicle* felt similarly inclined, and recorded the heavenly warning in classic hexameters:

> Sexagenus erat sextus millesimus annus,
> Quum pereunt Angli stella monstrante cometa.

As comets portended violent revolution, the contemporary chroniclers of our Continent saw it as a heavenly warning of the impending conquest of England. Indeed, even the annalists of the more distant countries of Europe, who had no knowledge of the quarrel between Harold and William over the crown of England, linked unhesitatingly the comet with the subsequent invasion in their chronicles.

Bishop Otto of Freisingn saw the comet as a harbinger of King Harold's death and the take-over of the British isles by the Normans; Ekkehard, the foremost contemporary German chronicler, wrote of 1066 as the year of the comet which saw the miserable subjugation of England by William the Norman; the Cambrai chronicle of St Andrew took the burning rays emitted by the comet as presaging war, famine and pestilence for the English, and noted that this came to pass when William of Normandy crossed the Channel with a big army; in the southern Italian city of Bari, Lupus Protospatarius linked the comet with the Norman duke's war on Harold, foretelling his victory over the English; Guillaume Godell, the Aquitanian monk, saw the red colour of the comet as a heavenly hint of a river of Christian blood the soil of England was to absorb; the *Lüttich Chronicle* of St James recorded that the appearance of the comet portended war for England, adding that the same year William of Normandy duly conquered the kingdom and maimed its king; even Dlugosz, the learned monk, writing in distant Poland, noted that the comet foretold much evil for England and Germany and subsequently King Harold was killed, as betokened by the heavenly sign.[1]

Closer to Britain, Orderic gave a most graphic account of the superstitious forebodings that seized the people on sighting the comet but could not resist to exploit it for a bit of pro-Norman propaganda:

> In the Year of Our Lord 1066, in the month of April, there appeared in the zodiac for fifteen days together, a star called comet, which, as clever astrologers who have keenly investigated the secrets of nature assert, portended a revolution. For Edward, king of England . . . had died just before, and Harold, Earl Godwin's son usurped the English throne. Guilty as he was of perjury, cruelty and other iniquities, he had now held it three months to the great injury of many persons, in as much as his unjust usurpation had occasioned violent animosities between different families, from which mothers had to bewail the loss of their sons, and wives of their husbands.

However, the English annalists' account, emphasizing the good justice of Harold's government, bring into question the pro-Norman writers' allegation of wholesale slaughter of the new king's enemies. Nevertheless, the weakness of his position would have made a purge of the more prominent opponents of his reign a prudent precaution.

In seizing the crown, he took very great risks, and he knew it. But having risen to the pinnacle of power against very great odds, he felt confident that he could cope with the situation. In shrewd moves, he divided his enemies, while at the same time he endeavoured to unite the country behind him with the help of the threat from across the Channel.

He bought off the most powerful of his challengers, the brothers Eadwin and Morcare, earls of Mercia and Northumbria, by marrying their sister, Ealdgyth. Less influential opponents he silenced in one form or another, and made determined efforts to strengthen the country's defences.

He made no move against Edgar, but then the aetheling was still only a child of about twelve; furthermore, he had a strong following among the more traditional magnates and, especially, among the burghers of London.[2] Any attack on the aetheling could have had very grave repercussions and Harold was clearly not in a position to chance that. So Edgar was allowed to move about freely in the country but there must have been a hint of menace implicit in King Harold's attitude to the aetheling that filled Agatha with fear for the life of her son. According to Boethius, the Scottish chronicler of St Margaret's life, 'Agatha, havand suspicioun of troubill eftir following, kepit hir son Edgair secretelie with grete diligence in her chalmer.'[3]

Harold worried about Duke William. The wretched oath of allegiance was clearly on his conscience and he was preparing for the inevitable day of reckoning. William had sent messengers to Harold right after his coronation, reminding him of his oath and demanding his allegiance. And he kept up the pressure with further warnings and reminders, at the same time mounting a clever public relations exercise to win sympathy for his case at the courts of Europe.

He proclaimed for the world and provided 'documentary proof' that Harold was a usurper, and in an astute move, sent special envoys to Pope Alexander II to convince the spiritual ruler of Christendom that the Englishman was a perjurer. As befitting a devout Christian prince, William further proposed that the usurper and perjurer must be punished and volunteered to go to war for Christendom.

The Pope, having for a long time wished to reform the English Church, approved William's invasion plan which, he reckoned, would allow the removal of some recalcitrant prelates. He therefore sent William a consecrated flag and this helped to lend William's intended conquest of England the character of a holy war.

Believing an attack from Normandy to be imminent, Harold kept an armada of ships and a good force of men throughout the summer on the south coast in readiness to repulse William. But as tension mounted more and more people began to see the wisdom of the late king's compromise succession plan, and the following of the aetheling grew with every passing day.

Harold was right, however, in assuming that the only real threat to his crown came from William, and so he failed to take note of the possible consequences of the changing mood in the country. He also left out of his plans the disastrous effects of medieval soldiering.

Like Edmund Ironside before him, Harold was confronted with the demand of his troops to be allowed to go home and harvest their land. The bread of the next year had to be gathered in if the people were not to starve, and so Harold's army dispersed just as Harold Hardrada, the warrior king of Norway, and Harold's exiled brother, Tosti, sailed up to England with a powerful battle fleet. This new, unexpected development in the fight for the crown of England greatly strengthened William's hand and improved his chances beyond measure.

Harold learned with dismay of the arrival of his brother with a Norse fleet. He set off at once with his housecarles and such troops as he could muster on his way to York, which was threatened by the invaders. He caught the Norsemen unawares at Stamford Bridge and in bitter fighting he won a resounding victory on 25 September. The Norwegian king and Tosti were among the dead. To the wounding appellations of him as a usurper and perjurer, his whispering detractors now added the accusation of fratricide.

William, determined to resolve his quarrel with Harold before the onset of the winter, sent a monk of Fécamp with a final offer to England.[4] The envoy was to remind Harold of William's 'legal right' to the kingdom and to propose three solutions: Harold should either relinquish his crown as he was pledged under his oath, or hold it for the Duke of the Normans. If, however, he would not accept either, the quarrel should be decided by single combat in the sight of the armies.

William's envoy was further empowered to state that his lord would also be prepared to submit the dispute to Pope Alexander and abide absolutely by his judgment, but in view of the Pontiff's patent partiality, this was not a feasible proposition.

Harold, however, would not even see William's envoy; as Malmesbury wrote:

> His unbridled rashness yielded no placid ear to the words of his advisers, thinking it base to turn his back on danger of any kind. And with similar impudence, or to speak more favourably, imprudence, he drove away the monk, who was the messenger of William, not deigning him even a complacent look, imprecating only that God would decide between him and the duke.

His intransigence in the face of superior forces sealed his and England's fate, in the opinion of the chronicler who proudly proclaimed in his writings his English and Norman heritage. 'For my part, as the blood of either people flows in my veins, I shall steer a middle course', Malmesbury wrote of the events of 1066, making his judgment of Harold's arrogant stand more damning.

After the rebuff to his envoy, William immediately prepared to sail against Harold with his invasion force, and the tragic events of 1066 were heading towards their inevitable conclusion. Two things were holding up the Norman invasion armada: one was the weather, the other William's hope for a favourable omen. As befitting a medieval prince, he employed a court 'sortilegus' – astrologer-cum-necromancer – without whose favourable horoscope he never engaged in battle or undertook any important decision.

On 28 September, the court soothsayer divined, by casting lots, that Harold would surrender without a fight and that Duke William's enterprise would be crowned by success. William's 50,000-strong invasion force, buoyed up and greatly reassured by the favourable omens, sailed from the mouth of the river Dives, where it had lain at anchor for over a month.

The Norman invasion fleet, heavily laden with horses, provisions and arms, was extremely vulnerable as it approached Pevensey Bay, but with the English fleet withdrawn from the south coast to London on 8 September and the army guarding the Sussex coast disbanded, William's troops landed without opposition.

A couple of strange incidents on the landing beach gripped the superstitious soldiery with apprehension, endangering William's enterprise. The court soothsayer, called to interpret the portents of the stars, was found to have drowned during the crossing. William retrieved the situation by pouring scorn on the foolishness of men whose will to fight apparently depended on the predictions of a diviner who could not even foretell his own fate.

William's words eased the atmosphere but could not dispel the chill felt in the face of the ominous death. And when William stumbled and fell on his hands as he was setting foot on English soil, his frightened men cried out: 'Mal signe est çi!'

But one of his quick-witted soldiers, pointing to the clod of earth which the duke had grasped, called out: 'You hold England, my lord, its future king.' As the kneeling and holding of a lump of earth formed part of the formal feudal act of taking possession of land, the soldiery accepted that what they saw was not the faltering first step of their duke but the symbolic seizing of England, and the invasion got under way.

On hearing of the Norman landing, Harold at once rode from York to London to collect fresh troops. Though his best housecarles and bowmen had been killed at Stamford Bridge, he wanted to confront his enemy at once. The euphoria of his recent great victory made him rash and, after a forced march through Kent and Sussex on 13 October, he took up a position on a spur of the South Downs 'at the spot which used to be called Senlac in ancient times', according to Orderic.

The size of his army is much debated. While Poitiers claimed that enormous forces of Englishmen had joined Harold's banner, Florence and Malmesbury asserted that his army was far too small to confront William. The decision of the fickle earls of Mercia and Northumbria to stay away with their seasoned troops would seem to bear out Florence's view that Harold joined battle with an inadequate and inexperienced force on 14 October.

The course of the battle of Hastings is too well known to require detailed description. Many eminent writers with a sense of history have, in the intervening centuries, analyzed it in depth and brooded over its consequences. Therefore the only contemporary English account of the battle, contained in the *Anglo-Saxon Chronicle*, suffices for the purposes of this narrative, as it is more concerned with the sudden change in Edgar Aetheling's fortunes than the grisly details of the fighting.

King Harold assembled a large army and marched to meet William at the hoary appletree. William attacked him before his troops were drawn up on formation. King Harold and all those who supported him resisted William strongly, and there were very big casualties on both sides. King Harold was killed in the battle, and so were his brothers, Earl Leofwine and Earl Gyrth, together with many brave men. The French remained masters of the field. God granted them this victory because of the people's sins.

The disaster of Hastings stunned the country. Harold's friends and foes alike saluted his bravery, and many lamented his terrible death if only because of the uncertainties it created. But on the whole, the feelings over the king's unexpected demise were rather mixed as his brief nine-month-long reign had exacerbated rather than healed the divisions brought about by his seizure of the crown.

In Mercia and Northumbria, few shed tears over the passing of Godwin's son, while in the south many people mourned him. But the great mass of traditionalist Englishmen both in Wessex and in the Danelaw rejoiced over the killing of the usurper, and greeted the new era ushered in by Hastings as liberation. They saw the Normans as a band of marauding raiders, of no greater significance than the Norsemen or the Danes in their time, and similarly misjudged Duke William's intentions.

The people of Wessex turned to Edgar Aetheling in a natural closing of ranks in a moment of danger. He was the living symbol of the Anglo-Saxon kingdom and his name became the rallying point of the country. The restoration of the right royal line held out fresh hope and the promise of better times for most Englishmen. The burghers of London were especially zealous supporters of Edmund Ironside's grandson and his appellation – 'Edgar Aetheling, England's darling' – can give an inkling of his great popularity.

The magnates and the leaders of the Church met in London in an attempt to resolve the crisis. Eadwin and Morcare appeared at the Witan and sought, in turn, the crown of Wessex. Their eminent birth and proven valour in battle, they argued, made them incomparably better suited for the throne than the foreign-born child Edgar, and urged the peers of the realm to choose one of them to lead the country in the fight against William.

But with no justifiable Mercian claim to the throne of Wessex and with the rightful descendant of Cerdic's royal house in the city, Eadwin and Morcare stood no chance. The burghers of London, who enjoyed by tradition a privileged position in the selection of the kingdom's monarchs, clamoured for Edgar. The seamen of London too came out in support of the aetheling. And as the constitutional machinery went through the time-honoured motions of Anglo-Saxon king-making, the Witan came to the decision that only Ironside's grandson could unite and save the country. Eadwin and Morcare did not oppose Edgar's election.

Fortune once again seemed to be smiling on the house of Aethelred the Unready. It was holding up the crown of England and beckoning approvingly to the aetheling in a gesture of goodwill it had denied Edgar's father, grandfather and great-grandfather. But even as it was radiating benign indulgence, Fortune made a wry face and the fleeting hope of better days was gone in a trice.

The bishops stubbornly withheld their support and without the Church's blessing Edgar could not be crowned king.[5] The Anglo-Saxons attached, like their forebears, a superstitious importance to the mystery of the anointment of their kings, and the uncrowned Edgar, though duly elected king of the English, lacked royal authority. His vulnerable position became desperate when Eadwin and Morcare, throwing national interests to the wind, withdrew with their forces to the north, letting it be known that they would welcome the partitioning of the country with William.

Edgar, deprived of a king's authority and his sword-arm, could hardly fulfil the expectations of the people and drive out the invaders. The chance to unite the country and counter the ruinous effects of a battle were lost. Though both Florence and Orderic recorded that the English intended to fight on under their youthful king, the dissent of the bishops and northern earls made the continuation of the fight hopeless – and the magnates of the Witan knew it. Submission to the alien became unavoidable. Orderic wrote:

> Stigand, the Archbishop, and other English nobles met the duke [at Berkhampstead] and, abandoning the cause of Edgar, came to terms with William, to whom they did homage and being received with favour were secured in all their honours and estates. The Londoners, also, being better advised, now transferred their allegiance to the duke, and delivered to him such and so many hostages, as required. Edgar Aetheling, therefore, who had been declared king by the English, having no means of resistance, humbly surrendered his person and his kingdom to William.

St Dunstan's prophetic vision of aliens subjugating the doomed kingdom of Aethelred the Unready was becoming a reality.

PART VI: THE 'LOST KING' OF ENGLAND

23. *A kingdom for a bag of silver*

There is something infinitely melancholy in the scene, so fondly portrayed by the Anglo-Norman chroniclers, of William the Conqueror magnanimously raising from his knees the last elected king of the Anglo-Saxons as he surrendered his kingdom, sealing the submission with the kiss of peace.

Though still only twelve, Edgar had known exile and royal splendour and through curious revolutions of fortune, had regained and lost his father's patrimony. And now he had to swear allegiance to the alien prince and plead for favours, instead of rallying the country against the invaders, all because of the dissension of the bishops and the treason of the northern earls. A king twice-elected but never crowned, Edgar was launched at Berkhamsted on a career that, in spite of some gallant actions and foolishly heroic undertakings, remained tied forever to the consequences of Berkhamsted. It was, in a sense, the progression of England's 'lost king' across countries, causes and revolutions to nowhere.

The lords spiritual and temporal, with no real allegiance to the nation-state forged in the crucible of battle against foreign invaders, showed greater concern for their personal privileges than for the fate of the kingdom.[1] Accordingly, they sought confirmation of their offices and tenures at Berkhamsted and in exchange offered their collaboration. Though, according to Anglo-Saxon tradition, Edgar was the kingdom's duly elected king, a choice affirmed by the Witan, the noble lords begged the Duke of Normandy to accept the crown of the realm. And to lend credibility to their offer, they swore oaths of allegiance to him and gave him hostages.

William was not only a farsighted statesman; he was an outstanding organizer and valiant soldier, and the boy Edgar was certainly no match for a ruler of his calibre. Nevertheless, he was still a foreign invader, while Edgar, the descendant of the royal house of Cerdic, was being forced by the peers of the realm to abdicate in the alien's favour. By offering to crown the Duke of Normandy, but not Edgar, the bishops were blindly following the Pope's pro-William policy, Harold's death notwithstanding, and using the authority of the Catholic Church to decide the fate of the Anglo-Saxon kingdom. With the sacred influence of the sacrament, they were proposing to metamorphose the Norman duke into an English king.

Duke William responded graciously. He promised to look after his defeated young rival and treat him as if he were his own son, and pledged upon his sword to the nobles that he would be a good lord to them.

His coronation at Westminster Abbey on Christmas Day, 1066, by Archbishop Ealdred of York and Geoffrei, the Norman Bishop of Coutances, was interrupted by an incident which was seen even by the loyal Norman chroniclers as an omen of future calamities.

When in response to Archbishop Ealdred's formal question the assembled nobles gave their assent to William's election a fraction too loudly, the Norman men-at-arms outside the abbey misunderstood the clamour of the English with awful consequences. As Orderic reported,

> The men-at-arms, suspecting some treachery, imprudently set on fire the neighbouring houses. With the flames quickly spreading, the people in the Abbey were seized with panic in the midst of the rejoicing and throngs of men and women eagerly struggled to escape from the church. The bishops, only with some few of their clergy and monks, maintained their post before the altar and trembling with fear completed the coronation with some difficulty, the king himself being much alarmed.

In the New Year, King William endowed Edgar with tracts of land in Hertfordshire, but when pressing affairs of state forced him to retire to Normandy, he took the aetheling with him, along with, along with other leading noblemen of England. In spite of the royal largesse, he clearly did not think it safe to leave Edgar in England in his absence. On the other hand, he did not have him murdered either, dangerous though he was as a living symbol of the vanquished Anglo-Saxon kingdom. And this is further evidence, however circumstantial, that it could not have been him who had the aetheling's father murdered in 1057.

In the coming months Edgar followed William about and was back in England before Christmas, disgruntled and rebellious, waiting for an opportunity to challenge the king. More and more people were taking to the woods, preferring the life of outlaws to William's rule. The fens, marshes and glens became their stronghold from whence they sallied forth to harass the Normans.

Many nobles fled northwards, first to Mercia and Northumbria, which were still only nominally under William's authority, and then on to Scotland, where King Malcolm Canmore welcomed the English fugitives with great hospitality. In the summer of 1068, Edgar, claiming that he had not been treated well by William, fled to Scotland with his family and Hungarian retainers to join the anti-Norman rebels gathering there. In so doing he broke his oath of allegiance to William.

According to Florence, the flight was at the instigation of the earls Marlesweyn and Gospatric and a handful of other Northumbrian lords who, 'fearing that they might be thrown into prison like others, and wishing to escape King William's tyranny, took with them Edgar Aetheling, his mother Agatha and his two sisters, Margaret and Christina'.

The English rebels gathering in Scotland needed a leader, while Edgar needed an army if he was to recover his crown.

In the circumstances, the flight to Scotland, as recounted by Florence, seems most plausible, especially as Malcolm, once himself a refugee at the English court, was indebted to the Confessor's family. While noted by the *Anglo-Saxon Chronicle*, this vital Scottish link has been overlooked by all later chroniclers, and they bridged the gap by claiming to see Divine Providence in the landing of Edgar in Scotland.

The source of this version of Edgar's post-Conquest peregrinations can be traced to Bishop Turgotus, myth-maker extraordinary and chaplain to Margaret in Edinburgh. Drawing on the bishop's biography, both Scottish and Anglo-Norman writers confidently asserted that Edgar, despairing of the state of England and his chance of recovering his throne, chartered a ship and sailed with his sisters for the Continent to return to Hungary, their native country. Fordun wrote:

> But the Sovereign Ruler, who rules the winds and waves, troubled the sea, and the billows thereof were upheaved by the breath of the gale. So while the storm was raging, they all, losing all hope of life, commended themselves to God, and left the vessel to the guidance of the waves.
>
> Accordingly, after many dangers and huge toils, God took pity on His forlorn children, for when no help from man seems to be forthcoming we must needs have recourse to God's help – and at length, tossed in the countless dangers of the deep, they were forced to fetch up in Scotland. So that holy family brought up in a certain spot which was henceforth called St Margaret's Bay by the inhabitants. We believe that this did not come about by chance, but that they arrived there through the providence of God Most High.

Malcolm's representatives who greeted the passengers of the unusually large ship driven to their shores were greatly impressed by the lordliness of the men, the beauty of the women and the good breeding of Edgar and his family. They were particularly taken by the matchless beauty of Margaret and the ready flow of her eloquence, and so was Malcolm, who fell in love with her at first sight, according to the progenitor of the St Margaret legend.

Malcolm, so the story goes, asked for Margaret's hand in marriage, and although the young princess would have preferred a virgin's life, Edgar Aetheling gave his consent. One has not to dig too deeply beneath the myth that shrouds the marriage of Margaret and Malcolm in order to uncover the truth.

The allegory of the tempest that tossed Margaret and her family to Scotland was convincing enough for a seafaring nation that saw storms at sea as manifestations of an inscrutable Divine Will. However, the likely reasons behind the royal family's flight to Scotland are less romantic.

Having broken his oath of allegiance to William, Edgar became an outlaw and his family's lands were forfeit. With his hopes of succession dashed and possessions lost, Edgar turned naturally to Malcolm, who not only welcomed all the English fugitives, but was personally indebted to the English royal family for giving him asylum in his hour of need.

That Agatha was heading with her children for Scotland, not Hungary, is borne out by the route her ship took. However, the possibility that she used some deception to allay the fears of William about the purpose of the journey cannot be excluded. Indeed, it seems quite plausible that she deliberately spread rumours of her intention of returning to Hungary in the hope that William would see the move as a natural solution for a poor widow left stranded in a strange land and not obstruct her departure. As far as William was concerned, the journey to Hungary must have looked like an anxious mother's decision to safeguard her dangerously-exposed young son, and the king could only have welcomed the painless removal overseas of his rival. Bishop Turgotus, told about the intended flight to Hungary by Margaret some twenty years later, appears to have taken the stratagem rather literally.

Early in 1069, the seething anti-Norman feeling erupted in a simultaneous insurrection in Northumbria, Wales and the earldom of Chester. Malcolm harried the border provinces, and the Danes of Mercia rallied to the rebels. Edgar Aetheling, accompanied by the exiled English nobles, left Scotland for York, the centre of the anti-Norman rising. He was given a rousing welcome by the population, and the mood of the Anglo-Saxons throughout the country indicated that they would welcome the aetheling as their liberator.

The fighting raged most fiercely at York, where the rebels besieged the Norman castle, that symbol of Norman dominance. William, however, replied to the hot-headed fury of the English with well-planned and cautious operations. He built forts as he advanced, left garrisons behind under experienced commanders and, with a secure hinterland, he devastated Northumbria and relieved York. Eadwin and Morcare, facing utter rout, surrendered, begging William's forgiveness. The revolt was crushed, and Edgar fled to Scotland again.

But the aetheling, now a mature fourteen- or fifteen-year-old could not accept defeat. In the autumn of 1069, when a Danish battle fleet, sent by King Sweyn Estrithson to aid the rebels, sailed up the Humber, he and his followers got together several warships and joined the Danes.

In an attempt to prove himself in battle, he sailed on a reckless, plundering raid with a single ship. His enterprise ended in tragedy when the Norman garrison of Lincoln caught him unawares, and destroyed his ship. Only the aetheling and two of his companions escaped. He then spent the winter with the Danish fleet, where he was joined by his mother and his sisters.

When William bribed Jarl Osbjern, the Danish fleet's captain, and he sailed for home in the spring of 1070, Edgar and his family headed for Scotland as Malcolm alone continued to fight against the Conqueror. However, unexpected complications set in and threatened to sour Edgar's relationship with his sole ally.

What neither Edgar, nor the rest of the English refugees could have foreseen was the passion aroused in the Scottish king by the beauty and style of Margaret. Malcolm was in love and he yearned for the princess with 'royal and even Imperial blood in her veins'. Margaret, however, was far from enamoured by her suitor and, as befitting a pious Christian maid, she intended to devote her days to the Church and 'lead a virgin's life'.

Malcolm was already married to Ingeborg, the widow of Thorfin, the lord of Orkney, but he quickly rid himself of this encumbrance, indicating that he would not take no for an answer.[2] The English nobles at the Scottish court fearing that Malcolm might withdraw his support for their cause if thwarted, urged the aetheling to give his consent to the marriage. In accordance with the customs of the time, it was up to him to decide his sister's fate, and he held out for a considerable time. But as the *Anglo-Saxon Chronicle* succinctly put it, in the end Edgar 'answered "Yea" and indeed he durst not otherwise because they were come into his power'.

Margaret and Malcolm's wedding took place with great pomp and circumstance at Dunfermline in that year. As her sister, Christina, became a nun and Edgar had no acknowledged offspring either, the children of Margaret, a lineal descendant of the Anglo-Saxon kings, became the sole heirs to the crown of England.

Malcolm kept his side of the bargain and continued to raid the neighbouring provinces of England. It was a hopeless fight, and though carried out in the name of the pretender to the English throne, it was no more than ordinary plunder. 'It was not that Malcolm supposed, by so doing, he could be of any service to Edgar, with respect of the kingdom, but merely to distress the mind of William', Malmesbury remarked.

William, however, did not take this new alliance lightly and he sent envoys to Malcolm with an ultimatum. He either delivered Edgar into his hands or else he would take him by force and destroy Malcolm's land with sword and fire.

According to Boethius, William was sent a brave reply:

King Macolme, seying grete troubill appering if he randrit nocht Edgare in his fayis handis, and perpetuall dishonour following if he so did, ansuerit that King Williamis desyris was nocht respondent to equite, and thairfor thai war nocht to be grantit.

In the end, Malcolm had no choice but to surrender and pledge fealty to the Conqueror of England. Edgar, forced to leave Scotland, first went to Flanders, then to France, where King Philip, an implacable opponent of William's, offered him the strategically-placed Montreuil Castle as a refuge.

But Edgar felt isolated and unhappy outside Britain, and he was beginning to have grave doubts about the future. The hopelessness of his position as a challenger without money, soldiers or friends must have been driven home, for in 1073 he put out peace feelers and became reconciled with William in the same year. As Malmesbury noted,

> They say this was extremely agreeable to the king that England should thus be rid of a fomentor of dissension. Indeed, it was his [the king's] constant practice, under the guise of high honour, to carry over to Normandy all the English he suspected, lest any disorders should arise in the kingdom in his absence.

He received Edgar Aetheling with honour at his court, and showed great magnanimity towards his youthful challenger. He gave him an allowance of a pound of silver a day but, prudently, insisted that he must live in Normandy.

So at the age of eighteen, Edgar became his adversary's pensioner, and for a bag of silver gave away his right to his kingdom.

24. *Tilting at Norman windmills: Edgar's progression from Berkhamsted to nowhere*

Cut off from his country and people, the 'lost king' of the Anglo-Saxons spent his early years of adulthood in search of a cause, a knight-errant *par excellence*, with a lance for hire.

He championed people and factions, espoused doctrines, only to drop them when the futility of the exercise became too obvious. In the mid 1070s he made one more attempt to recover his throne, but that too ended in a fiasco.

The chronology of this escapade is confused but the ascertainable facts indicate that it was King Philip of France who put heart once again into Edgar and, together with the Count of Flanders, launched him on a new campaign against King William.

He was given rich presents of gold and silver plates and cloaks of ermine to humour him, provided with soldiers and money and wished good luck by William's foes. But luck eluded him and he became ship-wrecked off the coast of England. He lost his ships and his treasures, and his soldiers fell into the hands of the Normans.

Edgar and his small band of survivors had to endure great hardships as they painfully made their way north to Scotland, 'some ruefully on foot, and some wretchedly riding', according to the Worcester writer of the *Anglo-Saxon Chronicle*. Challenging William on his home ground was not a course of action to be undertaken lightly, as all the rebels in the British isles had learnt at their expense, but Edgar's last restoration attempt merely ended on a note of ridicule.

Malcolm, uneasy about Edgar's presence in his country, advised his restless brother-in-law to approach William and plead for forgiveness. Showing remarkable forebearance, William once again forgave the aetheling. Whether he showed such magnanimity out of political calculations or genuine kindness towards his luckless rival, he certainly handled Edgar's defiance with great skill.

Through his moderation he managed to convey to the country that he did not take this Anglo-Saxon prince, or his challenges, too seriously and so deflate Edgar. He even acceded to the aetheling's request that he should be met with the honours due to his station upon entering England,

and sent the Sheriff of York to meet him at the Scottish border and escort him to Normandy. As a further proof of undiminished royal favour, the king returned to Edgar his lands in Hertfordshire and added to them another manor.

The aetheling stayed at the court of William for many years and, according to Malmesbury, 'silently sank into contempt through his indolence, or mildly speaking, through his simplicity'. He earned the Norman courtiers' scorn, and the monk's reproof, because of his unashamed hedonism in an age when everyone else was obsessed with saving their souls and mortifying their flesh. His reckless extravagance and passion for women and horses were seen as proof of his artless child-like *naïveté*, not the expressions of *ennui* of a thwarted and frustrated man.

One incident in particular served to underline his prodigality in the eyes of his contemporaries. When a magnificent charger took his fancy he did not hesitate to squander 365 pounds of silver – a whole year's pension he was drawing in exchange for abdicating his right to the throne – on the animal, anticipating by centuries Richard III's offer to swap his kingdom for a horse.

In the eyes of the frugal Normans this was a further demonstration of the aetheling's simplicity but others, who perceived different aspects of his character, were less bigoted in their judgement. Orderic, who could hardly be accused of pro-Anglo-Saxon sympathies, believed that Edgar was 'of a mild and ingenuous disposition', and many contemporaries saw him as the embodiment of knightly chivalry.

In 1085, Edgar Aetheling was about thirty, and the merry round of entertainments and courtly escapades began to pall. The joustings held no joy; the ladies of the many castles of Normandy were merely irksome with their insistence on chivalrous love. The senselessness of his existence made him seek fulfilment in new causes and wilder adventures, but the challenges and excitements could not hide the futility of it all. He was entering middle-age, an eternal aetheling without prospects, and life was passing him by. In England, certainly there was no way of turning the clock back: the Norman rule had been thoroughly consolidated.

His friendship with Robert Courte-Heuse, the perpetually discontented son of William the Conqueror, played a very important role in his life. Their sense of rejection and bitterness drew them closer and their shared diversions further cemented their friendship. And because he never married, friendships and other loyalties gained unusual importance in his life, involving him in extraordinary adventures.

Of course, like all men of his time, he fathered several children. One of them, born in Northumberland to an unknown mother, appears to have been named after him because the *Pipe Roll* of Northumberland mentions an 'Edgar Aetheling' in 1158 and 1167, when Edward the Exile's son would have been at least 112.

Getting more and more touchy with the passing of time, Edgar became convinced that the king was not treating him with the respect he felt entitled to as an Anglo-Saxon aetheling, and in 1086 he once again broke out of the claustrophobic world of the Norman court. This time, however, he did not flee to one of William's adversaries abroad to avenge the slight, but meekly sought William's leave to go abroad and fight with the Normans.

According to Florence, in the year of 1086, when his sister Christina took the veil and entered the Benedictine convent of Romsey in Hampshire, Edgar Aetheling sailed with a force of two hundred knights to Apulia in search of glory and adventure.

But the thrills of the fighting in Apulia quickly waned and when, after William the Conqueror's death in 1087, his friend Robert became Duke of Normandy, Edgar hurriedly returned to Normandy. His friendship with the duke assured him an eminent position, and Robert's generous gifts of land made him an integral part of the Norman feudal system. However, England appears to have been on his mind all the time.

Whether as a result of Edgar's manipulation, or prompted by his own well-developed sense of resentment, Duke Robert laid claim to the throne of England and openly challenged his brother, William Rufus, who had inherited the crown under their father's will. Edgar threw himself into the anti-William plot with a zeal that could not have been surpassed even if he had been seeking to recover the crown himself.

In 1091, he travelled to Scotland and invaded Northumbria with King Malcolm and a sizeable Scottish host to further his friend's – and perhaps his own – cause. In the end, the harrying and plundering did little to advance Duke Robert's claim and, as the *Anglo-Saxon Chronicle* records, William and Malcolm met, one flanked by Robert and the other by Edgar, at the Firth of Forth and peace was arranged between them. And so once again, Edgar Aetheling became reconciled with the ruler of England, and returned to Normandy to resume the social whirl and intrigue that helped to while away the tedium of court life.

Ingrigue, however, was a game that many could play simultaneously and in a court full of schemers and secret manipulators, whispering campaigns often had devastating results. In the mid-1090s, Edgar had found himself at the receiving end of a campaign of denigration launched and orchestrated by an English knight called Ordgar. He accused the aetheling of plotting against King William and, with the aid of wagging tongues, the king came to hear of it.

It is hardly surprising that, with Edgar's chequered record, the king believed Ordgar and the aetheling was asked to prove his innocence in Norman fashion by combat. Perhaps because of the nature of the charges, he found it difficult to get a champion. But in the end, a knight from Winchester, called Godwin, was moved by the plight of the last descendant of the house of Cerdic, and offered to do battle as his vindicator.

There is something nightmarish about an Anglo-Saxon royal prince, denounced by a fellow Englishman to the country's foreign conqueror for alleged plotting to seize the crown that is his by right, being forced to undergo an ordeal in foreign fashion to prove his innocence. But this weird incident also serves as a reliable indicator that, in spite of his dissipation and aimless adventure-seeking, Edgar Aetheling had not given up the hope of recovering his patrimony.

Though Ordgar and Godwin had to do battle Norman-style, surprisingly enough they fought on foot, not on horseback, according to the chronicles. The two English knights, formally dressed in coats of mail and in shining helmets, fought a long and desperate duel. Eventually, with a supreme effort, Godwin brought down the accuser who, contrary to the rules of combat, had a knife hidden in his boot and tried to stab his challenger. But knights observing the combat snatched the knife from him and, as he lay dying from his wounds, he confessed that he had falsely accused the aetheling. Edgar was vindicated and became, not for the first time, reconciled with his suzerain.

In piecing together the career of Edgar, it is not his involvement in so many plots and rebellions that is the most surprising thing, but the fount of loyalty and idealism that he succeeding in maintaining in spite of a lifetime of disappointments.

He showed more than ordinary family loyalty when, after the death of Malcolm, he mounted a military expedition against Donald, Malcolm's brother, and secured the Scottish throne for his young nephew, Edgar, in a hard-fought battle. Although the Scottish intervention was sanctioned by William, it was, in spite of its political usefulness for the king, a family affair, uncle coming to the rescue of his nephew in distress.

He displayed a similar attitude to Pope Urban II's crusade, which was espoused with fervour by his great friend, Duke Robert of Normandy. Though the spiritual purpose behind the crusaders' enterprise undoubtedly appealed to his own idealism, his decision to join at the age of forty-one the warriors of Christ seeking to recover the Holy Land from the Infidels must have been greatly influenced by the presence there of Duke Robert.

Duke Robert had pawned his duchy for 10,000 silver marks to King William Rufus in order to finance his crusade, and was sailing from Brindisi for the Holy Land in 1097 when Edgar Aetheling was still engaged in resolving the Scottish succession.

But soon afterwards he sailed for Constantinople and, after convincing Emperor Alexis Comnenus to finance his naval enterprise, he joined the crusade with an English fleet during the Syrian campaign in the summer of 1098. According to Orderic, Edgar and his English crusaders captured Lattakieh from the Turks. Edgar's role in the fighting is also noted by Malmesbury and the French chroniclers, who add that he was also involved in the siege of Irkah in the spring of 1099.[1]

Later that summer, Edgar was present at the siege of Jerusalem together with his friends Duke Robert and Robert Godwin, the son of his champion against Ordgar. But when the Turks captured and killed young Robert, the aetheling appears to have decided to return home. The flame of complex loyalties that had fired his crusading zeal had been extinguished.

England, the land of his father's forebears and the object of his abiding passion, was beckoning. He refused glittering offers of office from the Emperor of Byzantium and the King of Germany because of his 'silly desire' to be back in England, as Malmesbury put it rather uncharitably.

On his way home Edgar 'received many gifts from the Greek and German emperors who, out of respect for his noble descent, would also have endeavoured to retain him with them. But he gave up everything owing to his yearning for his native soil. Edgar, therefore, deluded by this silly desire, returned to England.

However deluded this emotional attachment to England by a prince born in Eastern Europe might have seemed to the Anglo-Norman keeper of records, it greatly commends Edgar. It was a powerful emotional bond with the land of his father which he viewed, after all, not merely as a source of advantages but the place where he belonged. This was the mature Edgar's commitment to the land of his forebears, a stand that helped to put in perspective, if not correct, his youthful indescretions – like the squandering of the silver received for his kingdom on a single horse – that Malmesbury and other near-contemporary chroniclers held against him.

In the autumn of 1100, he reached Normandy with Duke Robert, where the news of William Rufus's death and Henry I's election to the throne of England awaited them. Though his oath of allegiance to the crown of England clearly determined his formal position in the quarrel between the new king and his friend Robert, his emotions gained once again the upper hand, his friendship eclipsing the loyalty he owed his suzerain.

He faithfully backed Duke Robert throughout the escalating spiral of the internecine dispute between the brothers and gallantly took to the field, though he was now over fifty, when they decided to resolve their quarrel by the sword. On 28 September 1106, he was captured, together with Duke Robert, in the disastrous Battle of Tinchebrai.

King Henry had his brother imprisoned in the dungeons of Cardiff Castle, where he died twenty years later. The king's firm handling of the rebels seemed to signal the end of the road for Edgar Aetheling too, but with his customary luck in adversity he was soon pardoned and set free.

But after a lifetime of rebelliousness and adventures in support of quixotic causes, Edgar retired from public life and lived out his days in the tranquillity of his Hertfordshire estate. According to a contemporary chronicle (Spelman MS), he travelled to Scotland at a 'very advanced age' and allegedly died there in 1120, but there is strong evidence that he lived much longer.[2]

Malmesbury, who finished his *Gesta* in 1125, remarked about Edgar that, 'after various revolutions of fortune, he now grows old in the country [England] in privacy and quiet', indicating that the aetheling was still alive then.

He ended his days in peace and, as befitting an old soldier and crusader, just faded away, a forgotten symbol of a bygone world. With his passing the line of kings who had ruled the West Saxon kingdom (and later the whole of England) for close on six centuries came to an end.

Like his father and uncle Edmund before him, he had failed to save the realm or to live up to the expectations of his countrymen. Though he had lived most of his life under the new order of the conquering Normans, he remained an outsider and an anachronism, 'the lost king' of the Anglo-Saxons, without a country and without a role. And so his memory, like the hopes that were once pinned on him, faded:

> All things to nothingness descend,
> Grow old and die and meet their end;
> Man dies, iron rusts, wood does decay,
> Towers fall, walls crumble, roses fade . . .
> Nor long shall any name resound
> Beyond the grave, unless it be found
> In some clerk's book.[3]

EPILOGUE

The life story of Edmund and Edward the Exile, retrieved from the silt of history, leaves one with a vague sense of regret tinged with unease. It followed, it would seem, a predetermined course along which the real escape hatches had all been boarded up, and sham ones boldly displayed. In spite of one's secret hopes of seeing them overcome their destiny, their struggle to master their fate was clearly doomed from the outset.

Indeed, in following the aethelings' progression from ill-starred birth to tragic death, one cannot suppress a nagging suspicion that the conspiracy of hearts that saved them from Canute's henchmen had served no purpose, that the helping hands of Walgar, Onund Jacob, Yaroslav and Edward the Confessor had reached out across the frontiers in vain. Perhaps they could have escaped their destiny if they had had the superhuman strength and resolve to turn their backs on England, duty and the lure of kingship. But they were born victims of their circumstances and they died, after their allotted tribulations, prisoners of their condition.

The unease generated by this impression is heightened by the realization that, in spite of their move from country to country and the many promising new beginnings, the parameters of their world remained unchanged throughout: victors lived long to enjoy the spoils of their bloody wars and the vanquished were quickly forgotten; wickedness went unpunished and good unrewarded; and the innocents forced into exile remained outcasts to the end of their days.

Fate had dealt harshly with Edmund Ironside's children, but most cruelly with Edward because of the false hopes it had raised in him. For while Edmund's many narrow escapes and quaint adventures seemed merely pointless in view of his untimely demise, Edward's misfortunes plumbed the depths of a Greek tragedy. The sight of a good man struggling against incredible odds to fulfil his mission, only to be struck down as the dream of his life was about to come true, arouses pity. But there was no relief, no catharsis, as Edward was unceremoniously removed from the scene by the more ruthless contenders for the crown of England.

The hope that Fate would relent and make good the wrongs through Edward's son, Edgar, faded even before he had reached manhood. For a fleeting instant in 1066, the hopes of the country were pinned on Edgar, 'England's darling', but the short-sighted obstructionism of the bishops denied him – and the country – a last chance. The moment passed, and Edgar became England's 'lost king', who left no mark, no heirs, no monuments to be remembered by.

Like water in the sands of time, the aethelings' memory would have vanished without trace had it not been for Margaret, Edward's eldest daughter. Through her Edmund Ironside's progeny became reintegrated into the fabric of British society and, through her children's children, the ancient Anglo-Saxon line recovered the crown of England. Margaret made the aethelings' story complete, lending it an extra dimension that more than made up for the seemingly senseless tribulations of Edmund, Edward and Edgar.

But her claim to fame does not hinge on her genetic services to Aethelred's house, nor the historical accident of having provided a rounded end and fitting epilogue to her father's odyssey. By all accounts, she was a remarkable woman and she carved for herself a special and well-deserved niche in British history.

Archbishop Turgotus of St Andrews, Margaret's father-confessor, knew her intimately, and from his observations there emerges a woman of strong will-power and unusual intelligence, whose religious zeal was tempered by genuine compassion. Turgotus certainly idealized her and his account of her life and times was written as much for dynastic as didactic purposes. He openly acknowledges this in the 'Prologue' of his biography dedicated to Queen Matilda, Margaret's daughter, who 'commanded that I should narrate for you the particulars of the life of your mother, whose memory is held in veneration'. But he also adds that his evidence is 'especially trustworthy since – thanks to her great and familiar intercourse with me – you have understood that I am acquainted with the most part of her secrets'.

Cleansed of religious cant and the tendentious interpretations of a dynastic apologist, the incidents recounted by Turgotus make clearer the reasons for her popularity and why she captured the imagination of her contemporaries. Having arrived in this country aged about eight from Hungary with her foreign-born mother and exile-bred father, she began her life as a royal princess with distinctive handicaps. These were only accentuated by the murder of her father and the ineffectual support of her great-uncle, the king. But she took full advantage of the education provided for Edward's children by the Confessor and soon surprised even her teachers with her grasp of facts and the breadth of her knowledge.

Margaret 'employed herself in the study of the Holy Scriptures, and therein with joy to exercise her mind. Her understanding was keen to comprehend any matter, whatever it might be; to this was joined a great tenacity of memory, enabling her to store it up, along with a graceful flow of language to express it.'

Her keen intellect helped her, and the family whose brains she undoubtedly was, to cope with the difficult situations created by the Norman invasion of England. The flight to Scotland placed Margaret, who had hoped to become a nun, in an unenviable position: King Malcolm Canmore fell passionately in love with her, but she could not say no to her ardent suitor without jeopardizing her brother's restoration prospects and the English exile army's hopes of Scottish support.

Even Turgotus acknowledges that she acquiesced to the marriage plan 'rather in obedience of the will of her friends than to her own'. Having been compelled to submit to *force majeure*, she accepted her fate with good grace, a mark of her intelligence.

Margaret was clever, but still she was a woman. And since she could not change the ways of the world and was forced to do as the world does, she appears to have decided upon reshaping and remoulding her husband in her own image.

The force of her personality and reformist zeal can be gauged from her impact upon her husband. Malcolm was a simple warrior used to the wild ways of his country, and the sophistication of his wife deeply impressed him. In deference to her gentler ways, he now busied himself with almsgiving, charity and the notions of justice – occupations rather outside the usual interests of the rough and ready Highland chieftains of the period.

Margaret also taught him to spend his nights in constant prayers and vigils, rather than wenching and roistering with his men. Turgotus gives a graphic account of Margaret's sway over her illiterate but good-humoured husband and the unexpected forms this sometimes took.

> There was in him a sort of dread of offending one whose life was so venerable . . . and he readily obeyed her wishes and prudent counsels in all things. Whatever she refused, he refused also for the love of her. Hence it was that, although he could not read, he would turn over and examine books which she used either for her devotions or her study; and whenever he heard her express especial liking for a particular book, he also would look at it with special interest, kissing it, and often taking int into his hands . . .
>
> Now and then she helped herself to something or other out of the king's private property, it mattered not what it was, to give to a poor person; and this pious plundering the King always took pleasantly and in good part. It was her custom to offer certain coins of gold upon Maundy Thursday and at High Mass, some of which coins the Queen often devoutly pillaged, and bestowed on the beggar who was petitioning her for help. Although the King was fully aware of the theft, he generally pretended to know nothing of it, and felt much amused by it. Now and then he caught the Queen in the very act, with the money in her hand, and laughingly threatened that he would have her arrested, tried and found guilty.

Margaret also turned Malcolm's simple, scantily-furnished fort at Dunfermline into a royal court, where the royal couple ate off gold and silver dishes and entertained in style. English and Continental courtiers thronged its hall, doctors of theology called to consult the learned queen, and artists and architects waited upon her in hope of royal patronage.

Yet in spite of her accomplishments she was a stern woman who never laughed and had no sense of humour. In her presence no one dared to utter a frivolous remark or speak with levity. There was a gravity in her joy, and a quiet menace in her anger. With her, jollity never expressed itself in peals of laughter and vivaciousness was stifled. On the other hand, her fury too was similarly controlled and always tempered with justice. In fact, her perfectly-controlled emotions and staid character could well have served as a paragon for the troubadours and Minne-singers of the following century who admired 'Diu Maase' – moderation – in everything above all.

She brought up her children strictly, believing, according to Turgotus, that 'he that spareth the rod hateth his son'. The tutors and governesses of the royal children were under orders to whip them hard whenever they were naughty or frolicsome.

The noble ladied embroidering altar cloths, chasubles, stoles and other priestly vestments, she treated with similar heavy-handed firmness.

> No men were admitted among them, with the exception only of such as she permitted to enter along with herself when she paid the women an occasional visit. No giddy pertness was allowed in them, no light familiarity between them and men; for the queen united so much strictness with her sweetness of temper, so great pleasantness even with her severity, that all who waited upon her, men as well as women, loved her while they feared her, and in fearing loved her.

This severe mother and virtuous queen ruling the royal household with an iron rod was, at the same time, remarkable for her gentle charity. Her care of the poor and needy, carried out with humble piety, grew into a legend in her lifetime. She fed the hungry, comforted the orphans, defended the defenceless and looked after the widows. She never allowed anyone who came to her for help to go away empty-handed.

> Nor was it towards the poor of her own nation only that she exhibited the abundance of her cheerful and open-hearted charity, but those persons who came from almost every other nation, drawn by the reports of her liberality, were the partakers of her bounty.

The English especially benefited from her pious liberality. There were a great number of English prisoners, carried off in successive raids and sold into slavery in Scotland, who could not raise their ransom. Others again had escaped from serfdom or were simply sold into bondage in foreign lands by their own kinsfolk as the slave trade, denounced by Bishop Wulfstan, flourished in the unsettled circumstances of the time. Margaret offered help to all and paid their ransom.

Turgotus, himself of Saxon stock, recorded to what lengths Queen Margaret was prepared to go to secure freedom for these unfortunates.

> Spies were employed by her to go secretly through all the provinces of Scotland and ascertain what captives were oppressed with the

12. Illuminated pages from the Gospel of St Margaret of Scotland, the daughter of the 'Lost King of England', born in Hungary (Bodleian Library, Oxford).

most cruel bondage, and treated with the greatest inhumanity. When she had privately ascertained where these prisoners were detained, and by whom ill-treated, commiserating with them from the bottom of her heart, she took care to send them speedy help, paid their ransom and set them at liberty forthwith.

Impressive though her good works were, her reform of the Celtic Church became her most lasting – and fitting – memorial. The practices and customs of the Scottish Church were out of step with the Church of Rome, which Margaret had been brought up to regard as the True Church. These differences were deemed to be so serious by the monastic writer of the *Anglo-Saxon Chronicle* that he wrote that Margaret was destined 'to put down the evil customs which this nation practised'.

At her request, Archbishop Lanfranc of Canterbury sent her three English priest to act as her spiritual advisers and, with their help, she successfully combatted 'the defenders of a perverse custom with the sword of the Spirit, that is to say, with the word of God'.

In spite of the resistance of the Gaelic-speaking priesthood to the meddling of the English Queen in their affairs, the Celtic Church eventually agreed to the reforms Margaret proposed. As a result of her insistence that there could be no variations in the religious practices of those who served one God and belonged to the one universal faith, the Catholic Church of Rome, the Celtic Church was brought into line with the rest of Europe.

The first of her reforms was to restore the sanctity of the Sabbath. Sunday, which had become in Scotland a day for markets and fairs, was designated a day for fasting and prayer. Those who sullied the sanctity of the Lord's Day with worldly business of any sort now faced excommunication for two months. She also regulated the date of the start of Lent, forbade the Celtic-rite Masses and insisted that Holy Communion should be taken by everyone, even those who thought they were unworthy of receiving it. And in an enlightened act of social engineering, she prohibited marriage between a man and his step-mother or brother and deceased brother's widow.

Her sincere love of the Church earned her genuine popularity, in spite of the clergy's opposition to her reforms, and people came from far and wide to consult her on matters of religion. As Baronius, the eleventh-century church historian remarked, Margaret, 'having found the Church of Scotland like a wild desert, left it at her death in so flourishing a state that it resembled a well cultivated and beautiful garden'.

Margaret died on 16 November 1093, a few days after learning of the death of her husband and eldest son, Edward, in the battle of Alnwick. With her passing, the wheel of Aethelred's fated house had come full circle, and the story of a luckless generation ended on a hopeful note. The curse of St Dunstan had been expiated.

Such was the impact of her pious, prayerful life that it gave rise to a lore that has outlived Aethelred's house and endured to this day. Reports of miracles at her grave in Dunfermline proliferated, and in 1246 King Alexander II, her great-grandson, petitioned Pope Innocent IV that she should be included in the catalogue of saints. After an investigation into her miracles lasting three years, the Pope agreed to the canonization of Margaret, Queen of the Scots of blessed memory.

On 19 June 1250, with the solemn rite of canonization celebrated at Dunfermline, the lore of St Margaret was given a powerful fillip. Her bones, placed in a chest of silver adorned with precious stones, were reputed to have given out a fragrant odour not unlike the scent of spring flowers. Her relics became objects of veneration and mystic power as her saintly reputation spread across Britain and the Continent.

In the ensuing centuries the legends that grew up around Edward the Exile's daughter generated their own momentum, endowing her with superhuman traits and miraculous powers. Her relics drew multitudes of pilgrims to Dunfermline Abbey until the Reformation, 'when heretics stole into the Kingdome, trampled underfoot all divine and human lawes and seized the sacred moveables of [Dunfermline] Church; some things of greater veneration and value were saved from sacrilegious hands'.

And so the undignified peregrinations of Margaret's mortal remains began nearly four centuries after her death. According to Papebroch's appendix to his life of St Margaret, her head, still covered by a quantity of fine hair, was brought to Edinburgh Castle at the request of Queen Mary, who was living there in the 1560s. When she fled to England in 1567, the casket containing Margaret's head and other objects of reverence reputed to have belonged to her were taken for safe-keeping to the castle of the Laird of Drury, where they were guarded by a Benedictine monk.

In 1597, the growing fear of Scottish Catholics that St Margaret's relics might be profaned prompted a decision to take them abroad. Father John Robie, of the Society of Jesus, smuggled the chief relic to Antwerp, where Bishop John Malderus authenticated it as the saint's head. In his letter of 15 September 1620, attesting the relic's authenticity, he granted leave for its exposure to public veneration.

Seven years later, Margaret's head was transferred to the Scots College at Douay, where it was once again displayed for public veneration. On 4 March 1645, Pope Innocent X granted a plenary indulgence to all those who visited the college on the festival of St Margaret, and veneration of her relic continued for over two-and-a-half centuries at Douay. In 1785, the historian Carruthers saw it on display at the Scots College, but it disappeared in the upheaval of the French Revolution.

The rest of Margaret's and her husband's remains were taken after strange adventures, even further from their resting place in Dunfermline. According to the investigations of Papebroch, they were acquired by King Philip II of Spain, who deposited their urns in the Church of St Lawrence in the Escorial.[1] At the end of the eighteenth century they were still there, according to a report by Alban Butler. But when subsequently Bishop Gillies tried to recover the relics in order to restore them to a Scottish shrine, they could no longer be identified.

While Margaret's mortal remains might have turned to dust in a remote part of Europe, her legend has survived intact. An anonymous seventeenth-century Jesuit has provided a fitting epitaph for the daughter of a lifelong exile who, with the passage of time, became the 'Pearl of Queens' and the pride of the island race.[2]

> She eminently possest all the perfections of natural pearls; you will see their Candour in her Conscience as pure as Christal, their Splendour in her Spirit shining with divine illuminations in the government of her Kingdome, and their roundness, which is a figure that knowes no end, in her vigorous perseverance even unto death, which makes her obtain glorious victories over her passions, and obligeth her to submit all her desires to the will of God.

But it is just as well to remember that this 'perfect princess' of the British was born in Hungarian exile, tempered by the adversities of a cruel power struggle in England and steeled by the hardships of the turbulent years of the Norman takeover. Even if in reality she was not quite as perfect as her eulogists made her out to be, it is thanks to her that the Anglo-Saxon connection has endured.

Appendix 1. *Chronicon ex Chronicis ab initio Mundi ad Annum Domini 1118*

Florence of Worcester

1017: Then King Canute, by the advice of Eadric the traitor, outlawed Edwy the Aetheling, King Edmund's brother, and he was put to death, although innocent.

Eadric also advised him to make away with the young aethelings Edward and Edmund, King Edmund's sons; but as he thought it would be a foul disgrace to him if they were murdered in England, he sent them, after a short time, to the King of Sweden, to be put to death there. But though they were allies, that king was by no means disposed to execute his wishes, and he sent them to Solamon, King of Hungary, to spare their lives, and have them brought up at his court.

One of them, namely Edmund, in course of time died there; but Edward married Agatha, a daughter of the kinsman of the Emperor Henry, by whom he had Margaret, Queen of Scots, Christina, a nun, and Edgar the Aetheling.

1057: Edward the Aetheling, son of King Edmund Ironside, accepting the invitation of his uncle, King Edward (the Confessor) returned to England from Hungary, where he had been exiled many years before.

For the king had determined to appoint him his successor and heir to the crown, but he died at London soon after his arrival.

Appendix 2. *Leges Edovardi Confessori*

Iste praefatus Edmundus yren side habuit quendam filium Edwardum nomine, qui mox patre mortuo (timore Chnuti Regis) aufugit ad regnum Rugorum, quod nos melius vocamus Russiam. Quem Rex terrae Malesclotus nomine, ut cognovit quis esset, honeste retinuit. Qui de nobili progenie ibidem duxit uxorem de qua natus est ei Edgarus Ethelinge & Margareta que fuit postea Regina Scotiae & Christina soror ejus . . .

Fuit autem Margareta praedicta generosa valde, & optima, scilecet ex parte patris ex nobili genere & sanguine Regum Anglorum, & Britonum, ex parte vero matris ex genere & sanguine Regum Rugorum, sanctissimis antecessoribus, suis in bonis, & laudabilibus actibus consimilis, praeclara effulsit:

Erat enim de jure post decessum Edgari Athelinge fratris sui, verus haeres ultimi Regis Edwardi de corona totius regni praedicti, sed instinctu, petitione, & voluntate boni Regis Edwardi propinqui nostri, aliter mutatum est, qui coronam nobis totius regni praedicti dedit, & regnum praedictum nobis jurare fecit, qui peroptime aequitatem, & scientiam, justitiam, probitatemque nostram novit. Princeps vero Albaniae duxit eam in uxorem casu fortuito. Picti enim a Picto duce vocantur, Scotti vero Albania pars Monarchiae regni hujus, quod olim vocabatur regnum Brytanniae.

Cui Christinae Eadwardus dedit terram, quam habuit postea Radulphus de Limiseia [alias Lunesi]. Fuit enim praedicta Christiana soror Edgari Ethelinge, propter quem misit Rex Edwardus avunculus ejus, & fecit eum venire ad se, qui postquam venit non multum vixit, & uxor illius in brevi temporis curriculo defuncta est.

Rex vero Edwardus Edgarum filium eorum secum retinuit, & pro filio nutrivit. Et quia cogitavit ipsum haeredem facere, nominavit Ethelinge, quod nos Domicellum; i.e. damisell:

Sed nos indiscrete de pluribus dicimus, quia Baronum filios vocamus Domicellos.

Angli vero nullos nisi natos Regum. Quod si expressius volumus dicere in quadam regione Saxoniae, Ling, imago dicitus, Athel Anglice nobilis est, quae conjuncta sonant, nobilis imago.

Unde etiam occidentales Saxonici, scilicet Excestrenses, habent in Proverbio summi despectus, hinderling; i.e. omni honestate dejecta, vel recedens imago.

Rex autem Edwardus ut cognovit gentis suae nequitiam, & praecipue superbiam filiorum Godwini, scilicet Haraldi, qui postea regnum invasit, Tosti, Gurti Leofwini, & aliorum fratrum suorum, comperit non posse fore stabile vel ratum quod proposuerat de Edgaro Ethelinge, adoptavit Wilhelmum ducem Normannorum in regnum, Wilhelmum dico Nothum, i.e. Badtardum, filium Roberti avunculi sui, videcelet fratris, matris suae, virum strenuum, bellicosum & fortem qui postea annuente Deo debellando supradictum Haraldum Godwini filium, regnum Anglorum victoriose adeptus est.

Appendix 3. William of Poitier's account of the Norman Conquest: *Gesta Guillelmi Ducis Normannorum et Regis Anglorum*

Edward, King of the English, loved William [of Normandy] as much as if the duke had been his brother or his son, and he had long before appointed him as his heir. It was at this time that Edward gave William a pledge even more binding than any which he had proffered so far. By the very sanctity of his way of life he was a man constantly preoccupied with the next world. He now felt that his own hour was fast approaching, and he therefore determined to make all possible preparations for his death. In order to confirm his promise by an oath, he sent Harold to William, Harold, the wealthiest of all his subjects, the most powerful and the most highly honoured. Some time before, Harold's brother [Wulfnoth] and his nephew [Hakon] had been handed over to William as hostages, in an attempt to secure this same succession. In sending Harold, King Edward behaved with the utmost wisdom, for, with his wealth and his authority, Harold was the man to contain any revolt of the English, if, with that perfidy and restlessness which they so often display, they were to rise in revolt.

On his way to carry out the business entrusted to him, Harold experienced some danger during the crossing. He landed on the coast of Ponthieu, but there he fell into the hands of Count Guy. He and his party were seized and thrown into prison. I have no doubt that so great a nobleman would have preferred shipwreck to such ignominy. Their lust for gain had led certain local groups of French people to adopt an execrable custom, which is quite barbarous and devoid of any touch of Christian justice. They seize the persons of men who are in high place or who are very wealthy. They throw them into prison, heap insults upon them and even torture them. When their victims are almost at death's door as the result of the miseries which they have endured, they let them go, but only in exchange for an enormous ransom.

When Duke William discovered what had happened to the envoys who were on their way to him, he sent his own messengers with orders that they should free Harold by simple request or, if necessary, by threats. Count Guy behaved very well. He could have tortured Harold, and either cut his throat or ransomed him, just as the fancy took him; but he resisted these temptations and rode with him to Eu castle, where he handed him over to William. Guy was rewarded amply enough, for William conveyed to him several vast and valuable estates, adding a considerable sum of

money into the bargain. William received Harold with great honour, taking him off to the city of Rouen, which was the capital of the Duchy. There
he treated Harold and his party most hospitably, for he wanted to cheer
them up and make them forget the hazards of their journey. William had
every reason to congratulate himself on this important guest, who had
come to him as the envoy of his close relation and dearest friend. He
naturally hoped that Harold would mediate faithfully between himself
and the English people, who held him second only to their king.

A council was convened at Bonneville-sur-Touques and there, according to the sacred rite of Christian people, Harold swore an oath of fidelity
to William. A number of extremely famous men who are not given to
lying, whose word can be trusted and who, moreover, were present and
witnessed the event, have told how, freely and distinctly, as the last article
of his oath, Harold made the following deposition: that he would act as
William's representative at the court of his master, King Edward, as long
as that king remained alive; that after Edward's death he would do everything in his power, by exercising his authority and by using his vast
wealth, to confirm William in his succession to the throne of England; that
in the meantime he would entrust to the duke's military representatives
Dover Castle, to the fortification of which he would give his own personal
attention, paying for it with his own funds; and finally that he would
hand over other castles in such district of that country as the duke might
wish to fortify, and that he would provide the garrisons with all the food
they needed. The duke took Harold's two hands in his and received his
homage. Then, just before Harold made his oath, the duke received his
petition, and confirmed him in the possession of his lands and all his
functions. Edward was already ill and he was not expected to live long.

William knew that Harold was keen on fighting and only too ready to
add to his laurels, so he fitted him and his party out with the weapons of
war, provided them with mettlesome horses, and led them off to take part
in the war in Brittany. Harold was William's guest and he had come as an
envoy: now the duke made him his comrade-in-arms, in the hope that, by
doing him this honour, he might ensure that he remained faithful and
obedient. In its overweening arrogance the whole of Brittany had risen in
arms against Normandy. . .

Conan, the son of Alan, was the leader in this rash enterprise. As he
grew to man's estate, he became more and more arrogant. For a long time
he had been under the guardianship of his uncle Eudo, but he freed
himself, clapped Eudo in chains and threw him into prison. Then with
great truculence he started to rule over the province which he had inherited from his father. He stirred up again the revolt which his father had
once led, for he had made up his mind to be the enemy of Normandy and
not its vassal. By ancient right William was not only ruler of the Normans
but Conan's overlord as well. William ordered a castle called Saint James
to be constructed on the frontier where Normandy faces Brittany, for he

was determined to prevent starving pillagers from crossing over to rob and ravage the unprotected churches and the far-flung village communities of these borderlands. It was Charles [the Simple], King of the Franks, who bought peace and the alliance of Rollo, the first Duke of the Normans and the progenitor of all the other dukes who were to come after him. Charles gave his daughter Gisela to Rollo in marriage and handed Brittany over to him for the Normans to rule for ever. The Franks actually asked for this Treaty [of Saint-Clair-sur-Epte], for, even with the sword of the Gauls to assist them, they could no longer resist the Danish axe. There is plenty of evidence for this in the pages of our Annals. On the number of occasions the Counts of Brittany strove their hardest to shake off the yoke of Norman domination, but they never succeeded. Alan and Conan were close blood-relations of the Dukes of Normandy, and as a result they resisted those dukes with even greater courage. In the end Conan became so arrogant that he had the nerve to announce the actual day on which he proposed to cross the frontiers of Normandy. By nature he was a very savage man, and he was at the height of his physical strength. His lands stretched far and wide, his men were devoted to him, and Brittany produced an incredible number of warriors.

In those parts each fighting-man fathers another fifty, for according to their barbarous ways of going on, he is apportioned ten or more women. They say that the same was true of the Moors in ancient times, for they knew nothing of God's law or of personal restraint. The immense hordes of people which result show little interest in cultivating the fields or developing the arts of civilization, for they spend all their time rushing about on horseback and practising with their weapons. They drink a lot of milk, but they do not have much bread to eat. Their extensive meadow-lands, which hardly know what harvest means, offer rich pasture to their flocks. When they are not actually at war they occupy their time in robbery, brigandage and family feuds, to keep their hands in, as it were. In battle they engage the enemy with savage alacrity: and when they are actually fighting they rage like lunatics. They are used to driving all before them, but they themselves rarely give in. They rejoice in victory and in honour won on the battlefield, and on these subjects they are given to endless boasting. They take great pleasure in quarrelling over the booty which they have stripped from the dead: with them this is an honourable pastime and one which they enjoy immensely.

Duke William cared not a straw for all this horribleness. On the very day which, as he well recalled, Conan had appointed for his own advance, he himself invaded Brittany. Like a man who sees the lightning-flash come perilously near, Conan fled at full speed to the positions which he had prepared, abandoning the siege of Dol, which was one of his own castles. Dol played no part in the rebel uprising, for it remained faithful to the just cause. Rivoallon, the lord of the castle, tried to hold Conan. Sarcastically he called him back, begging him to wait for forty-eight hours, for that would be enough for him to pay his ransom. The poor man was terrified: he continued his retreat and would not stay his course: everything he heard made him more frightened still. Meanwhile the awesome battle-leader who pursued him would have pressed on behind him in his flight had he not perceived the obvious danger of leading so large an army through this open countryside, where there were no supplies and no known roads. In this barren land, if anything at all remained from the previous year's harvest, the local inhabitants had hidden it away in safe retreats, together with their flocks. The corn was green and still stood in the ear. William therefore turned his army back, harassed as it was by this lack of provisions. He was afraid that his troops might be encouraged to plunder church lands, if they came to any, and, in his magnanimous way, he imagined that Conan would soon beg grace and pardon for the crime which he had committed. William had no sooner withdrawn from Breton territory than it was reported to him unexpectedly that Geoffrey of Anjou had joined Conan with an immense force, and that both leaders were preparing to attack him the very next day. The prospect of battle filled Duke William with delight, for he realized that it would be all the more glorious to triumph in a single fight over two separate enemies, each of them so formidable. What is more, the advantages of such a victory would be immense.

However, Rivoallon, in whose territory they pitched their tents, was loud in his complaints. He would have been grateful to William, he said, for rescuing him from his enemy, if the damage which he was doing had not cancelled out all the gain. If William were to make his stand there to meet the enemy army, this tract of land, which was not very fertile anyway, and which had already been sadly ravaged, would be completely ruined. What difference would it make to the local peasantry if they lost the labour of a whole year through a Norman army instead of through a Breton one? The expulsion of Conan had brought Rivoallon some measure of fame, but it had done nothing to preserve his property. The duke replied that Rivoallon must realize that any hasty withdrawal would be a disgrace. He promised full payment in ready money for any damage which might be done. He forbade his troops to do any harm to Rivoallon's crops or his cattle. They obeyed this order with such scrupulous care that a single stook of corn would have sufficed as recompense for all the harm which they did. They waited in vain for the enemy onslaught; but Conan continued his retreat.

Duke William returned to his base. He kept Harold with him as his guest for some time. Then he loaded him with presents and sent him on his way. By doing this he paid his respects both to King Edward, at whose order Harold had come, and to Harold himself, who had undertaken the mission. What is more, one of the two hostages, Harold's nephew [Hakon], went back with him, for to please his guest Duke William gave him his liberty.

These, then, are the reproaches made against you, Harold. After all these kindnesses, how could you dare to deprive Duke William of his inheritance and to make war on him, you who, by an oath so sacrosanct, had bound yourself and all your people to him, placing your hands in his and swearing fealty? It was for you to hold the Englishmen in check. Instead you most perniciously encouraged them in their revolt. The following winds which swelled your coal-black sails as you journeyed homewards brought nothing but unhappiness. You horrid man! The calm sea-waters which permitted you to cross back to your native shore must ever be accursed. The quiet harbour where you landed must bear its brunt of shame, for with you came the most disastrous shipwreck ever suffered by your fatherland . . .

The news was received quite unexpectedly of an event which turned out to be true: England had lost King Edward and Harold had been crowned in his place. This headstrong Englishman had not waited for the result of a public election. With the backing of a number of blackguardly partisans, he had broken his plighted word and occupied the royal throne by popular acclamation, on the very day when, in the midst of mourning and with all his people plunged in grief, the good king was being laid to rest. Harold was crowned by Stigand, in a ceremony which was not acceptable to God, for the archbishop had been deposed from his priestly ministry and excommunicated by the Pope in his wisdom and zeal.

Duke William sought the advice of his supporters, and then decided to avenge this insult and lay claim to his inheritance by force of arms.

Notes to text

1. Of auguries and thingmen and Anglo-Saxon attitudes

[1] The Jómvikings embodied a new breed of well-disciplined professional soldier. They derived their name from a community of soldiers living in the fortress of Jómsborg, at the mouth of the river Oder. Membership of this community was limited to warriors of proven valour. Apart from Thorkill the Tall, Sweyn and his son Canute were Jómvikings who came to play important roles in English history.

[2] Geoffrey of Monmouth, writing at the beginning of the twelfth century, recorded the continuing popularity of Merlin's prophecies. They were being talked about so much that, 'from all sorts of places people of my own generation kept urging me to publish his prophecies', and so he translated them from the British tongue into Latin.

[3] St Dunstan's prophecy was prompted by the murder of Aethelred's brother Edward by their mother at Corfe Castle in 978. As a result, Aethelred, raised to the throne thereafter, was cursed by St Dunstan.

[4] *La Estoire de Seint Aedward le Rei*, Ms. Cantab, Ee III 59, from Bishop Moore's Library, 11. 195–218.

[5] The Encomiast gave the size of Canute's fleet as 200, while Adam of Bremen, usually well informed and reliable, thought it comprised 960 craft. It is likely that the Hanseatic chronicler of Nordic events also included a Norwegian fleet that joined Canute's campaign against the English.

[6] *La Estoire*, op. cit., 11. 245–63.

2. Odin's bird of battle flaps its wings

[1] The raven lore was so widespread in eleventh-century England that the embroiderers of the Bayeux Tapestry showed Odin's bird on William the Conquerer's banner before the Battle of Hastings.

[2] *La Estoire*, op. cit., 11. 263–357.

[3] William of Malmesbury, *Chronicle of the Kings of England*, Bohn's Antiquarian Library.

3. *Murder royal in the privy*

1 Nocte siquidem sequentis diei festivitatis sancti Andreas Lundoniae perimitur insidiis Edrici Strioni. Cotton Library Ms., p.30.
2 Heidrekr Striona het ein rikr madr, er fe tok till þess af Knuti Konungi, et hann sviki Jatmund Konung, oc draepi hann med mordvigi, oc þetta var hans bani: Heidrekr var þo fosti Jatmundor Konungs, oc trudi hann honom sem sialfun ser. *Knytlingasaga*, in Fornmana Sögur XI, 177–446 (Copenhagen 1828).
3 Geoffroi Gaimar, *L'Estoire des Engleis*, ed. T.Wright (1844), pp.141–52.
4 The reverberations of this scandal were such that William of Malmesbury, writing in the following century, found it necessary to record the facts in his chronicle. He gave as the source of the story – which includes secret visits to Sigeferth's widow, acts of deliberate deception, and a secret marriage – the archives of Frideswide's church in Oxford, where the chronicler 'read the history of this transaction'.
5 The chroniclers of the period seem to be confused about the ages of Edmund's two boys. Most agree, however, that Edmund was the elder, although Florence of Worcester believed they were twins. The reason for this confusion could be that Edmund married Ealdgyth in 1015, and was dead by 16 November 1016. This left little time for the birth of two children, though Edward could well have been born in the late summer of that year, or possibly posthumously.
6 The *Knytligasaga* states that the crown would only pass to the other contracting party if a sworn-brother should die without children.
7 John Stow, *Generall Chronicle of England*, p.92.

4. *A 'letter of death'*

1 Gaimar, op. cit., 11. 4507–19.
2 Ibid., 11. 4445–80.
3 E.B.Everitt, *Six early plays related to the Shakespeare Canon Anglistica*, XIV (1965) 331–6.
4 Eric Sams, *Shakespeare's Lost Play: 'Edmund Ironside'*, Fourth Estate (London 1986).

5. *The resentful English look to the aethelings for deliverance*

1 *Enconium*, op. cit., 1. 1040.
2 In his *Chronicon*, Brompton wrote:
   Praetera rex Kanutus quadam vice Emmam consortem suam consuluit, quid de duobus filiis regis Edmund Irenside, Edmundo videlicet Edwardo, foret melius faciendum. Quae respondens dixit: Domine, recti sunt regni Angliae haeredes, qui vita et sanitate comitibus non minimam vobis guerram in brevi parabunt. Ideo vobis consulo quatinus eos ad partes longinguas alicui destinetis, qui eos ab amorem vestri secrete interficiat, ed. R. Twysden, *Historiae Anglicanae Scriptores X*, 19 (1652).
3 Gaimar, op. cit., 11. 4548–70.
4 Snorri Sturluson, *Heimskringlasaga*, vol. II, pp. 193–200; 'The "Togdraþa" on Canute', *English Historical Documents c. 500–1042*, London (1979), pp. 337–340.

6. Twenty-nine false leads and a cold trail

1 *The Anglo-Saxon Chronicle*, Ms. D, ed. D. Whitelock, p.133.
2 The identity of Edward's wife, and the ramifications of the Hungarian link are considered in greater detail in Part IV, chapter 3.
3 The key phrases in the two works are almost identical. Florence's 'ad regem Suavorum occidendos misit' becomes 'ad regem Suavorum eos interficiendos transmisit' in Ailred's. Florence's reference to the aethelings' young age 'sed illos ad regem Hungarorum Salomonem nomine, misit nutriendos, vitaque reservandos' is rendered by Ailred as 'Rex vero Suavorum nobilium puerorum miseratus aerumnam, ad Hungariorum regem eos destinat nutriendos', and so on.
4 Turgotus, Life of St Margaret, trans. A.O.Anderson, *Early Sources of Scottish History*, AD 500–1286, II, pp.59–88. Simeon of Durham questioned Turgotus's authorship, believing that it was compiled by the monk Theodoric, also of Durham. Later medieval Scottish historians, however, established without any doubt that the author who wrote in the first person singular and clearly identified himself as Margaret's confessor, could only have been Bishop Turgotus.

7. The Russian connection

1 Gaimar, op. cit. 11. 4580–4.
2 She was a daughter of King Olaf's concubine, Aedla of Vendland.
3 'Filii ejus /Edmundi regis/ in Ruzziam exilio damnati', Adam of Bremen, *Gesta Hammaburgensis Ecclesiae Pontificarum*, II, chap. 51, in MGH, ss, VII, p.324.
4 Adam named them as Sigafried, Grimkil, Bernard and Rudolph.
5 Gaimar, op. cit., 11. 4582–8.

8. The 'Polish red herring'

1 J.Steenstrup, *Normannerne, Danske og Norske Riger paa de Britiske Øer i Danevaeldens Tidsalder*, Vol. III (1882); Laurence M.Larson, *The Heritage of Canute the Great* (1902); and William Stubbs' commentary on Roger de Hoveden's *Chronica* in the Rolls Series (1869).
2 Stubbs identified the King of the Suebi as Duke Gottschalk of the Vends.
3 *Leges Anglo-Saxonicae* (1721), cap.: *Leges Edovardi Confessoris Regis*, s. 35, p.208.
4 See Part IV, chapter 3.
5 Roger of Hoveden must have come across a copy of the *Leges* late in his life, for he included verbatim the aethelings' Kievan exile in the *Legal Appendix* to his *Chronicon* with the apparent intention of correcting its Swedish-Hungarian route. But the Latin text refers to the kingdom of 'Dogorum' instead of 'Rugorum'. It reads: 'Iste praefatus Eadmundus [Ferreum-latus] habuit quemdam filium Eadwardum nomine, qui mox, patre mortuo, timore Regis Cnuti aufugit ad regnum Dogorum, quod nos melius vocamus Russiam. Quem Rex terrae Malesclotus nomine, ut cognavit quis esset, honeste retiniut.'
6 Karamzin, op. cit., II
7 Among the more notable historical works referring to the aethelings' stay were Ivan Andreyevsky, *O pravakh inostrantsev v Rossiyi do vstuplenya Ioanna III* (Moscow 1954); A. Sinyavsky, *Otnoshenya drevne-russkoy tserkvi i obshchestva k latinskomu zapadu* (Moscow 1899); and I.P.Kozlovsky, *Vnesnye snoshenya drevney Rusi* (Moscow 1930).

9. At Yaroslav the Great's hospitable court

1 Gaimar, op. cit., 11. 4587–4604.
2 The democratic Kievan period upon which the Russians now look back with nostalgic yearning began with the coming of the Viking Varangians in the ninth century and ended in the holocaust of the Mongol invasion in the middle of the thirteenth century. Kiev's leading role was taken over by Moscow whose princes borrowed the tools of statecraft from the tyrannical Mongol system.
3 An anatomical analysis of his skeleton, contained in Dr D.G.Rokhlin's book *Itogi Anatomicheskogo i Rentgenicheskogo Izucheniya Skeleta Yaroslava* (Leningrad 1940), confirmed that he had been lame from childhood and later had broken his leg.

10. Anglo-Saxon counters in a Continental battle for dominance

1 Saxo wrote: '1040: Rex in festo sancti Andree in Altstide placitum habuit, ubi et legatos Ruzorum cum muneribus suscepit', *Chronicon*, MGH, 55, VI, p.684.
2 '1043: Legati quoque Ruzorum magna dona tulerunt, sed majora recipientes abierunt', *Annales Altahenses maiores*, MGH, 55, XX, p.798.

11. Hungarian princes join Kievan refugee colony

1 N.Maffei, 'Life of St Stephen', in *Fuga Saecoli*, (Paris 1632).
2 The biography of St Gellert: A contemporary bishop of the country, stated clearly that Andrew, Béla and Levente were Vazul's sons.
3 Simon de Kéza, *Kézai Simon Kronikája* (1283) II. Cap. 3–55 and 170–8; cf. *Gesta Hunnorum et Hungarorum*, ed. Endlicher (Rerum Hungaricarum Monumenta Arpadiana, Pest 1849).
4 Joannes Turóczy, *Chronica Hungarorum* (1488), ed. Schwandtner, Scriptores rerum Hungaricarum (Vindobonae 1746) p.43.
5 Gaimar's chronicle contains a tantalizing claim that after Harthacanute's death the English did actually seriously consider the recall of Edmund and Edward from Hungary. But since the aethelings were still in Kiev in 1042, according to the ascertainable documentary evidence, this claim must be received with caution. This reservation is dictated not only by Gaimar's confusion over the geographical position of Gardorika-Gardimbre and the placing of his narrative thereafter in Hungary, but because he further asserts that Edward (The Confessor) had joined his cousins in Hungary before his recall from Normandy 'to help them in a war they had'. While Edmund and Edward were certainly involved in Hungary's war of succession in 1046, there is no documentary evidence to back up the claim that Edward (the Confessor), not particularly noted for martial qualities, had travelled to the distant country of Hungary at all, let alone to lend a hand to his cousins fighting for a totally unknown Hungarian prince. But because of the inclusion of later historical events amidst the jumble of probably misunderstood hearsay, it is worth quoting the relevant lines in full:

> [In 1042, the English] discussed what they should do
> For which heirs they should send.

If they sent to Hungary
It would be too far, they have little aid.
In the end they agreed
That they should send to Normandy
For Edward and Aelfred.
Edward was the elder brother
He had gone into Hungary
To help his cousins
In a war they had.
The people of Velcase caused it. (II. 4779–4790)

12. A call from Hungary

1 *Chronica Hungarorum*, op. cit., p.38.
2 According to another version, the symbolic act of Hungary's submission to the Holy Roman Emperor took place in 1045, and involved the presentation of a golden lance; ibid., p.43.
3 Ibid., pp.44–5.

13. In the rebel camp

1 St Gellert, *Legend* (minor) and *Legend* (major) (12th c.); *Scriptores Rerum Hungaricarum tempore ducum regumque stirpis Arpadianae gestarum* II, 47–506 (Budapest 1938); cf. Maffei, *Fuga Saecoli* (Paris 1632).

14. Signs of royal favour

1 Judge Sarchas, in L. Závodszky, *A St István, St Lászlo és Kálmán korabeli törvények forrásai* (Budapest 1904)
2 See Joseph Koller, *Historia Episcopatus Quinqueecclesiarum* (1782), II, pp.86–93.
3 György Fejér, *Codex Diplomaticus* (1829), III/2, p.421; it is now known as Somogyvári Transsumptum, 76/1404, Magyar Országos Levéltár, Budapest.
4 József Holub, 'Határper Baranya es Tolna között', *Yearbook of the Janus Pannonius Museum*, Pécs (1969).
5 'An. Christi 1235: Idem Andrea donationes priorum regum Aeclesiae Quinque-Ecclesiensi factas, recenset et confirmat; in compensationem vero sumtuum a Bartholomeo Episcopo Quinque-Ecclesiensi in Aragoniam suscepta legatione factorum, adiectis terris auget quoque.' Fejér, op. cit.
6 Ibid.
7 Dezsö Csánki, *Magyarország történelmi földrajza a Hunyadiak korában*, vol. 3 (1897).
8 The more noteworthy scholars who addressed themselves to this issue include: János Xántus, Kik voltak az angolszász hercegek St István udvarában? *Századok* XIII (Budapest 1878); Lajos Kropf, 'Ágotha Királylány származása', *Turul* (Budapest 1896); Jenö Horváth, *Az Árpadok Diplomáciája 1001–1250*, II (Budapest

1935); Béla Malcolmes, *St István unokájà, St Margit Skocia Királynéjà magyar származása* (Budapest 1938); Sándor Fest, *Skóciai St Margit magyar származása* (Budapest 1939); Janos Herzog, *Skóciai St Margit származása kérdése*, Turul (Budapest 1939).

9   György Györffy, *István Király ás miive* (Budapest 1972) p.514.
10   *Anglo-Saxon Chronicle*, Ms 'E', Bodleian Ms Land 636, formerly E. 80; ibid., Ms Cottonian, Domitian A. VIII.
11   Prokopius, *Bell Goth.*, IV 20.
12   'Cometes stella in occidentem facem dirigens apparuit, plura mala quibus et Almaniae et *Britanniae* regiones afflictae fuerunt designans. In *Britannia, quae nunc Anglia dicitur*, Rex Eraldus occiditur', *Historia Polomica* (11th c.) (Dobromigli 1615) I, 238.
13   About the thirteenth-century Count Cletus, Béla Malcomes, a student of St Margaret's origins, had the following to say: 'Ivan Nagy and Gyorgy Pray and many other eighteenth century genealogists, had researched the reputed link between the Nádasdy Family and the Anglo-Saxon princes but with little success. But one of their positive starting points was that a Nádasdy forebear had "Britanicus" as his middle-name. One wonders whether, after all, there was not a connection between the above mentioned Count Cletus and the Britons whose lands he owned in the thirteenth century?... Is there, perhaps, after all, some link between the departed Anglo-Saxon princes and the family of Count Nádasdy that unquestionably originates from there? As yet it cannot be ascertained. One of the reasons is that the origins of Count Cletus cannot be uncovered; another is that the Nádasdy family archives provide only scant data about the origins of Cletus and his relationship with the Nádasdys. Ivan Nagy is attempting to deny the existence of a certain link between the British princes and the subsequent owners of [the Nádasd] lands, but cannot give an acceptable explanation why had one of the forebears of the Count Nádasdys the middle-name "Britanicus"?' Béla Malcolmes, op. cit., pp. 60–90.
14   Ibid., p.60.
15   Lászlo Papp, 'Rékávár és 1963. évi felderitö ásatása', *Yearbook of the Janus Pannonius Museum* (Pécs 1967).

15. Scandal at court

1   Gaimar, op. cit., ll. 4618–56.
2   'Porro Edmundo filiam suam dedit uxorem.'

16. Edward's marriage to a 'lady of royal descent'

1   '... Eadwardus vero Agatham filiam germani imperatoris Henrici III in matrimonium accepit, ex qua Margaretam reginam Scotorum, et Christianam virginem, et clitonem Eadgarum suscepit.'
2   The Oxford University Press's *Medieval Latin Word List* also gives a wider but closely related meaning of the word, formed from *germanus*: this is *germanitas*, which in British and Irish sources means 'brotherliness'.
3   'Haec [Margarita] nimirum filia fuit Eduardi Regis Hunorum, qui fuit filius Edmundi cognomento Irnesidae, fratris Eduardi Regis Anglorum, et exsul conjugem accepit cum regno *filiam Salomonis Regis Hunorum*', *The Ecclesiastical History of England and Normandy*, p. 457.

4   '. . . Ubi dum benigne aliquo tempore habiti essent, major [Edmund] diem obit, minor [Edward] *Agatham reginae sororem* in matrimonium accepit', Malmesbury, op. cit., p. 90.

5   John Pinkerton, author of *Vita Antique Sanctorum* (1789), and Dr John Geddes, author of *The Life of St Margaret of Scotland* (1794), were the most outstanding British champions of Bruno's paternity. Both relied on the authority of Papebroche, the editor of Theodoric's Ms on Margaret, who had examined all the Anglo-Saxon sources and accepted the aethelings' direct exile route from Sweden to St Stephen's court in Hungary. He knew nothing of the aethelings' Kievan sojourn, and consequently his followers had come to their conclusion without the benefit of the facts.

17. *Two tell-tale insertions in a Norman law collection*

1   'Iste praefatus Edmundus Irenside habuit quendam filium Eadwardum nomine, qui mox patre mortuo (timore Chnuti Regis) aufugit ad regnum Rugorum, quod nos melius vocamus Russiam. Que Rex terrae Malesclotus nomine, ut cognavit quis esset, honeste retinuit, Et ipse Eadwardus accepit ibi uxorem ex nobili genere, de qua natus est ei Eadgarus Athelinge et Margareta regina Scotie et Cristina soror eius.' *Leges Anglo-Saxonicae*, op. cit.

2   According to the Domesday Book, she owned lands in four localities – Bradwell, Oxfordshire; Wolverley [Hulverley]; Arley; Long Itchington in Warwickshire – and houses in Warwick.

3   Szabolcs de Vajay, *Duquesne Review* (1962).

18. *The shadow of the Bastard of Normandy over England*

1   Harleian Collection Ms. 526. The work changes direction abruptly after Harold's death, indicating that the part dealing with the Confessor's life up to his death was written *before* the Norman Conquest.

2   *La Estoire*, op. cit.

3   The Witan – the 'Meeting of the Wise' – while not a formally constituted body with clearly defined powers, was a very influential council. Freeman in his monumental *History of the Norman Conquest* saw it as England's 'legislature'.

4   Malmesbury's account of the events of 1054 reads: 'Rex Edwardus, pronius in senium, quod ipse non susceperat liberos, et Godwini videret invalescere filios, misit ad Regem Hunorum ut filium fratris Edmundi, Edwardum, cum omni familia sua mitteret; futurum ut aut ille aut filii sui succedant regno hereditario Angliae; orbitatem suam cognatorum suffragio sustentari debere.' Op. cit., *Patrologiae Curs*, p. 179. See also Bohn's *Antiquarian Library*, pp. 276–7.

19. *An innocent abroad*

1   The Domesday Book says that the lands in Huntingdonshire were granted to Abbot Aelfwine in recognition of his services in Germany. There were no other

missions sent by the Confessor to Germany for which he could have been thus rewarded.

2 1054: 'On tham ylean geare ferde Ealdred biscop suth ofer sae into Sexlande, and wearth taer mid mycelre arwarthnesse underfangaen.'

3 1057: 'Daes ilcan geres for Aldred biscop to Colne ofer sae thaes kynges aerende, and wearth thaer underfangen mid mycclan werthscipe fram tham Casere, and thaer he wunode wel neh an ger; and him geaf aegther teneste, ge se Biscop on Colone and se Casere', in Petrie's *Monumenta Historia Brit.*, p. 453.

4 1054: 'Aldredus Wigorniensis Episcopus ... magnis cum xeniis Regis fungitur legatione ad Imperatorem, a quo simul et ab Herimanno Coloniensi archipraesule magno susceptus honore, ibidem per integrum annum mansit, et Regis ex parte Imperatori suggesit ut, legatis Ungariam missis, inde fratuelem suum Eadwardum, Regis videlicet Eadmundi Ferrei Lateris filium, reduceret, Angliamque venire faceret', *Chronicon ex Chronicis*, op. cit., p. 607.

5 The Italian chronicler Bonfini gave the following account of Henry III's obsession to punish and destroy Hungary: 'Dann Keiser Heinrich der dritt begert den todt und schmach künig Peters zu rechen uund die Ungern von wegen ihrs meyneyds uund Conspiration zu Straffen. Darumb er dann allenthalben vyl Volcks versamlet und disen horzug mitt einem söllichen gemutt genommen, auff das er das Ungerland eintweders dem Römischen Reych zinsbar machte oder sie an ihr macht gar schwecht und zegrunt richt', *Des Aller Mechtigsten Künigreichs inn Ungern warhafftige Chronick und anzeigung wie das anfang auff und abgang genummen* (Basle 1545).

20. *A tragic end to Edward's Continental odyssey*

1 Florence: '1057: Ut ei mandarat suus patruus Rex Eadwardus, de Ungaria ... Angliam venit. Decreverat enim Rex illum post se regni haeredem constituere', op. cit., p. 608.

2 *ASC*: 'Her ... com Aedward aetheling, Eadmundes sunn cynges, hider to lande, and sona thaes gefor.'
Ingulph: 'Edwardus etiam patruelis regis Edwardi vocatus de Hungaria, ubi Angliam attigit, informatus obiit, spesque regii sanguinis deinceps deficere coepit.'
Florence: 'Ex quo venit parvo post tempore vita decessit Lundoniae.'

3 According to textual studies, this work was written or rewritten between 1066 and 1079, i.e. within the lifespan of a man who could have witnessed both Edward the Exile's return and death, and its consequences for England.

21. *Edward's son groomed for the throne*

1 'Rex vero Edwardus Edgarum filium eorum secum retinuit, et pro filio nutrivit. Et quia cogitavit ipsum haeredem facere, nominavit Ethelinge', op. cit., p. 208.

2 For the full version of the Norman side, see Appendix 3.

3 In contrast with the claim of the weavers of the tapestry that Harold took his oath at Bayeux, Orderic Vitalis puts the events at Rouen. 'Moreover', he wrote, 'Harold had taken the oath of allegiance to Duke William at Rouen, in the presence of the nobles of Normandy, and doing him homage had sworn on the holy relics to all that was required of him', op. cit., p. 456.

22. 1066: the comet of revolution over England

1 Otto, Bishop of Freising, *Chronicon* (11th c.), in M. Bouquet, *Recueil des Historiens des Gaulles et de la France* XI (Paris 1738);
St Andrew of Cambrai, *Gesta pontificarum Camacensium* (11th c.), ed. Bethman (Paris 1853);
Lupus Protospatarius of Bari, *Annales*, (11th c.), ed. G. H. Pertz, *Monumenta Germaniae Historica* V.59;
Guillaume Godell of Aquitania, *Chronicon* (11th c.), in M. Bouquet, *Recueil des Historiens des Gaulles et de la France*, XI, 284;
St James, *Lüttich Chronicle* (11th c.), ed. G. H. Pertz, *Monumenta Germaniae Historica* XVI, 639;
Jan Dlugosz, *Historia Polonica* (11th c.) I, 238 (Dobromigli 1615).
2 Bishop Ealdred describes him as 'puer', confirming that he could not have been older than twelve.
3 The *Chronicle of Scotland*, Book 12, p.168, Canon John Bellenden's 1540 translation.
4 Some chroniclers put the Monk of Fécamp's mission in the first week of October, after William's landing.
5 In his *Chronica Gentis Scotorum* (Book V, chap. XII), John of Fordun, the learned Scottish chronicler, takes to task the clergy for opposing Edgar. 'But it seems to me that they did wrong in this, both before God and the people: before God, because on one of whom He had preferred for the kingship by his birth, from so many kings, his forebears, begotten, as he was in the rightful line of descent; it was *not lawful* for them to reject, nor unjustly to rob him of his patrimony – guiltless, as he was – with their tongues sharper than any sword . . . To their eternal reproach and scandal of the inhabitants of the kingdom, they raised above themselves, not according to the justice of law but following their hearts' desires, a man *without* the least right to reign.'

23. A kingdom for a bag of silver

1 Among those submitting to William at Berkhamstead were, according to the *Anglo-Saxon Chronicle* and other contemporary sources, Archbishop Stigand, Archbishop Ealdred of York, Bishop Wulfstan of Worcester, Walter of Hereford, the earls Eadwin and Morcare and many nobles and leading burghers of southern England and London. In a curious aside, the chronicler remarks that 'it was very unwise that they had not submitted before'.
2 *Spelmani Codex legum veterum statutorem regni Angliae*, ed. David Wilkins, *Leges Anglo-Saxonicae* (Oxford 1721).
3 Some accounts claim that Malcolm was a widower, but others specifically state that he badly wanted to marry Margaret 'for the sake of her ancient and noble descent'.

24. Tilting at Norman windmills

1 Nicholas Hooper, in his 'Edgar Aetheling, Anglo-Saxon prince, rebel and Crusader', asserts that it would have been chronologically impossible for Edgar to

have participated in the Crusade, claiming that his Crusader exploits were mixed up with his actual journey to the Holy Land in 1102; *Anglo-Saxon England*, no. 14 (1985).

2 Robert Wace wrote his *Roman de Rou* within a generation of the aetheling's death.

Epilogue

1 The investigation carried out in the 1740s is based on a statement of one George Conlon which is recounted in considerable detail in *De Duplici Statu Religionis apud Scotos.*

2 *The Idea of a Perfect Princesse in the Life of St Margaret of Scotland* (Paris 1661).

Bibliography

Adam of Bremen, Gesta Hammaburgensis ecclesiae pontificarum (1050), ed. G. H. Pertz, *Monumenta Germaniae Historica* II, 74–334 (Hanover 1826)

Alberic des Trois Fontaines, *Chronicon* (13th c.), ed. G. G. Leibniz (Hanover 1698)

Ailred of Rievaulx, *De Genealogia Regum Anglorum* (1154), ed. R. Twysden in *Historiae Anglicanae Scriptores X* (London 1652)

Mikhail P. Alekseyev, *Anglo-Saksonskaya parallel k poucheniyu Vladimira Monomakha*, Akademia Nauk SSSR, Trudy Otdely Drevney Russkoy Lityeratury II, 14–49 (Leningrad 1935)

Ivan Andreyevsky, *O pravakh inostrantsev v Rossiyi do vstuplenya Ioanna III* (Moscow 1954)

Amiens, *see* Guy

Anglo-Saxon Chronicle (11th c.), *Two of the Saxon Chronicles Parallel*, ed. C. Plummer & J. Earle (Oxford 1892–9)

Antiquités Russes (Copenhagen 1852), II

Arnulph (Archbishop of Rheims) *Historia*, in C. Duchesne, *Historia Francorum Scriptores IV* (Paris 1636)

Baronius (11th c.), *Annales ecclesiastici* II (Rome 1590)

N. Baumgarten, 'Généalogie et mariages occidentaux des Rurikides Russes du Xe au XIIIe s.', *Orientalia Christiana* IX, 8 (1927)

Hector Boethius, *The Chronicle of Scotland* (1526) Lib. XII (translation 1540)

Antonius Bonfinius, *Des Aller Mechtigsten Künigreichs inn Ungarn, Warhaftige Chronick und Anzeigung* (Basle 1545)

Bremen, *see* Adam

Brompton, *see* John

George Buchanan, *The History of Scotland* (16th c.) I–II, Lib VII, 287–693 (Edinburgh 1821)

John Capgrave, *Chronicon* (15th c.), ed. F. C. Hingeston (Rolls Series, London 1858)

Chronicle of Melrose Abbey (13th c.), tr. J. Stevenson, *The Church Historians of England*, IV.i 79–242 (London 1853)

D. Cornides, *Regum Hungariae qui seculo XI regnavere, genealogiam illustrat* (1778)

Dezsö Csánki, *Magyarország Történeti Földrajza a Hunyadiak Korában*, III (Budapest 1890–1913); cf. *Árpád és az Árpádok* (Budapest 1908)

Csaba Csapódi, *A St István korára és a korai kereszténységre vonatkozó irodalmi feldolgozások* (Budapest 1938)

A. Duchesne, *Historiae Normannorum scriptores antiqui* (Paris 1619)

Jan Dlugosz, *Historia Polonica* (11th c.) (Dobromigli 1615) I

Durham, *see* Symeon

Abbot Ekkehard of Urau, *Chronica* (late 11th c.), ed. J. P. Migne, *Patrologia Latina cursus completus*, CXIV (Paris 1844)

Encomium Emmae Reginae (11th c.), ed. A. Campbell, Camden Third Series LXXII (London 1949)

E. B. Everitt, 'Six early plays related to the Shakespeare canon', *Anglistica*, XIV (1965)

György Fejér, *Codex Diplomaticus* (Pécs 1829), III/2, 421

Sándor Fest, *Skociai St Margit magyar származása* (Budapest 1939)

Florence of Worcester, *Chronicon ex Chronicis* (11th c.), ed. W. Howard (London 1592); *The Chronicle of Florence of Worcester*, tr. T. Forester (London 1854)

John of Fordun, *Chronica Gentis Scotorum* (14th c.), ed. W. F. Skene in *Historians of Scotland* (Edinburgh 1871–2)

Edward Freeman, *The History of the Norman Conquest* (Oxford 1870), I–III

Geoffroi Gaimar, *L'Estoire des Engleis* (12th c.), ed. T. D. Hardy and C. T. Martin (Rolls Series, London 1885); cf. *The Anglo-Norman Chronicle of G. Gaimar* (London 1884) lines 4415–4655

Geoffrey of Monmouth, (Bishop of Asaph), *The History of the Kings of England* (12th c.), tr. Lewis Thorpe (London 1969)

Guillaume Godell (of Aquitaine), *Chronicon* (11th c.), ed. M. Bouquet, *Recueil des Historiens des Gaules et de la France* XI

Guillaume de Jumièges, *Gesta Normannorum Ducum* (11th c.), ed. J. Marx (Rouen 1914) VII

Guillaume de Poitiers, *Histoire de Guillaume le Conquérant* (11th c.), ed. R. Foreville (Paris 1952)

Guy of Amiens, *Widonis Carmen de Hastingae proelio* (11th c.), ed. F. Michel, *Chroniques Anglo-Normandes* III (Rouen 1836)

György Györffy, *István Király és Müve* (Budapest 1977)

Bishop Hartvik (of Györ), *Life of St Stephen* (12th c.) in Maffei, *Fuga Saecoli* (Paris 1632)

Henry of Huntingdon, *Historia Anglorum* (12th c.), ed. T. Arnold (Rolls Series, London 1879)

Andreas Hess, *Chronica Hungarorum* (Buda 1473)

Higden, *see* Ranulph

Metropolitan Hilarion, *On the law of Moses* (11th c.)

József Holub, 'Határper Baranya és Tolna között', *Yearbook of the Janus Pannonius Museum* (Pécs 1960)

Nicholas Hooper,'Edgar Aetheling, Anglo-Saxon Prince, Rebel and Crusader', *Anglo-Saxon England* XIV (1985)

Jenö Horváth, *Az Árpádok Diplomáciája 1001–1250*, II (Budapest 1935)

Hoveden, *see* Roger

Abbot Ingulph, *Chronicle of Croyland Abbey* (11th c.), ed. W. Fulman, *Rerum Anglicanum Scriptores* (London 1684)

Ipatyevskaya Letopis (1420)

John of Brompton, *Chronicon* (12th c.), ed. R. Twysden, *Historiae Anglicanae Scriptores* X, (London 1652)

Jumièges, *see* Guillaume

Nikolai M. Karamzin, *Istoriya Gosudarstva Rossiyskogo* (18th c.) (St Petersburg 1815–24) II

István Katona, *Historia Critica Regum Hungariae* I–II (Pestini 1779)

Simon de Kéza, *Kézai Simon Krónikája* (1283), II cap 3–55; cf. *Gesta Hunnorum et Hungarorum*, ed. Endlicher (Rerum Hungaricarum Monumenta Arpadiana, Pest 1849)

Henry Knyghton, *Chronica de Eventibus Angliae*, ed. R. Twysden, *Historiae Anglicanae Scriptores* X (London 1652)

Knytlingasaga in *Fornmanna Sögur* XI, 177–446 (Copenhagen 1828)

I. P. Kozlovsky, *Vnesnye snoshenya drevney Russi* (Moscow 1930)

Lajos Kropf, *Ágotha Királylány Származása* (Turul 1896)

La Estoire de Seint Aedward le Rei (1245), ed. H. R. Luard in *Lives of Edward the Confessor* (Rolls Series, London 1858)

Johan M. von Lappenberg, *Geschichte von England* (19th c.) (Hamburg 1834); cf. *Geschichte der europäischen Staaten*, I

Felix Liebermann, *Über die Leges Edwardi Confessoris*; cf. *Die Gesetze der Angelsachsen* (Halle 1896–1912), II

Lavrentyevskaya Letopis (1377)

Leges Edovardi Confessoris (1134), *Leges Anglo-Saxonicae* (London 1721) XXV

John Leslie, *De Origine, Moribus et Rebus Gestis Scotorum* (1578)

Erpold Lindenbrog, *Historia Daniae Regum* (1629); cf. *Scriptores rerum Germanicarum Septentionalium* (1706)

A. I. Lyashchenko, *Eymundar Saga; Russkiye Letopisi*, Izd. Akademii Nauk SSSR, XII (Moscow 1926), 1010–1071

Lupus Protospatarius (of Bari), *Annales* (11th c.), ed. G. H. Pertz, *Monumenta Germaniae Historica* V

G. P. Maffei, 'The Life of St Edward', *Fuga Saecoli* (Paris 1632)

Béla Malcolmes, *St István unokája, St Margit Skócia Királynéja magyar származása és magyarországi szülöhelye* (Budapest 1938)

William of Malmesbury, *De Gestis Regum Anglorum*, ed. W. Stubbs (Rolls Series, London 1887)

Walter Map, *De Nugis Curialium* (12th c.), ed. M. R. James (Oxford 1914)

Georges B. Manteyer, 'Les origines du Dauphiné de Viennois', *Bulletin de la Société d'Etudes Hautes-Alpes* (1925)

Alajos Markovits, *Az Árpádkirályok családi összeköttetései Europa különféle udvaraival* (Szombathely 1888)

Johan Messenius (Bishop of Lund 16th c.), *Scondia Illustrata* I (1700)

Monmouth, *see* Geoffrey

Thomas More, *History of the Reign of Richard III* (16th c.), ed. R. S. Sylvester (New Haven & London 1963)

Nestor, *Nachalny Svod* (1095); cf. *La Chronique de Nestor*, ed. Louis (Paris 1834) II

Novgorodskaya Letopis (13th c.)

Orderic Vitalis, *Historia Ecclesiastica* (early 12th c.), ed. A. Le Prévost (SHF, Paris 1838–55) BR VIII

Otto (Bishop of Freising 11th c.), *Chronicon* in M. Bouquet, *Recueil des Historiens des Gaules et de la France*, XI (Paris 1738)

Francis Palgrave, *The History of Normandy and of England* (London 1851); *Scotland's Documents and Records Illustrating the History of Scotland and the Transactions between the Crowns of Scotland and England* (London 1837)

Carolus F. Palma, *Notitia Rerum Hungaricarum* (Rome 1785)

Lászlo Papp, *Rékavár és 1963. évi felderitö ásatása* (Pécs 1967)

C. H. Pearson, *The History of England during the Early Middle Ages* (London 1867)

Pelbartus de Temesvár (late 15th c.), *Sermones pomerii fratris Pelbarti de Themesvár* (Hagenau 1498)

John Pinkerton, *Vita Antiquae Sanctorum qui habitarerunt Scotia* (London 1789)

Poitiers, *see* Guillaume

Joannes Pontanus, *Rerum Danicarum Historia Libris* X (1631)

Povest Vremyonnykh Lyet (12th c.)

Georgio Pray, *Annales Regum Hungariae ab Christi ad annum* MDLXIV (Vienna 1764) 27–59; *Dissertationes Historico-criticae de Sanctis Salamone Rege et Emerico Duce Hungariae* (1775)

Prosper (of Aquitaine), *Chronicon* in A. Duchesne, *Historiae Francorum Scriptores* I (Paris 1619)

Protospatarius, *see* Lupus

Ranulph of Higden, *Polychronicon* (14th c.), ed. C. Babington & J. R. Lumby (Rolls Series, London 1865–86)

Rheims Chronicle (11th c.), *Ex brevi Chronico Remensi*, ed. M. Bouquet, *Recueil des Historiens des Gaules et de la France*, IX–XII (1738)

Jozsef Rézbányai, *Magyarországi St Margit, Katholikus Szemle* (Budapest 1896)

John Robie (signed J. R.), *The Idea of a Perfect Princesse in the Life of St Margaret, Queen of Scots* (Paris 1661)

Roger of Hoveden, *Chronicon* (12th c.), ed. W. Stubbs (Rolls Series, London 1868–71)

Roger of Wendover, *Flores Historiarum* (13th c.), ed. F. Liebermann in *Monumenta Germaniae Historica Scriptores* XXVIII

G. Rokhlin, *Itogi anatomicheskogo izuchenya skeleta Yaroslava* (Leningrad 1940)

Saxo Grammaticus, *Danica Historia* (1576); cf. *The First Nine Books of Danish History*, tr. O. Elton III (London 1894)

Eric Sams, *Shakespeare's Lost Play: Edmund Ironside* (London 1986)

Mária Sándor, 'A mecseknádasdi St István templom', *Yearbook of the Janus Pannonius Museum* (Pécs 1971)

Judge Sarchas in L. Závodszky, *A St István, St Lászlo es Kálmán korabeli törvények forrásai* (Budapest 1904)

Sigebert of Gembloux, *Chronico ab anno 381 ad 1113* (12th c.) (Paris 1513)

Sighvat the Scald, *Tograpa* (up to 1042), ed. D. Whitelock in *English Historical Documents* I (London 1979)

Symeon of Durham, *Opera omnia*, ed. T. Arnold (Rolls Series, London 1882–5)

A. Sinyavsky, *Otnoshenya drevnye Russkoy tserkvy i obshchestva k latinskomu zapadu* (Moscow 1899)

Henry Spelman,'Spelmani Codex legum veterum statutorem regni Angliae', ed. David Wilkins, *Leges Anglo-Saxonicae* (Oxford 1721)

J. Steenstrup, *Normannerne, Danske og Norske Riger paa de Britiske Øer i Danevaeldens Tidsalder* (Copenhagen 1882)

Frank M. Stenton, 'The Danes in England', *Proceedings of the British Academy* (1927) 203–246; *Anglo-Saxon England* (London 1947)

John Stow, *Annales, or General Chronicle of England* (London 1616)

Snorri Sturluson, *The Heimskringlasaga* (early 12th c.) (London 1844)

Peter F. Suhm, *Geschichte Dänmarks, Norwegen und Holsteins* (Liepzig 1777)

Imre Szentpétery, *Scriptores rerum Hungaricarum tempore ducum regumque stirpis Arpadianae gestarum*, II (Budapest 1937); *Az Árpádházi királyok okleveleinek kritikai jegyzéke*, II (Budapest 1927)

St Andrew of Cambrai, *Gesta pontificarum Camaracensium* (11th c.), ed. Bethmann (Paris 1853)

St James, *Lüttich Chronicle* (11th c.), ed. G. H. Pertz, *Monumenta Germaniae Historica* XVI

St Gellert, *Legend (minor)* & *Legend (major)* (12th c.), *Scriptores Rerum Hungaricarum tempore ducum regumque stirpis Arpadianae gestarum* II, 47–506 (Budapest 1938); cf. Maffei, *Fuga Saecoli* (Paris 1632)

Joannes Thuróczy, *Chronica Hungarorum* (1488), ed. Schwandtner, *Scriptores rerum Hungaricarum*, I (Vienna 1746)

Joannes Tomcus / Ivan Tomcus Marnavic / (Bishop of Bosnia 11th c.), ed. G. H. Pertz, *Monumenta Germaniae Historica*, VI

Turgotus (Bishop of St Andrews 11th c.), *Vita Margaretae* (1789)

Szabolcs de Vajay, 'Agatha, mother of St Margaret Queen of Scotland,' *Duquesne Review* (1962)

Orderic Vitalis, *see* Orderic

Robert Wace, *Le Roman de Rou* (11th c.), ed. A. Holden (Société des Anciens Textes Français, Paris 1970–71) I–II

Gusztav Wencel, *Árpádkori Uj Okmánytár* (Pest 1860–74) X, 233

Mór Wertner, *Az Árpádok családi története* (Temesvár 1892)

Florence of Worcester, *see* Florence

János Xantus, 'Kik voltak az angloszász hercegek St István udvarában?' *Századok* XII (Budapest 1878)

INDEX

Aba, Samuel, king of Hungary, 80, 107
Abaujvar, 84
Adam of Bremen, archbishop of
    Hamburg, 53–4, 56, 57, 67, 71, 118
Adelheid, daughter of Andrew I, 105
Aelfwine, abbot of Ramsey, 132, 134,
    197
Athelred II the Unready, king of
    England, 3, 4, 5, 6, 7, 10, 23, 129, 130
Agatha, wife of Edward the Exile, xi,
    143, 153, 163, 164; origins, 109–21
Agnes of Poitiers, 135
Ailred of Rievaulx, 49, 107, 108, 110,
    114, 130
Alekseyev, M.P., 57
Alexander II, king of Scotland, 180
Alexander II, Pope, 153, 154
Alexis Comnenus, emperor of
    Byzantium, 170
Alfred, son of Aethelred, 6, 26, 126,
    127, 141
Alnwick, battle of, 180
Amleth, 27, 28
Anastasia, queen, wife of Andrew I,
    70, 75, 104
Andrew I, king of Hungary, 48, 70, 71,
    72, 74–5, 80–1, 82, 91, 102, 118, 134,
    135; military intervention in
    Hungary, 83–8
Andrew II, king of Hungary, 93
Andrew of Cambrai, St, Gesta Pontifi-
    carum Camacensium, 151
Anglo-Saxon Chronicle, 17, 20, 24, 30–1,
    45, 47, 110, 132, 133, 137, 138, 146,
    155–6, 165, 169, 179
Annales Altahenses Majores, 74
Anne, daughter of Yaroslav the Great,
    70, 76, 118
Apulia, 169
Arnulph, 111
Árpád dynasty, 71, 102, 107
Ashington, Essex, 16

Baronius, 180
Bartholomew, bishop of Pécs, 93
Bayeux Tapestry, 146
Béla, prince, 72, 74–5, 88
Beneta, bishop, 85
Berkhamsted, 161
Bestrik, bishop, 85
Bjorn, earl, 126
Boethius, 153, 165–6
Boleslaw I, king of Poland, 55
Bridge of the Three Princes, 100
Brindisi, 170
'Britons', use of term, 96–7
Bruno, bishop of Augsburg, 114
Bruno of Brunswick, 119
Bua, magnate, 80, 81
Budli, bishop, 85
Buhna, magnate, 80, 81
Burke's Peerage, x
Butler, Alban, 181
Byzantium, 52, 65, 97

Canute, king of the English, Danes and
    Norwegians, x, 5, 32, 33, 129, 175;
    punitive campaign against Eng-
    land, 7–9; proclaimed king by
    Witan, 10–11; single combat with
    Edmund Ironside, 12–16; division
    of kingdom, 17–18; possible role in
    Edmund Ironside's murder, 19–22;
    rule of England, 23, 37; executes
    Eadric, 29–31; invasion of Scandin-
    avia, 39– 41; Baltic empire, 68–70;
    death, 75
Capgrave, John, 22
Cardiff Castle, 171
Carruthers, 181
Castle Mound, Mecseknádasd, 98–101
Catholic Church, Hungary, 79, 80, 81,
    104
Celtic Church, 179–80
Cerdic, House of, 4, 10, 150, 161
Chester, 164

chivalry, 104
Christina, daughter of Edward the
   Exile, 114, 116, 118, 143, 165, 169
Chronica Hungarorum, 79
Chronicle of Melrose Abbey, 110
chroniclers, working methods, 44–9
chronology, uncertainty of in chron-
   iclers, 44–5
churches, Kiev, 66–7
Cletus, count, 98, 196
Cnut, king *see* Canute
Cologne, 133–4
combat, trial by, 169–70
comet, 151–2
Conrad, duke of Bavaria, 134
Constantine Monomachos, emperor of
   Byzantium, 70
Cornides, Daniel, 111
Csánki, Dezsö, 94
Csepel, 103
Csupor, Miklos, 98
Cymbeline, 33

danegeld, 3, 8, 17, 23
Danelaw, 4
Danes, 164; raids, 3–9; behaviour in
   England, 37–8
Darabos family, 98
David I, king of Scotland, 49, 117
Denmark, 28–9, 39, 51
Dictionary of National Biography, x
Dives river, 155
Dlugosz, Jan, 97, 152
Dombai, János, 100
Domesday Book, 116
Donald, king of Scotland, 170
Douay, Scots College, 181
Dover, 126–7, 146
Dunfermline, 177, 180, 181
Dunfermline Abbey, 180–1
Dunstan, St, 4, 18, 142, 157, 180

Eadric Streona, ealdorman of Mercia,
   11, 12, 16, 18, 20, 21–2, 24; death of,
   29–31
Eadwig, brother of Edmund Ironside,
   26, 38
Eadwin, earl of Mercia, 152, 155, 156–
   7, 164
Ealdgyth, wife of Edmund Ironside,
   24, 53, 192
Ealdgyth, wife of king Harold, 152
Ealdred, archbishop of York, 31, 47–8,
   132–5, 162

Edgar Aetheling, xi, 105, 111, 116, 117,
   119, 136, 143–5, 146, 149–50, 152–3,
   155, 156–7, 161, 175, 199; flight to
   Scotland, 162–4; campaign against
   William the Conqueror, 164– 6, 167;
   at William's court, 168–9; friendship with Robert Courte-Heuse,
   168, 170, 171; accused of plot
   against William Rufus, 169– 70;
   campaign against Donald of Scotland, 170; crusade, 170–1; retire-
   ment from public life, 171–2
Edgar, king of Scotland, 170
Edinburgh Castle, 181
Edith, queen, wife of Edward the
   Confessor, 126, 127, 148
Edmund Aetheling, x, xi, 24–5, 116,
   118, 175, 176, 192; discussion of
   status at Gemot, 26–7; proposed
   murder, 26, 27–8, 30–3, 39, 40; exile,
   28–9; enmity of Emma, 38–9; supposed flight to Hungary from
   Sweden, 43–9; flight to Russia, 51–
   4, 56– 8; refuge at Kiev, 61–70, 75,
   76, 193; joins military intervention
   in Hungary, 81– 8; possible lands in
   Hungary, 91–101; sexual scandal,
   104–8; death, 108
Edmund Ironside, 32–3
Edmund Ironside, king of England, 24,
   29, 32, 38, 175, 176; fighting against
   Canute, 8–11; single combat with
   Canute, 12–16; division of kingdom, 17–18; murder, 18–22, 53, 126
Edmund, St, 6
Edward, son of St Margaret, 180
Edward the Confessor, king of
   England, x, xi, 6, 26, 42, 47, 69, 70,
   75–6, 115, 116, 128, 129, 134, 135,
   137, 139–40, 143, 147, 175; Norman
   influence at court of, 125–7; recalls
   Edward the Exile, 130–1, 132;
   choice of Edgar for throne, 144–5,
   146; deathbed, 148–9
Edward the Exile, x, xi–xii, 24–5, 147,
   175, 176, 192; discussion of status at
   Gemot, 26–7; plan to murder, 26,
   27–8, 30–3, 39, 40; exile, 28–9; enmity of Emma, 38–9; role in succession to Edward the Confessor, 41–2;
   supposed flight to Hungary from
   Sweden, 43–9; return to England,
   45, 135, 136–8; flight to Russia, 51–
   4, 56–8; refuge at Kiev, 61–70, 75,

76, 193; in Russia, 75, 76, 115–16,
117; joins military intervention in
Hungary, 81–8; possible lands in
Hungary, 91–101; marriage, 109–21;
suggested return, 130–1; death and
possible murder, 138–42, 145
Edwin, 26
Ekkehart, 114, 151
Eleanor of Provence, queen, 126
Emeric, son of king Stephen, 72, 73, 111
Emma of Normandy, wife of
Aethelred and Canute, 6, 12, 23–4,
27, 37, 118; attempts to ensure the
succession, 38–9; enmity to
aethelings, 51
Encomiast, 7, 11–12, 20, 22, 23, 29, 30,
38, 55
Encomium Emmae Reginae, 7
Encyclopaedia Britannica, x
England, 68–9; Danish raids, 3–9; div-
ision of, 17–18; Norman influence,
125–7; succession to throne, 129–
31; Norman invasion, 154–5
English Virgin's Hill, 100
La Estoire de Seint Aedward le Rei, 5–6,
14–16, 22, 126
Eustace II, count of Boulogne, 126–7
Everitt, E.B., 32
Evlia, Chelebi, 98–9

Fejér, György, 93, 94
Feng of Jutland, 27–8
Fitzwimark, Robert, 148
Florence of Worcester, 11, 17, 20–1, 22,
26, 27, 30, 31, 45, 47, 49, 110–11, 114,
130, 133–4, 136, 145, 155, 157, 162–3,
169, 183, 192
Fordun, John of, 130, 163
Freeman, Edward, 139

Gaimar, Geoffroi, 12, 14, 22, 24, 27, 28,
29, 30, 31, 32, 38–9, 40, 48, 50–1, 53,
54, 56, 61, 62, 105–8, 194–5
Galicia, 68
Gardorika-Gardimbre, 54, 61, 62, 63,
107
Gellert, bishop, 85
Gemot, 26–7, 132, 135
Geoffrey, bishop of Coutances, 162
geographical terms, unreliable use by
chroniclers, 44
Germany, 134
Geysa, father of king Stephen, 79
Gillies, bishop, 181

Gisela, queen, wife of king Stephen,
55, 72, 74, 78, 110, 111, 112, 114, 119
Godell, Guillaume, 152
Godwin, earl of Wessex, 125–8
Godwin, knight, 169–70
Goslar, 118
Gospatric, earl, 162
Greek Orthodox Church, 65
Guillaume of Jumièges, 57
Gunhild, daughter of Emma and
Canute, 38, 118
Gunhild, wife of Henry III, 133
Gunhilde, queen, wife of Sweyn
Forkbeard, 55
Guy, bishop of Amiens, 107
Guy, count of Ponthieu, 146
Györffy, György, 95
Gyrth, earl, 156

Hanseatic cities, 53
Harold II, king of England, 117, 126,
129, 139–40, 141, 144, 147, 152–3;
becomes earl of Wessex, 128; oath
to Duke William, 145–6, 153, 198; at
Edward the Confessor's deathbed,
148–50; accession to throne, 149–50,
152; campaign against Tosti and
Harold Hardrada, 153–4; at Hast-
ings, 155–6; death, 156
Harold Hardrada, king of Norway, 70,
153–4
Harthacanute, king of England and
Denmark, 38, 70, 75, 82, 144
Hartvik, bishop, 71–2
Hastings, battle of, xi, 155–6
Heimskringlasaga, 6, 20, 54
Henry II, emperor, 110, 112, 114, 118,
119
Henry III, emperor, 69, 70, 76, 79–80,
88, 110, 114, 119, 130, 132–5, 198
Henry I, king of England, 51, 115, 171
Henry I, king of France, 57, 70, 76
Hermann, archbishop of Cologne, 134
Hilarion, Metropolitan, 65–6
Holub, József, 93
horses, 103–4
Hugolin the Treasurer, 141
Hungarian National Archives, 96
Hungary, x, 130, 131, 132; aethelings
supposed flight to, 43–9; succession
to king Stephen, 71–7; after king
Stephen's death, 78– 82; Andrew
and Levente's military intervention,

83–8; aethelings in, 91–101; court
  life, 102–8
hunting, 103
Huntingdon, Henry of, 12, 17, 21, 23,
  31, 49

Iam, tribe, 68
Ingeborg, wife of Malcolm Canmore,
  165
Ingegerd, queen, 53, 54, 56, 61, 64
Ingulph, abbot of Croyland, 23
Innocent IV, Pope, 180
Innocent X, Pope, 181
Ipatyevskaya Letopis, 56
Irkah, siege of, 170

James, St, *Lüttisch Chronicle*, 152
Jerusalem, siege of, 171
Johannes Tomcus, 111
John of Brompton, 22, 38, 108
Jómvikings, 3, 4, 5, 83, 191
justice, Yaroslav the Great, 66

Karamzin, N.M., 57, 75
Kazimir I, king of Poland, 70
Kent, 7
Kéza, Simon de, 73–4
Kiev, 52–4, 63–4, 66–7; aethelings
  refuge at, 61–70
King John, 33
knights errant, 84
Knytlingasaga, 17, 20
Korogyi, Philip, 98
Koronchaya Kniga, 66

Ladoga, 54
Lake Ladoga, 54, 61
land deeds, mentioning 'Lands of
  Britons', 91–101
Lanfranc, archbishop of Canterbury,
  179
Lappenberg, Johann Martin von, 139
Larson, Laurence, 55
Lászlo the Bald, 73, 74
Lattakieh, 170
Lavrentyevskaya Letopis, 56
laws, Yaroslav the Great, 66
Leges Edovardi Confessoris, 56, 57, 96,
  115–18, 184–5
Leofwine, earl, 156
letters of death, 26, 27, 33
Levente, prince, 71, 72, 74–5, 80–1, 82;
  military intervention in Hungary,
  83–8

Liber Vitae, 37
Liebermann, Felix, 117
Limezy, Ralph de, 116
Lincoln, 165
Lithuania, 68
Liudolf, margrave of West-Friesland,
  119
London, 7, 17, 152, 155, 156; siege of,
  11–12
Lupus Protospatarius, 152
Lüttich Chronicle, 152

Magnus I, king of Norway, 40, 64, 69,
  144
Malcolm III Canmore, king of
  Scotland, 144, 162, 163–4, 165–6,
  167, 169, 176, 180
Malcomes, Béla, 100–1, 196
Malderus, bishop John, 181
Malmesbury, William of, 21, 22, 23–4,
  31, 48–9, 110, 112, 128–9, 130, 133,
  140, 146, 147, 149–50, 154, 165, 168,
  170, 171, 172, 192
Manors, 103
Map, Walter, 12
Margaret of Scotland, St, x, xi, 49, 100,
  105, 111, 112, 115, 116, 117, 118, 130,
  143–4, 153, 163–4, 165, 175–82
Maria, sister of Yaroslav the Great, 70
Marianus Scotus of Fulda, 47, 48
Marleswyne, earl, 162
Marothi family, 98
marriages, political, 70, 75, 76
martial arts, learning, 64
Mary queen of Scots, 181
Matilda, queen, wife of Henry I, 176
Máza, 93, 96, 100, 101
Mazovians, 68
Mecseknádasd, 'Lands of Britons', 91–
  101
Ménfö, battle of, 80
mercenaries, Andrew and Levente's
  forces, 81
Mercia, 17, 156, 162
Merlin, 3–4, 11
Messenius, Johan, bishop of Lund, 41
Mieczyslav, king of Poland, 55, 75
Montreuil Castle, 166
Morcar, earl, 20
Morcare, earl of Northumbria, 152,
  155, 156–7, 164
More, Sir Thomas, 32

Nachalny Svod, 54

Nádasd, 93, 94, 96, 98, 108
Nádasdy, counts, 97–8, 196
Nestor, 56, 65
nobility, English, William of Malmes-
bury's views on, 128–9
Norman Conquest, x, 41–2, 112, 154–7,
161–2
Normandy, 169
Normans, 129; influence in England,
125–7; invasion of England, 154–6
northdael, 17
Northumbria, 156, 162, 164, 169
Norway, 52; Canute's campaign
against, 39–41
Novgorod, 52, 63
Novgorodskaya Letopis, 56

Olaf, king of Norway, 40, 41, 52, 53, 64
Olney, accord of, 17, 24–5
Onund Jacob, king of Sweden, 40, 52,
175
Orderic Vitalis, 28–9, 48, 57, 110, 111,
147, 152, 155, 157, 162, 168, 170, 198
Ordgar, knight, 169–70, 171
Orthodox Christianity, 65–6
Orthodox Church, 107
Osbjern, Jarl, 165
Ottar the Black, 8
Otto, bishop of Freising, 151
Oxford, 20

paganism, Hungary, 79, 80, 81, 84–6
Palgrave, Sir Francis, 139
Papebroch, 181
Papp, Lászlo, 101
Pearson, C.H., 139
Pechenegs, 63, 75, 94
Pécs, 93, 94, 97, 100
Pécsvárad abbey, 102–3
Pelbartus, 111
Pest, 85
Peter Orseolo, king of Hungary, 72, 78–
81, 84, 86, 111–12, 134
Pevensey Bay, 155
Philip I, king of France, 166, 167
Philip II, king of Spain, 181
Poitiers, William of, 145–6, 186–90
Poland, 55–6, 74–5
Poles, 63
Poole, 10
princes in the Tower, 32–3
Prokopius, 97
prophecies, 3–4
Prosper, 97

Ralph, earl of Hereford, 130, 143
Ranulf of Chester, 31
Ranulph of Higden, 108
Raven Banner, 10, 191
Réka Castle, 99–101, 102
religion, Yaroslav the Great and, 65–6
restoration, Anglo–Saxon line,
attempts at, 38–9
revolt, anti–Norman, 164
Rézbányai, Jozsef, 95
Rheims Chronicle, 151
Richard I, duke of Normandy, 6, 23–4
Richard III, king of England, 33
Richard III, 32–3
Robert II Courte–Heuse, duke of
Normandy, 168, 169, 170–1
Robert, archbishop of Canterbury, 147
Robert, count of Gloucester, 51
Robert Godwin, 171
Robert the Deacon, 141
Robie, Father John, 181
Roger of Hoveden, 31, 193
Roger of Wendover, 22
Rorik, 28
Rouen, 146, 198
Rurik, 52, 54, 56, 64, 65
Russia: flight of aethelings to, 51–4, 56–
8; aethelings in, 61–70, 75, 76, 115–
16, 117
Russian Orthodox Church, 66
Russkaya Pravda, 66

St Sophia, Kiev, 67
St Stephens church, Mecseknádasd, 93,
95, 101
Salamon, king of Hungary, 47, 48, 110,
111, 112, 119, 121
Sams, Eric, 32
Sándor, Mária, 95, 101
Sandwich, 7, 8
Saxo Grammaticus, 27–8, 40, 52, 69,
114, 139–40, 146, 149
Scotland, 162–4, 171–2
Scots College, Douay, 181
Scottish Church, 179–80
Senlac, 155
Shakespeare, William, 32–3
shamans, 79
Sherstone, battle of, 11
Sigebert, 114
Sigeferth, earl, 20, 24, 192
Sighvat, 20, 40–1
Sigrid, queen, wife of Sweyn
Forkbeard, 55

single combat, Canute and Edmund
Ironside, 12–16
Slavs, 66
Slessick, 7
Sophie, wife of king Salamon, 119
Southampton, 10
Stamford Bridge, battle of, 154, 155
Steenstrup, J., 55
Stephen, St, king of Hungary, x, 47, 55,
61, 78, 86, 107, 111, 112; succession
to, 71–7
Stigand, archbishop of Canterbury,
127, 148, 157
Stow, John, 25
Sturlusson, Snorri, 6, 20
succession, Edmund Ironside and
Canute, 17–18
Suebi, 55
Sveyn Godwinson, earl, 126
Svyatopolk, brother of Yaroslav the
Great, 63
Sweden, x, 28, 39, 40, 41, 52, 61
Sweyn I Forkbeard, king of Denmark,
4, 5, 6, 23, 55
Sweyn Estrithson, king of Denmark,
164
sworn brothers, Edmund Ironside and
Canute, 17–18
Symeon of Durham, 31, 110
Syria, 170
Székesfehérvár, 80, 85

thingmen, 7
Thorkill the Tall, 3, 4–5, 16, 55
Thuróczy, 85, 114
Tinchebrai, battle of, 171
Tolna, priory, 98
Tosti, earl, 147, 153–4
trial by combat, 169–70
Turgotus, archbishop of St Andrews,
49, 144, 163, 164, 176, 177, 178–9

Udalrik, Czech king, 74

Vajay, Szabolcs de, 94–5, 119
Varangians, 52, 63, 64, 66, 81, 83–4
Vata, 84, 85
Vazul, 72, 73, 74
Vikings, 52, 83
Villeins, 103
Viska, magnate, 80, 81
Vita Aedwardi Regis, 126, 148
Vita Eberhardi, 111
Vizer, Father, 93
Vladimir I, king of Russia, 63

Wales, 164
Walgar, earl, 28, 40, 41, 43, 49, 51, 52,
53, 54, 56, 61, 62, 68, 69, 76, 109, 175
Washingborough Chronicle, 51
Wessex, 7, 17
William I the Conqueror, king of Eng-
land, xi, 116, 117, 127, 129, 139, 140–
1, 149; claim to throne, 145–7, 153,
154; invasion, 151–2, 154–6; coron-
ation, 161–2; defeats Malcolm
Canmore, 165–6
William II Rufus, king of England, 169,
170, 171
William, bishop of London, 141
Witan, 3, 6, 10–11, 126, 127, 131, 140,
141, 156–7, 161, 197
Wulfstan, archbishop of York, 6–7,
129, 133, 178

Yaroslav the Great, Grand Duke of
Kiev, 52–3, 56, 57, 61, 63–7, 75, 104,
116, 117–18, 175; foreign policy, 68–
70, 76, 82
Yelisaveta, daughter of Yaroslav the
Great, 70
York, 155, 164